Getting to the Core of Writing

Essential Lessons for Every Second Grade Student

Richard Gentry, Ph.D.
Jan McNeel, M.A.Ed.
Vickie Wallace-Nesler, M.A.Ed.

Shell Education

Publishing Credits

Dona Herweck Rice, *Editor-in-Chief*; Robin Erickson, *Production Director;*
Lee Aucoin, *Creative Director;* Timothy J. Bradley, *Illustration Manager*;
Sara Johnson, M.S.Ed., *Senior Editor*; Jodene Lynn Smith, M.A., *Editor*;
Melanie Green, M.A.Ed., *Associate Education Editor;* Tracy Edmunds, *Editor*;
Leah Quillian, *Assistant Editor*; Grace Alba, *Interior Layout Designer;*
Corinne Burton, *M.A.Ed., Publisher*

Standards

Shell Education
5301 Oceanus Drive
Huntington Beach, CA 92649-1030
http://www.shelleducation.com

ISBN 978-1-4258-0916-4

Reprinted 2013

Table of Contents

Table of Contents *(cont.)*

The Importance of Writing

In recent years, many school districts and teachers referred to writing as the "Neglected R" and viewed reading as the path to literacy success. Today, as research has revealed more information about the fundamental connection between reading success and writing competency, we are realizing that the road to literacy is a two-way street (Graham and Hebert, 2010). While working as literacy consultants, we encountered numerous, capable teachers struggling with the complexity of implementing rigorous writing instruction. We wrote this book to enable all teachers to implement a successful writing program with a high degree of teaching competency. The success enjoyed by many of the teachers using the materials in this book has relieved frustrations, rejuvenated careers, and rekindled enthusiasm for teaching.

This book was written to fulfill two major objectives. The first objective involves motivating teachers to value and incorporate writing instruction as an essential element of literacy development. It should help them implement best practices and simplify the planning of writing instruction. New writing standards have been applied by education leaders at every level. Ultimately, the responsibility for implementing these standards is placed on the classroom teacher. Historically, the lack of emphasis on writing instruction in teacher education programs has left teachers feeling woefully unprepared to teach primary students to write, particularly at a level which meets the expectations of the standards for writing. The burden of this responsibility and feelings of inadequacy have left both experienced and novice teachers feeling empty-handed and unprepared.

Since 2010, most states have adopted the Common Core State Standards (CCSS), which are designed to provide teachers and parents with a clear understanding of what students are expected to learn. Since the CCSS are newly adopted, many teachers have not received professional development to become familiar with the standards nor have they received resources for their instruction, particularly in the area of writing. Therefore, the second objective of this book is to assist teachers in becoming familiar with these standards for writing and provide resources to support the implementation of these standards in their classrooms. *Getting to the Core of Writing* provides lessons outlining four key areas of writing: Text Types and Purposes, Production and Distribution of Writing, Research, and Range of Writing. It offers suggestions to meet those standards in instruction during Writer's Workshop. It also addresses how speaking and listening standards are easily practiced by engaging students in an interactive lesson format.

It is no secret that students become better writers by writing every day. This book contains the foundational structure and best practices that will guide teachers as they establish a daily Writer's Workshop that includes consistent, structured instruction to engage students in the writing process. Beyond that, a flexible pacing guide is provided to aid in planning writing instruction.

It is our hope that this book provides teachers with all the tools needed to inspire and equip young writers in today's classrooms.

—Richard, Jan, and Vickie

Traits of Quality Writing

The traits of quality writing continue to gain recognition as the language of successful writers. Educators at the Northwest Regional Educational Laboratory, now Education Northwest, searched for an accurate, reliable method of measuring student writing performance. Six attributes of good writing are identified in *Seeing with New Eyes* (Bellamy 2005). These characteristics are used to inform and guide writing instruction.

- **Ideas** are the heart of the message, the content of the piece, and the main theme.
- **Sentence Fluency** is the rhythm and flow of the language, the sound of word patterns, and the way in which the writing plays to the ear, not just to the eye.
- **Organization** is the internal structure, the thread of central meaning, and the logical and sometimes intriguing pattern of ideas within a piece of writing.
- **Word Choice** is the use of rich, colorful, precise language that moves and enlightens the reader.
- **Voice** is the heart and soul, the magic, and the wit, along with the feeling and conviction of the individual writer that emerge through the words.
- **Conventions** are how the writer uses mechanical correctness in the piece—spelling, paragraphing, grammar and usage, punctuation, and capitalization.

Knowing and understanding the traits of quality writing supports teachers, students, and parents in thinking about writing and understanding what makes for writing success. Even in the early grades, students can communicate and recognize the characteristics of quality writing. The works of Ruth Culham (2008) and Vicki Spandel (2008) emphasize the value and benefits of using these traits to provide a common language—"a writer's vocabulary for thinking, speaking, and working like writers" (Spandel 2008, 7)—to enrich instruction and assessment in primary classrooms.

The value and importance of using this trait language in writing instruction is well supported by research (Gentry 2006). It is particularly important when working with students in the early grades to provide instructional tools to support students' different learning styles. In *Getting to the Core of Writing*, the traits are personified through student-friendly characters. Each of the characters represent a different writing trait, and collectively they are referred to as the Traits Team (traitsteam.pdf). Students are introduced to the individual team members through the mini-lessons. The Traits Team becomes a valuable tool for a Writer's Workshop experience. A more detailed description and poster of each Traits Team member is provided in the introduction to each trait section.

The Reading and Writing Connection

For years, researchers have acknowledged the reciprocal nature of the reading and writing process. For example, researchers have reported that beginning reading and writing are intricately connected and develop hand-in-hand in five early phases (Ehri 1997; Gentry 2006). Researchers such as P. David Pearson suggest that rather than teach and assess bits and pieces of reading skills and writing skills, teachers should provide deep and broad exposure to these processes, "in their more global, not their more atomistic aspect." As Richard Gentry (2006) writes, "Early writers use knowledge about sounds, letters, syllables, words, word parts like onsets and rimes, and phonics patterns, so early writing advances reading. But we haven't taken full advantage of it. Too often early reading and writing are not connected; they are treated separately."

Getting to the Core of Writing approaches Writer's Workshop from this global perspective, honoring the links between reading and writing and connecting them to the Common Core State Standards. Taken from this approach, Writer's Workshop will be an orchestra in concert—not the screeching sounds of the orchestra tuning up in bits and pieces.

When beginning readers and writers advance from nonreaders to independent, automatic, fluid readers in kindergarten through second grade, there is evidence that reading and writing develop in tandem. This is illustrated in the *Phases of Writing* chart (pages 8–9) and is adapted from a developmental monitoring process called Tracking Five Phases of Code Breaking (Gentry 2006, 2010). Beginners in a particular phase approach word reading and word writing with similar understandings and strategies. The sub-skills and cross connections of reading, writing, and spelling strengthen naturally as students explore and become engaged in both reading and writing processes at each successive phase. There are five phases of writing development that can be observed in students as they practice writing. At each of these phases, reading and writing brain circuitry is intricately connected, and the student's responses while writing, reading, and spelling mirror each other and fit the patterns observable in the phase. Thinking about development globally rather than taking an atomistic view of isolated skills instruction will give teachers a unified perspective for monitoring progress and targeting instruction as they work with beginning writers and readers (Gentry 2006).

Phases of Writing

	Description	Writing Sample
Phase 0	• Begins at birth • Advances with widespread age discrepancies depending upon the exposure that children receive with literacy at home or in preschool • Writing is characterized by marking, drawing, and scribbling which leads to letter-like forms • First words and easy books may be mastered through reading aloud • Repeated exposure to books eventually leads to first experiences with memory reading of words and phrases	
Phase 1	• Begins when the child writes his or her name and begins using letters • Attempts to write messages and stories using letters • Imitates the reading of easy books • Does not know that letters represent sounds and has little capacity to "sound out" when reading words • Relies on pictures, logographic memory, or guessing	 A flock of butterflies
Phase 2	• Expanding knowledge of the alphabet and ability to match beginning and prominent letters to sounds • Labels drawings or writes messages with a few letter-sound matches • Begins to make the voice-to-print match through finger-point reading • Can respond as writers with more elaborate pieces with appropriate instruction • Number and sophistication of books read from memory grows in Phase 2, often reaching level C (Fountas and Pinnell) or 3 (Reading Recovery; DRA) • Begins to attend to letter-sound matches at the beginning of words and write unknown words in what looks like abbreviated spelling	 Humpty Dumpty

Phases of Writing *(cont.)*

	Description	Writing Sample
Phase 3*	• Reading, writing, and spelling occur by attending to one letter for each sound and by employing growing conventionally-spelled, word recognition vocabulary • Can read many books from memory • Scores of words are recognized on sight, often enabling the child to move into mid-first grade reading levels and beyond • Child is on the cusp of being an independent reader and has new strategies for figuring out unknown words, such as using word families and analogy as in *mat, cat, sat, fat, hat, rat*	
Phase 4*	• Writers show awareness of phonics patterns • Words are spelled in "chunks" for example, *billdings* for *buildings* • Able to read easy chapter books • Can recognize 100 or more words on sight and spell many words correctly • Transitioning into second grade reading levels • Replaces memory reading with fluid decoding ability and automatic independent reading	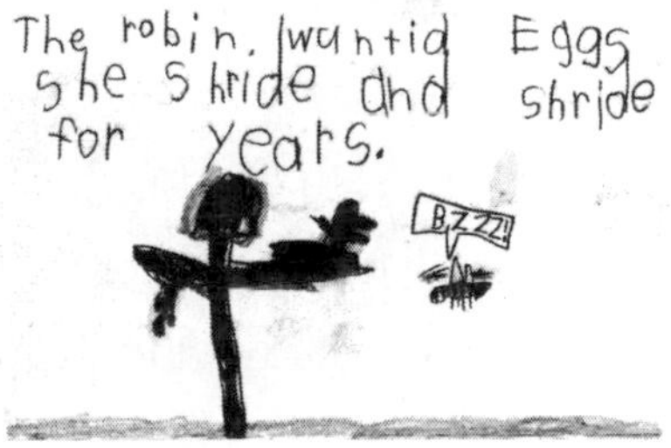

adapted from *Raising Confident Readers: How to Teach Your Child to Read and Write—from Baby to Age 7* (Gentry 2010).

*For a full student writing sample, please see the Teacher Resource CD (samples.doc)

The Purpose of Assessment

Assessment plays an integral role in writing instruction. It may occur at the district or state level to measure the student's ability to meet specific standards. Many classrooms include self-assessment where students use rubrics and checklists to score and reflect on their own work. Writing assessment can also take place informally as we sit and confer with young writers, taking anecdotal notes. Maintaining student writing portfolios comprised of both spontaneous and directed writing provides assessment information of a student's writing development and performance over a specific time. No matter the type or form of assessment, it should enable you to determine students' strengths and weaknesses so you may revise your instruction to meet the needs of your writers.

> *Assessment must promote learning, not just measure it. When learners are well served, assessment becomes a learning experience that supports and improves instruction. The learners are not just the students but also the teachers, who learn something about their students.*
>
> —Regie Routman (1999, 559)

Monitoring students' writing over time provides valuable information about their growth and development. The samples, collected periodically throughout the year into student portfolios, reflect where the Writer's Workshop journey began and the student's ongoing progress and achievement relative to the instructional goals. Portfolios, along with your anecdotal notes, not only inform parents of their child's growth but also show students the variety of concepts and skills learned during Writer's Workshop.

In addition to ongoing classroom assessment, it is valuable to conduct benchmark assessments at the beginning, middle, and end of the year. The beginning of the year benchmark provides you with a baseline of data that represents the foundational skill level of the student writer. The middle and end of the year benchmarks show areas of achievement and needs as well as identify effective instructional strategies. *Getting to the Core of Writing* refers to these benchmarks as Benchmarks 1, 2, and 3 respectively. After each benchmark, it is important to analyze the student's work using the grade-level rubric (page 244; secondgradewritingrubric.pdf) in order to identify the additional support needed for the student.

Collaborating with other teachers encourages targeted conversations about student work and helps build confidence as you become more knowledgeable in interpreting and evaluating student writing. Although *Getting to the Core of Writing* includes a Suggested Pacing Guide (pages 12–13; pacingguide.pdf) and a Year-at-a-Glance plan of instruction (yearataglance.pdf) that provide benchmark prompt suggestions, it is not a one-size-fits-all classroom writing map. Your assessments and observations provide essential information to guide instructional decisions designed to meet the needs of all your students. For additional assessment resources, including benchmark support information, a rubric, a scoring guide, a classroom grouping mat, and scored student writing samples, see Appendix A.

Planning Writing Instruction

Essential in any literacy development is planning and scheduling. *Getting to the Core of Writing* supports teachers as they learn and grow as writers along with their students while at the same time implementing Writer's Workshop. Growing requires nurturing like writing requires practice. The provided plan of instruction is based on the conviction that Writer's Workshop happens each and every day throughout the school year. Mini-lessons may be retaught when necessary. Some mini-lessons may require more than one day for students to fully grasp an understanding of the writing concept. Additionally, teachers proficient in writing instruction may select individual mini-lessons and teach them in an order that meets the specific needs of their students.

When writing is shared consistently and enthusiastically, students learn, love, and choose to write. As always, instruction must also be guided by the developmental needs of the students as revealed through their daily writing. The structure provided by Writer's Workshop and the lessons in this book allow both students and teacher to recognize themselves as successful writers. Once the routines of Writer's Workshop are in place, it is much easier for the teacher to focus on a quality daily writing time. Things become so routine that teachers will find themselves feeling motivated and passionate about writing instruction instead of overwhelmed.

The pacing guide found on pages 12–13 provides a suggested sequence for when to teach the lessons in this book. It serves as a guide for consistent practice in the writing process and incorporates the traits of quality writing. It is suggested that some lessons be taught more than once throughout the year. When this occurs, if desired, the content of the student writing pieces can be modified slightly to provide students with opportunities to practice writing **opinion-**, **informative-/explanatory-**, and **narrative-**based texts. By doing this, students get to write different genres in formats that are familiar to them. For example, in Ideas lesson 1, students can change the content about which they brainstorm to create an opinion piece on why dogs are the best pet, a narrative on their summer vacation, and an informative piece on the types of plants around the school.

Planning Writing Instruction *(cont.)*

Suggested Pacing Guide

Month	Lesson
August/September	• Managing WW Lesson 1 (page 31) • Managing WW Lesson 2 (page 33) • Ideas Lesson 1 (page 55) • Conventions Lesson 1 (page 207) • Managing WW Lesson 4 (page 39) • Word Choice Lesson 1 (page 157) • Ideas Lesson 2 (page 58) • Managing WW Lesson 5 (page 41) • Managing WW Lesson 6 (page 43) • Conventions Lesson 2 (page 217) • Sentence Fluency Lesson 1 (page 83) • Managing WW Lesson 7 (page 46) • Word Choice Lesson 2 (page 161) • Ideas Lesson 3 (page 61) • Organization Lesson 1 (page 113) • Conventions Lesson 3 (page 220) • Organization Lesson 2 (page 115) • Sentence Fluency Lesson 2 (page 87) • Organization Lesson 3 (page 118) • **Administer Benchmark 1:** Draw a picture and write a story about you and your friend.

Month	Lesson
October	• Review Managing WW Lessons 1–7 as needed. • Ideas Lesson 1 (page 55) • Ideas Lesson 3 (page 61) • Sentence Fluency Lesson 3 (page 89) • Word Choice Lesson 1 (page 157) • Conventions Lesson 2 (page 217) • Managing WW Lesson 8 (page 49) • Organization Lesson 4 (page 120) • Conventions Lesson 4 (page 223) • Word Choice Lesson 3 (page 165) • Sentence Fluency Lesson 4 (page 94) • Ideas Lesson 4 (page 63) • Organization Lesson 5 (page 126) • Word Choice Lesson 4 (page 168)

Month	Lesson
November	• Review Managing WW Lessons 1–8 as needed. • Ideas Lesson 1 (page 55) • Ideas Lesson 3 (page 61) • Word Choice Lesson 5 (page 170) • Sentence Fluency Lesson 5 (page 97) • Conventions Lesson 3 (page 220) • Ideas Lesson 5 (page 66) • Organization Lesson 4 (page 120) • Sentence Fluency Lesson 6 (page 99) • Word Choice Lesson 6 (page 173) • Organization Lesson 5 (page 126) • Conventions Lesson 5 (page 226)

Month	Lesson
December	• Review Managing WW Lessons 1–8 as needed. • Ideas Lesson 1 (page 55) • Ideas Lesson 3 (page 61) • Sentence Fluency Lesson 7 (page 102) • Word Choice Lesson 1 (page 157) • Organization Lesson 7 (page 133) • Organization Lesson 8 (page 136) • Conventions Lesson 6 (page 229) • Ideas Lesson 6 (page 69) • Word Choice Lesson 7 (page 183) • Organization Lesson 4 (page 120) • Conventions Lesson 5 (page 226)

Planning Writing Instruction (cont.)

Suggested Pacing Guide (cont.)

Month	Lesson
January	• Review Managing WW Lessons 1–8 as needed. • Ideas Lesson 1 (page 55) • Ideas Lesson 3 (page 61) • Sentence Fluency Lesson 6 (page 99) • Word Choice Lesson 4 (page 168) • Organization Lesson 7 (page 133) • Organization Lesson 8 (page 136) • Conventions Lesson 7 (page 231) • Ideas Lesson 7 (page 72) • Sentence Fluency Lesson 8 (page 104) • Word Choice Lesson 8 (page 185) • Organization Lesson 9 (page 141) • Conventions Lesson 5 (page 226) • **Administer Benchmark 2:** Draw and write about one season of the year. Make sure to add lots of details.

Month	Lesson
February	• Review Managing WW Lessons 1–8 as needed. • Ideas Lesson 1 (page 55) • Ideas Lesson 3 (page 61) • Sentence Fluency Lesson 2 (page 87) • Conventions Lesson 3 (page 220) • Word Choice Lesson 2 (page 161) • Ideas Lesson 4 (page 63) • Sentence Fluency Lesson 7 (page 102) • Organization Lesson 6 (page 131) • Organization Lesson 10 (page 145) • Organization Lesson 11 (page 147) • Conventions Lesson 6 (page 229) • Organization Lesson 9 (page 141)

Month	Lesson
March	• Review Managing WW Lessons 1–8 as needed. • Ideas Lesson 1 (page 55) • Ideas Lesson 3 (page 61) • Word Choice Lesson 5 (page 170) • Sentence Fluency Lesson 5 (page 97) • Ideas Lesson 8 (page 77) • Sentence Fluency Lesson 9 (page 107) • Organization Lesson 11 (page 147) • Word Choice Lesson 10 (page 193) • Conventions Lesson 5 (page 226) • Conventions Lesson 7 (page 231)

Month	Lesson
April	• Review Managing WW 1–8 as needed. • Ideas Lesson 1 (page 55) • Ideas Lesson 3 (page 61) • Ideas Lesson 7 (page 72) • Word Choice Lesson 7 (page 183) • Organization Lesson 2 (page 115) • Sentence Fluency Lesson 8 (page 104) • Organization Lesson 3 (page 118) • Conventions Lesson 4 (page 223) • Word Choice Lesson 9 (page 188) • Organization Lesson 12 (page 151) • Conventions Lesson 7 (page 231)

Month	Lesson
May	• Revisit mini-lessons based on students' needs and interests. Plan a celebration of writing to recognize the wonderful writers in your classroom. You may wish to have children write a narrative connected to Mother's Day or Father's Day. Also consider informational writing like a report about insects, plants, or life cycles, or a how-to-book about making a healthy snack or planting a garden. Don't forget opinion writing. Write letters stating opinions about next year's lunch or recess program. Students also have opinions about favorites with reasons and examples to support that topic. The possibilities are endless. • **Administer Benchmark 3:** All of us have had special times and adventures in second grade this year. It might be something you learned, a trip, or even meeting new friends. Write a story about your adventures in second grade. Be sure to give details to show what it was like and what made it so memorable/special. As you plan your story, think about how you will organize your story with a brilliant beginning, middle, and excellent ending, and what details and examples you will add to make the story interesting.

Components of Writer's Workshop

Writer's Workshop entails common characteristics that are essential to developing enthusiastic and successful student writers (Graves 1994, 2003; Fletcher 2001; Calkins 1994, 2005; Ray 2001, 2004; Gentry 2000, 2004, 2010). The guidelines that follow have been time-tested by years of classroom practice and collaboration with master writing teachers. The framework of this structure includes the following: the mini-lesson, writing practice time, and sharing time.

The Mini-Lesson

The mini-lesson is 5–15 minutes in length and begins the workshop. It is an opportunity to review past learning, introduce new writing strategies through modeling, and engage students in practicing those strategies through oral rehearsal. Each mini-lesson is focused on one specific topic that both addresses the needs of writers and reflects these skills as practiced by real authors. The mini-lesson is always energetic and challenges students to participate while building their confidence as writers. Students gather in a common area and become part of a comfortable, safe environment that provides guidance and encouragement.

In the appropriate mini-lessons, introduce the Traits Team poster as a visual reminder for students of the writing traits. The Traits Team includes *Ida, Idea Creator* (page 54); *Simon, Sentence Builder* (page 82); *Owen, Organization Conductor* (page 112); *Wally, Word Choice Detective* (page 156); *Val and Van Voice* (page 198); and *Callie, Super Conventions Checke*r (page 206). These characters work as a team to show students that good writing is not built one skill at a time but with a team of strategies. The Traits Team can be displayed in the classroom and referred to often to refresh students' memories of the importance for good writing.

Writing Practice Time

During the 15–30 minute writing practice, students apply the skill, strategy, or craft taught in the mini-lesson. This part of the lesson gives students practice necessary in becoming proficient writers as they compose a message to share with a reader. Simultaneously, the teacher helps individual students or small groups of students compose through conferencing. These conferences provide teachers the opportunity to praise students for applying a strategy, followed by a short teaching point. Teachers document observations in a Conferring Notebook to be used for evaluating students' progress, planning new instruction, and meeting with parents. An important part of the writing practice time is the *Spotlight Strategy*. It calls attention to one or two students briefly each day by spotlighting their work, especially when attempting the focus skill presented in the mini-lesson.

Sharing Time

The 5–15 minutes of sharing echoes the mini-lesson across Writer's Workshop and provides an additional opportunity for student talk time. At the end of the writing practice time, students are invited to spend several minutes sharing with partners, in small groups, or individually in the Author's Chair. Teachers select students to share based on their observations during writing time. A variety of sharing methods is used to promote motivation and excitement. At the end of Writer's Workshop, homework suggestions are made to help students follow up on the mini-lesson ideas. Homework can be shared on the next workshop day.

Implementing the Lessons

Each lesson supports teachers in their writing instruction and encourages students to write like published authors. Consistent language builds a commonality between students as well as across grade levels. Talking about writers, studying other writers, and practicing the craft of writing give students the gift of being an author. While the focus of the lesson may change each day, the lesson routine remains constant. Building routines in any instruction yields smooth transitions between activities and fewer opportunities for distractions. Some mini-lessons may be taught daily while others might be explored across several days. Several mini-lessons can easily be adapted to multiple themes and various pieces of literature, including those listed in the Common Core State Standards Suggested Works. It is important to consider the specific developmental levels and needs of the students. The lesson format provides structure, support, and a framework for instruction for the busy classroom teacher.

Using consistent language during each section of Writer's Workshop is one structure that students will recognize and that will be helpful for smooth transitions. Suggested language for each section of Writer's Workshop is provided in the lessons that follow. Each Writer's Workshop lesson includes the following sections:

- Think About Writing
- Teach
- Engage
- Apply
- Write/Conference
- Spotlight Strategy
- Share
- Homework

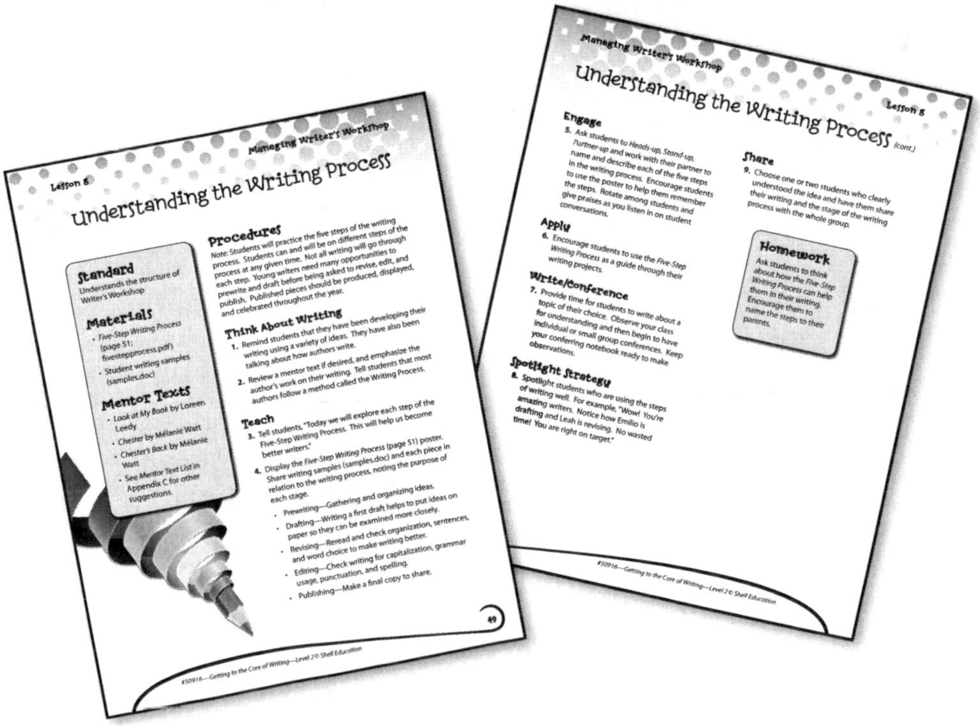

Managing Writer's Workshop

Lesson 8

Understanding the Writing Process

Standard
Understands the structure of Writer's Workshop

Materials
- *Five-Step Writing Process* (page 51; fivestepprocess.pdf)
- Student writing samples (samples.doc)

Mentor Texts
- *Look at My Book* by Loreen Leedy
- *Chester* by Mélanie Watt
- *Chester's Back* by Mélanie Watt
- See *Mentor Text List* in Appendix C for other suggestions.

Procedures
Note: Students will practice the five steps of the writing process. Students can and will be on different steps of the process at any given time. Not all writing will go through each step. Young writers need many opportunities to prewrite and draft before being asked to revise, edit, and publish. Published pieces should be produced, displayed, and celebrated throughout the year.

Think About Writing
1. Remind students that they have been developing their writing using a variety of ideas. They have also been talking about how authors write.
2. Review a mentor text if desired, and emphasize the author's work on their writing. Tell students that most authors follow a method called the Writing Process.

Teach
3. Tell students, "Today we will explore each step of the Five-Step Writing Process. This will help us become better writers."
4. Display the *Five-Step Writing Process* (page 51) poster. Share writing samples (samples.doc) and each piece in relation to the writing process, noting the purpose of each stage.
   - Prewriting—Gathering and organizing ideas.
   - Drafting—Writing a first draft helps to put ideas on paper so they can be examined more closely.
   - Revising—Reread and check organization, sentences, and word choice to make writing better.
   - Editing—Check writing for capitalization, grammar usage, punctuation, and spelling.
   - Publishing—Make a final copy to share.

49

#50916—Getting to the Core of Writing—Level 2 © Shell Education

Managing Writer's Workshop

Understanding the Writing Process (cont.)

Lesson 8

Engage
5. Ask students to *Heads-up, Stand-up, Partner-up* and work with their partner to name and describe each of the five steps in the writing process. Encourage students to use the poster to help them remember the steps. Rotate among students and give praises as you listen in on student conversations.

Apply
6. Encourage students to use the *Five-Step Writing Process* as a guide through their writing projects.

Write/Conference
7. Provide time for students to write about a topic of their choice. Observe your class for understanding and then begin to have individual or small group conferences. Keep your conferring notebook ready to make observations.

Spotlight Strategy
8. Spotlight students who are using the steps of writing well. For example, "Wow! You're amazing writers. Notice how Emilio is drafting and Leah is revising. No wasted time! You are right on target."

Share
9. Choose one or two students who clearly understood the idea and have them share their writing and the stage of the writing process with the whole group.

Homework
Ask students to think about how the *Five-Step Writing Process* can help them in their writing. Encourage them to name the steps to their parents.

Implementing the Lessons *(cont.)*

Procedures and Notes—Special information and teaching tips, followed by the explicit directions for teaching the lesson.

Think About Writing—Students reconnect to past mini-lessons and teachers make authentic connections between reading and writing.

Standards and **Materials**—Indicates the areas of focus for the lesson and all materials needed.

Mentor Texts—Published writing that contains explicit and strong examples of the concepts addressed in the lesson. Use the recommended mentor text as a read-aloud during your reading block or quickly review it during Writer's Workshop. During writing block, focus on small samples of text that match the mini-lesson skill. Recommended mentor texts are suggested as part of each lesson. Alternative suggestions can be found in Appendix C (page 250) or on the Teacher Resource CD (mentortextlist.pdf).

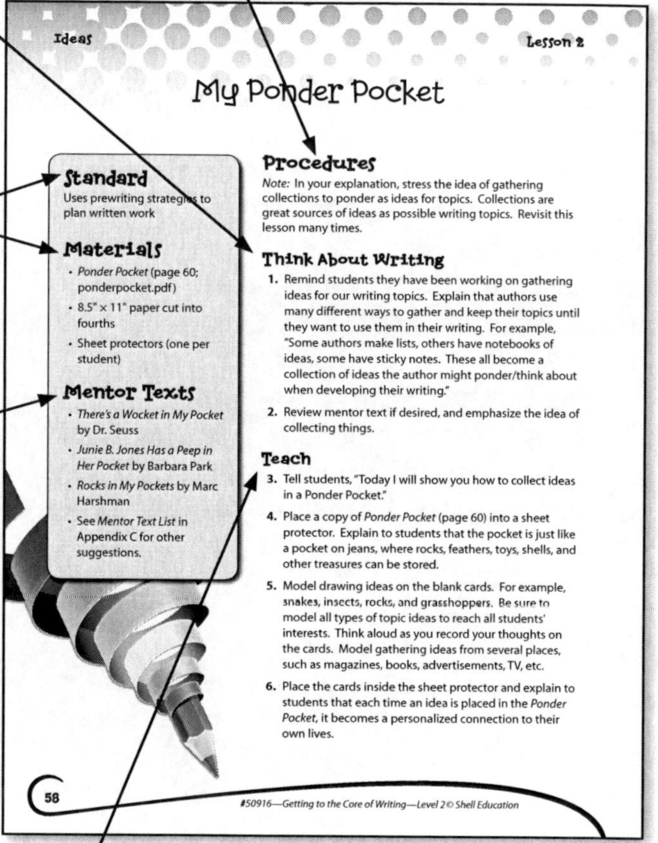
Ideas Lesson 2

My Ponder Pocket

Standard
Uses prewriting strategies to plan written work

Materials
- *Ponder Pocket* (page 60; ponderpocket.pdf)
- 8.5" × 11" paper cut into fourths
- Sheet protectors (one per student)

Mentor Texts
- *There's a Wocket in My Pocket* by Dr. Seuss
- *Junie B. Jones Has a Peep in Her Pocket* by Barbara Park
- *Rocks in My Pockets* by Marc Harshman
- See *Mentor Text List* in Appendix C for other suggestions.

Procedures
Note: In your explanation, stress the idea of gathering collections to ponder as ideas for topics. Collections are great sources of ideas as possible writing topics. Revisit this lesson many times.

Think About Writing
1. Remind students they have been working on gathering ideas for our writing topics. Explain that authors use many different ways to gather and keep their topics until they want to use them in their writing. For example, "Some authors make lists, others have notebooks of ideas, some have sticky notes. These all become a collection of ideas the author might ponder/think about when developing their writing."
2. Review mentor text if desired, and emphasize the idea of collecting things.

Teach
3. Tell students, "Today I will show you how to collect ideas in a Ponder Pocket."
4. Place a copy of *Ponder Pocket* (page 60) into a sheet protector. Explain to students that the pocket is just like a pocket on jeans, where rocks, feathers, toys, shells, and other treasures can be stored.
5. Model drawing ideas on the blank cards. For example, snakes, insects, rocks, and grasshoppers. Be sure to model all types of topic ideas to reach all students' interests. Think aloud as you record your thoughts on the cards. Model gathering ideas from several places, such as magazines, books, advertisements, TV, etc.
6. Place the cards inside the sheet protector and explain to students that each time an idea is placed in the *Ponder Pocket*, it becomes a personalized connection to their own lives.

58 #50916—Getting to the Core of Writing—Level 2© Shell Education

Teach—Supports students through demonstration and modeling to help students elevate their level of writing.

Implementing the Lessons *(cont.)*

Engage—Students will talk to each other about what they will apply in their writing. Talk time is short, intense, and focused. Teacher monitors, observes, and offers supportive comments.

Spotlight Strategy—Teacher points out students' efforts and successes, emphasizing a skill or specific task to further student understanding.

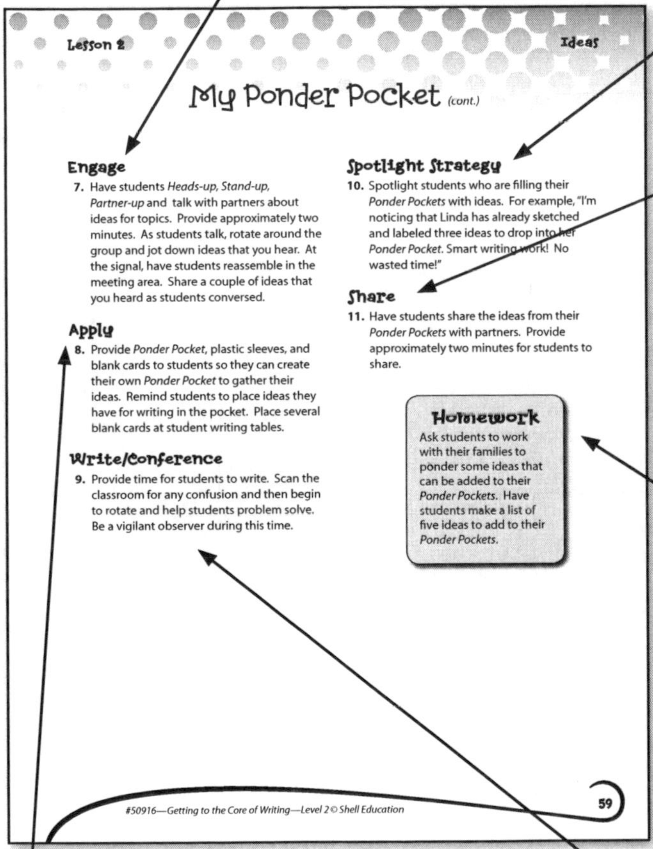
Lesson 2 Ideas

My Ponder Pocket *(cont.)*

Engage

7. Have students *Heads-up, Stand-up, Partner-up* and talk with partners about ideas for topics. Provide approximately two minutes. As students talk, rotate around the group and jot down ideas that you hear. At the signal, have students reassemble in the meeting area. Share a couple of ideas that you heard as students conversed.

Apply

8. Provide *Ponder Pocket*, plastic sleeves, and blank cards to students so they can create their own *Ponder Pocket* to gather their ideas. Remind students to place ideas they have for writing in the pocket. Place several blank cards at student writing tables.

Write/Conference

9. Provide time for students to write. Scan the classroom for any confusion and then begin to rotate and help students problem solve. Be a vigilant observer during this time.

Spotlight Strategy

10. Spotlight students who are filling their *Ponder Pockets* with ideas. For example, "I'm noticing that Linda has already sketched and labeled three ideas to drop into her *Ponder Pocket*. Smart writing work! No wasted time!"

Share

11. Have students share the ideas from their *Ponder Pockets* with partners. Provide approximately two minutes for students to share.

Homework

Ask students to work with their families to ponder some ideas that can be added to their *Ponder Pockets*. Have students make a list of five ideas to add to their *Ponder Pockets*.

#50916—Getting to the Core of Writing—Level 2 © Shell Education 59

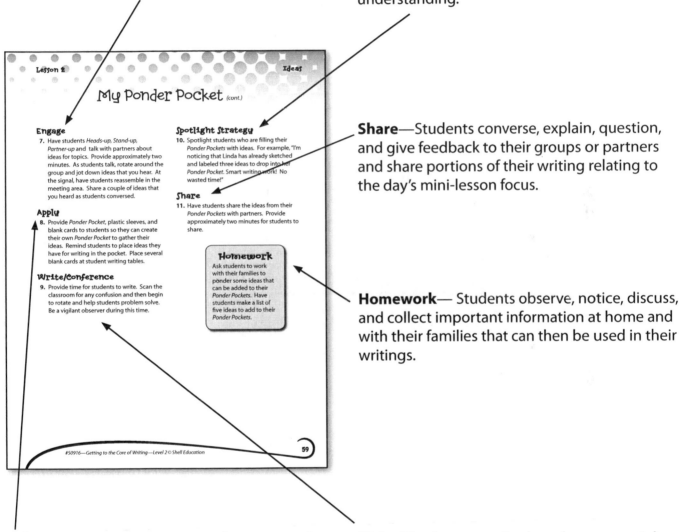

Share—Students converse, explain, question, and give feedback to their groups or partners and share portions of their writing relating to the day's mini-lesson focus.

Homework— Students observe, notice, discuss, and collect important information at home and with their families that can then be used in their writings.

Apply—Students will practice what was taught in the mini-lesson, develop independence, and take ownership of their writing. Teacher restates the mini-lesson concept to solidify it for students.

Write/Conference—Students have essential, independent practice time. Teacher confers with students in one-on-one or small-group settings.

Implementing Writer's Workshop

Writer's Workshop-at-a-Glance

This chart provides an at-a-glance overview of the Writer's Workshop format provided in *Getting to the Core of Writing*. It can be a helpful tool to use when planning instruction.

Component	Time	Description
Mini Lesson	5–15 minutes	Lesson plan subsections include: • Think About Writing • Teach • Engage • Apply

Writing Practice	15–30 minutes	Lesson plan subsections include:
		• Write/Conference
		    • Praise accomplishments
		    • Make a teaching point
		    • Use Conferring Log
		• Spotlight Strategies

Sharing	5–15 minutes	Lesson plan subsections include:
		• Share
		    • Whole/small group
		    • Partners
		    • Compliment and comment
		• Homework

The Writing Conference

Writing conferences are most successful when they occur as a conversation between two writers who are simply talking about writing. It is a time to value students as writers, to differentiate instruction, to teach new strategies, and to gather information for forming instructional decisions. Anderson (2000) notes that a conference conversation basically includes two parts: conversation based upon the student's current writing and conversation based on what will help him or her become a better writer. Katie Wood Ray (2001) and Lucy Calkins (2003) tell us conferring is hard! It is one part of the day that is a bit unknown. When conferring one-on-one with young writers, there is no script—no specific plan developed prior to the meeting. That is a strong deterrent that can keep many teachers from stepping into the conferring role during Writer's Workshop.

Following Calkins' dictum: "Conferring is the heart of Writer's Workshop" (2003, VIII), the sharing of information in conference conversation over the development of a specific writing piece is the very heart of teaching writing. Although difficult at times, especially at first, even the smallest conversation lets your students know you are interested in them as writers and helps nudge them forward in their writing development. Just as students become better writers by writing, you will only become better at conferring by conferring. The sincerity with which you approach this task will not only affect your students' writing future but also your sense of accomplishment as a teacher.

Although the content of the conference conversation is unknown, the conference structure is predictable. The four phases of a conference structure are:

1. Observe
2. Praise
3. Guide
4. Connect

First, study to determine what the writer knows, what the writer is trying to do, and what the writer needs to learn. Next, provide praise. Then, develop a teaching point and guide and encourage the writer to practice that teaching point. Lastly, stress the importance of using what was learned in future writing.

The Writing Conference *(cont.)*

Included in Appendix A and on the Teacher Resource CD are additional resources dedicated to the subject of conferring with students.

- **Essential Materials**—Use this list to assemble a "toolkit" of items you can carry with you as you conference with students.
- **Mini-Lesson Log**—Keep a record of the mini-lessons taught to serve as a reminder of writing strategies and crafts students have been exposed to during whole-group instruction (minilessonlog.pdf).
- **Conference Log**—This conference form serves as a good starting point and makes it easy to view your entire class at one glance. It is a simple summary of the conference listing the name, date, praise, and teaching point. See pages 235–241 in Appendix A for more information on conferring steps. Some teachers prefer a separate conference page for each student as they become more familiar with the conferring process (conferencelog.pdf).
- **Conference Countdown**—This page lists simple reminders of salient points to consider during writing conferences (conferencecountdown.pdf).

When you take the time to have a conversation, you are sending a message that you care enough to listen and communicate. With so much emphasis on testing achievement, it is important to stay committed to teaching the writer and not just the work of the writer. Carl Anderson (2000) tells us that student efforts and achievements are most likely not due to the questions we ask, the feedback we give, or our teaching. He states, "In the end, the success of a conference often rests on the extent to which students sense we are genuinely interested in them as writers—and as individuals."

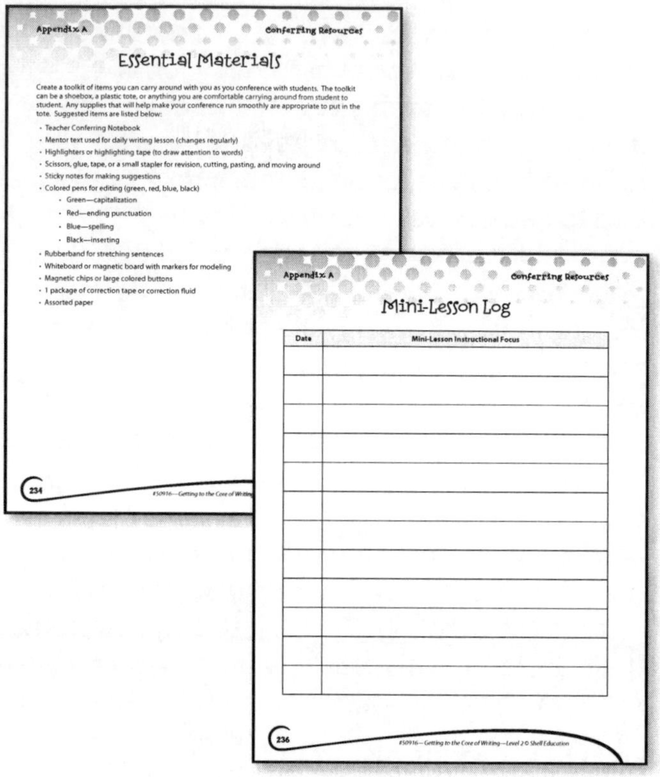
Appendix A — Conferring Resources

Essential Materials

Create a toolkit of items you can carry around with you as you conference with students. The toolkit can be a shoebox, a plastic tote, or anything you are comfortable carrying around from student to student. Any supplies that will help make your conference run smoothly are appropriate to put in the tote. Suggested items are listed below:

- Teacher Conferring Notebook
- Mentor text used for daily writing lesson (changes regularly)
- Highlighters or highlighting tape (to draw attention to words)
- Scissors, glue, tape, or a small stapler for revision, cutting, pasting, and moving around
- Sticky notes for making suggestions
- Colored pens for editing (green, red, blue, black)
  - Green—capitalization
  - Red—ending punctuation
  - Blue—spelling
  - Black—inserting
- Rubberband for stretching sentences
- Whiteboard or magnetic board with markers for modeling
- Magnetic chips or large colored buttons
- 1 package of correction tape or correction fluid
- Assorted paper

234

Appendix A — Conferring Resources

Mini-Lesson Log

Date	Mini-Lesson Instructional Focus

236 #50916—Getting to the Core of Writing—Level 2 © Shell Education

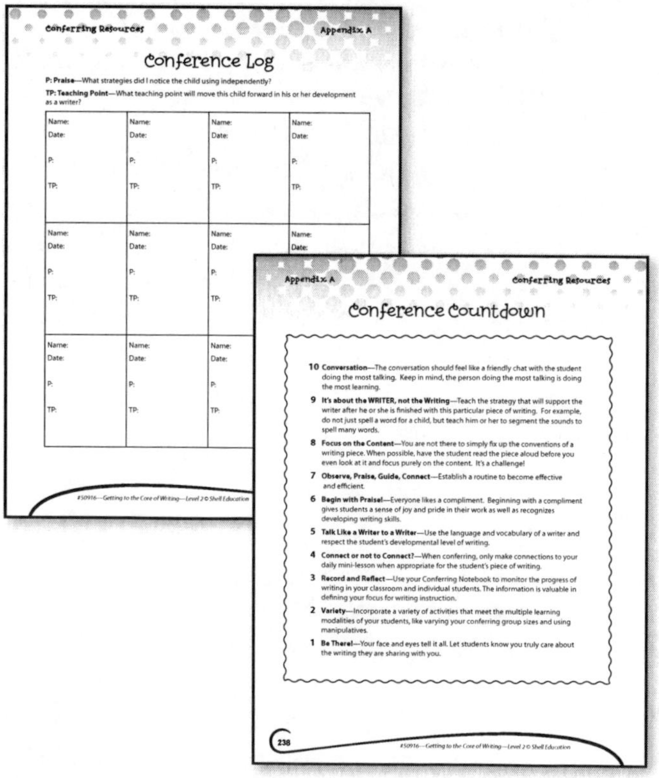
Conferring Resources — Appendix A

Conference Log

P: Praise—What strategies did I notice the child using independently?

TP: Teaching Point—What teaching point will move this child forward in his or her development as a writer?

Name: Date: P: TP:	Name: Date: P: TP:	Name: Date: P: TP:	Name: Date: P: TP:
Name: Date: P: TP:	Name: Date: P: TP:	Name: Date: P: TP:	Name: Date:
Name: Date: P: TP:	Name: Date: P: TP:	Name: Date: P: TP:	

#50916—Getting to the Core of Writing—Level 2 © Shell Education

Appendix A — Conferring Resources

Conference Countdown

10 **Conversation**—The conversation should feel like a friendly chat with the student doing the most talking. Keep in mind, the person doing the most talking is doing the most learning.

9 **It's about the WRITER, not the Writing**—Teach the strategy that will support the writer after he or she is finished with this particular piece of writing. For example, do not just spell a word for a child, but teach him or her to segment the sounds to spell many words.

8 **Focus on the Content**—You are not there to simply fix up the conventions of a writing piece. When possible, have the student read the piece aloud before you even look at it and focus purely on the content. It's a challenge!

7 **Observe, Praise, Guide, Connect**—Establish a routine to become effective and efficient.

6 **Begin with Praise!**—Everyone likes a compliment. Beginning with a compliment gives students a sense of joy and pride in their work as well as recognizes developing writing skills.

5 **Talk Like a Writer to a Writer**—Use the language and vocabulary of a writer and respect the student's developmental level of writing.

4 **Connect or not to Connect?**—When conferring, only make connections to your daily mini-lesson when appropriate for the student's piece of writing.

3 **Record and Reflect**—Use your Conferring Notebook to monitor the progress of writing in your classroom and individual students. The information is valuable in defining your focus for writing instruction.

2 **Variety**—Incorporate a variety of activities that meet the multiple learning modalities of your students, like varying your conferring group sizes and using manipulatives.

1 **Be There!**—Your face and eyes tell it all. Let students know you truly care about the writing they are sharing with you.

238 #50916—Getting to the Core of Writing—Level 2 © Shell Education

Top 10 Tips for Creating Successful Writers

1. **Schedule Writer's Workshop Daily.** Scheduling Writer's Workshop daily grants valuable, necessary time for students to practice and grow as writers.
2. **Establish and Commit to Routines.** Life is good when everyone knows what to do and when to do it. Take the time to establish foundational routines that will impact your Writer's Workshop throughout the year. Revisit Managing Writer's Workshop lessons as the need arises.
3. **Model, Model, Model!** Modeling gives direct instruction while scaffolding for young writers. Use these steps to model specific skills and behaviors with students (*I* is the teacher and *you* is the student) (Pearson and Gallager 1983):
   - I do, you watch.
   - I do, you help.
   - You do, I help.
   - You do, I watch.
4. **Read, Read, Read!** Reading a variety of texts through the eyes of a writer exposes students to the craft of the author and encourages students to explore new avenues of writing.
5. **Display and Celebrate!** Walking down the hallway in a school setting, you can usually get a good idea of the writing that is going on in each classroom. The more students write, the more comfortable they become, and they will want to show off their work. Celebrate student writing and recognize students as writers.
6. **Confer Weekly.** This is your opportunity to learn about each student's writing development. Encourage, guide, and listen.
7. **Share, Share, Share!** Young children love to share everything. Sharing during Writer's Workshop enhances their sense of importance as a writer.
8. **Involve and Inform Parents.** Writing work is an automatic means of connecting with parents. Wall displays of writing samples show parents how you value their child's writing effort. Hold an Author's Tea and invite parents so they can see first-hand the important writing work of their child.
9. **Be Flexible and Reflect.** A well-planned lesson may fall flat. So, go back to the drawing board and ask yourself, "Why?" "What happened?" How can you reteach to make the right connections for students? Take time to reflect on your teaching and student learning.
10. **Set High Expectations.** Be specific with your expectations and articulate clearly what you would like the students to accomplish. Believe in your students' abilities and challenge them to succeed. Every child can be an author.

Correlation to Standards

Shell Education is committed to producing educational materials that are research- and standards-based. In this effort, we have correlated all of our products to the academic standards of all 50 United States, the District of Columbia, the Department of Defense Dependent Schools, and all Canadian provinces. We have also correlated to the **Common Core State Standards**.

How To Find Standards Correlations

To print a customized correlation report of this product for your state, visit our website at **http://www.shelleducation.com** and follow the on-screen directions. If you require assistance in printing correlation reports, please contact Customer Service at 1-877-777-3450.

Purpose and Intent of Standards

Legislation mandates that all states adopt academic standards that identify the skills students will learn in kindergarten through grade twelve. Many states also have standards for Pre-K. This same legislation sets requirements to ensure the standards are detailed and comprehensive.

Standards are designed to focus instruction and guide adoption of curricula. Standards are statements that describe the criteria necessary for students to meet specific academic goals. They define the knowledge, skills, and content students should acquire at each level. Standards are also used to develop standardized tests to evaluate students' academic progress. Teachers are required to demonstrate how their lessons meet state standards. State standards are used in the development of all of our products, so educators can be assured they meet the academic requirements of each state.

McREL Compendium

We use the Mid-continent Research for Education and Learning (McREL) Compendium to create standards correlations. Each year, McREL analyzes state standards and revises the compendium. By following this procedure, McREL is able to produce a general compilation of national standards. Each lesson in this product is based on one or more McREL standard. The chart on the following pages and on the Teacher Resource CD (standards.pdf) lists each standard taught in this product and the page number(s) for the corresponding lesson(s).

TESOL Standards

The lessons in this book promote English language development for English language learners. The standards listed on the Teacher Resource CD (standards.pdf) support the language objectives presented throughout the lessons.

Common Core State Standards

The lessons in this book are aligned to the Common Core State Standards (CCSS). The standards on pages 25–26 and on the Teacher Resource CD (standards.pdf) support the objectives presented throughout the lessons.

Correlation to Standards (cont.)

McREL Standards

Standard	Lesson
Understands the structure of Writer's Workshop	My Writing Folder (page 31); Looks Like, Sounds Like, Feels Like (page 33); Guidelines for Writer's Workshop (page 36); Posture and Pencil Grip (page 39); Two-Inch Voices (page 41); Turn and Talk (page 43); Sharing (page 46); Understanding the Writing Process (page 49)
Prewriting: Uses strategies to plan written work	Ideas Thinking Chart (page 55); My Ponder Pocket (page 58); Getting Ideas from Literature (page 61); Important People in My Life (page 63); Important Places (page 66); My Heart Treasures (page 69); Amazing Animals (page 72); Things I know List (page 77)
Drafting and Revising: Uses strategies to draft and revise written work	Super Sentence Stems (page 83); Growing Sentences (page 87); Parts of a Sentence (page 89); What's Missing? (page 94); When and Where? (page 97); Rubber Band Sentences (page 99); And Then... (page 102); Fun with Sentence Variety (page 104); Writing Detective: Sentences (page 107)
Editing and Publishing: Uses strategies to edit and publish written work	Capital Rap (page 220); Rockin' Editors (page 223); My Editing Tools (page 226); Proper Punctuation (page 229); Editing with CUPS (page 231)
Uses strategies to organize written work	Poetry—Simple Acrostic (page 113); Poetry—Triante (page 115); Making Alphabet Books (page 118); My Hand Plan (page 120); Now, That's a Story! (page 126); Brilliant Beginnings (page 131); Excellent Endings (page 133); Telling, Sketching, and Writing Narrative Text (page 136); Writing a Letter (page 141); Addressing an Envelope (page 145); Informative: My 1-2-3 Report (page 147); I Know How To… (page 151)
Uses writing and other methods to describe familiar persons, places, objects, or experiences	Using Our Senses (page 161); Word Power (page 168); A Rainbow of Words (page 170); Sparkling Synonym Stars (page 185); Lucky Me Similes (page 193)
Writes in a variety of forms or genres	Poetry—Simple Acrostic (page 113); Poetry—Triante (page 115); Making Alphabet Books (page 118); My Hand Plan (page 120); Now, That's a Story! (page 126); Telling, Sketching, and Writing Narrative Text (page 136); Writing a Letter (page 141); Addressing an Envelope (page 145); Informative: My 1-2-3 Report (page 147); I Know How To… (page 151)

Correlation to Standards (cont.)

McREL Standards (cont.)

Standard	Lesson
Writes expressive compositions (uses an individual, authentic voice)	More Than Happy, Sad, and Mad (page 199); Voice Times Two (page 202)
Uses descriptive words to convey basic ideas	Using Our Senses (page 161); More Action Words (page 165); Word Power (page 168); A Rainbow of Words (page 170); Sounds All Around from A to Z (page 173); Awesome Adjectives (page 183); Sparkling Synonym Stars (page 185); Transition Words (page 188); Lucky Me Similes (page 193)
Uses complete sentences in written compositions	Parts of a Sentence (page 89); What's Missing? (page 94); When and Where? (page 97); Rubber Band Sentences (page 99); And Then... (page 102); Fun with Sentence Variety (page 104); Writing Detective: Sentences (page 107)
Uses verbs in written compositions	More Action Words (page 165)
Uses adjectives in written compositions	Awesome Adjectives (page 183)
Uses conventions of spelling in written compositions	Using High Frequency Words (page 157); Using Our Sound Charts (page 207); Count and Spell (page 217)
Uses conventions of capitalization in written compositions	Capital Rap (page 220); Rockin' Editors (page 223)
Uses conventions of punctuation in written compositions	Rockin' Editors (page 223); Proper Punctuation (page 229)

Correlation to Standards (cont.)

Common Core State Standards

The stated purpose of the Common Core State Standards (standards.pdf) is to guarantee that all students are prepared for college and career literacy as they leave high school. These standards indicate that all students need the ability to write logical opinions and informational texts with sound reasoning to support their findings. Previously, instruction in the primary grades focused primarily on narrative writing, limiting students' exposure to other forms of writing. *Getting to the Core of Writing* provides the fundamental writing skills to support students in their continued growth as writers, thus enabling them to enjoy continued success as the challenges presented by the spiraling curriculum become increasingly complex.

The structure of Writer's Workshop and the lessons in this book not only address the CCSS for writing, but Speaking and Listening Standards are also practiced during one-to-one, small-group, and whole-group class settings through the engaging and sharing components of the lesson format. Due to the reciprocal nature of reading and writing, *Getting to the Core of Writing* naturally meets many of the Common Core State Standards for Reading and for Language.

Standard	Lesson
Writing: Text Types and Purposes, W.2.1	Getting Ideas from Literature (page 61); Making Alphabet Books (page 118); My Hand Plan (page 120); Writing a Letter (page 141)
Writing: Text Types and Purposes, W.2.2	Getting Ideas from Literature (page 61); Amazing Animals (page 72); Making Alphabet Books (page 118); My Hand Plan (page 120); Writing a Letter (page 141); Informative: My 1-2-3 Report (page 147); I Know How To... (page 151)
Writing: Text Types and Purposes, W.2.3	Getting Ideas from Literature (page 61); My Hand Plan (page 120); Now, That's a Story! (page 126); Brilliant Beginnings (page 131); Excellent Endings (page 133); Telling, Sketching, and Writing Narrative Text (page 136); Writing a Letter (page 141)
Writing: Production and Distribution of Writing, W.2.5	All lessons
Writing: Research to Build and Present Knowledge, W.2.7	Getting Ideas from Literature (page 61); Making Alphabet Books (page 118); My Hand Plan (page 120); Informative: My 1-2-3 Report (page 147)
Writing: Research to Build and Present Knowledge, W.2.8	Getting Ideas from Literature (page 61); Amazing Animals (page 72); Things I Know List (page 77); My Hand Plan (page 120); I Know How To... (page 151)
Speaking and Listening: Comprehension and Collaboration, SL.2.1	All lessons

Correlation to Standards *(cont.)*

Common Core State Standards *(cont.)*

Standard	Lesson
Speaking and Listening: Comprehension and Collaboration, SL.2.2	All lessons
Speaking and Listening: Comprehension and Collaboration, SL.2.3	All lessons
Speaking and Listening: Presentation of Knowledge and Ideas, SL.2.4	My Hand Plan (page 120); Now, That's a Story! (page 126); Telling, Sketching, and Writing Narrative Text (page 136)
Speaking and Listening: Presentation of Knowledge and Ideas, SL.2.5	Telling, Sketching, and Writing Narrative Text (page 136); I Know How To... (page 151); More Than Happy, Sad, and Mad (page 199)
Speaking and Listening: Presentation of Knowledge and Ideas, SL.2.6	All lessons
Language: Conventions of Standard English, L.2.1	Super Sentence Stems (page 83); Growing Sentences (page 87); Parts of a Sentence (page 89); What's Missing? (page 94); When and Where? (page 97); Rubber Band Sentences (page 99); And Then... (page 102); Fun with Sentence Variety (page 104); Writing Detective: Sentences (page 107); Using High Frequency Words (page 157); More Action Words (page 165); Word Power (page 168); Awesome Adjectives (page 183)
Language: Conventions of Standard English, L.2.2	Using High Frequency Words (page 157); Using Our Sound Charts (page 207); Count and Spell (page 217); Capital Rap (page 220); Rockin' Editors (page 223); My Editing Tools (page 226); Proper Punctuation (page 229); Editing with CUPS (page 231)
Language: Vocabulary Acquisition and Use, L.2.3	All lessons
Language: Vocabulary Acquisition and Use, L.2.5	Using Our Senses (page 161); More Action Words (page 165); Word Power (page 168); A Rainbow of Words (page 170); Sounds All Around from A to Z (page 173); Awesome Adjectives (page 183); Sparkling Synonym Stars (page 185); More Than Happy, Sad, and Mad (page 199)
Language: Vocabulary Acquisition and Use, L.2.6	All lessons

Acknowledgments

We stand on the shoulders of national and world-renowned teachers of teachers-of-writing, such as our friend the late Donald Graves, Lucy Calkins, Ralph Fletcher, Donald Murry, Vicki Spandel, Ruth Culham, Katie Wood Ray, Carl Anderson, Charles Temple, Jean Gillet, Stephanie Harvey, Debbie Miller, Regie Routman, Marissa Moss, Steve Graham, and Connie Hebert to name a few, as well as the educators at Northwest Regional Educational Laboratory. Thank you. We are also truly grateful to the faculty at Auckland University, workshop leaders, and experiences with the teachers in New Zealand some 20 years ago who got us started.

While writing this series and in the past, there were frequent chats about writing and words of wisdom from Dona Rice, Sara Johnson, Jean Mann, Lois Bridges, and Tim Rasinski. Scores of teachers who read our manuscripts, praised our work, gave us confidence, and adjusted our missteps. We could not have succeeded without two super editors, Dona and Sara, and the great staff at Teacher Created Materials/ Shell Education.

We attribute much of what's good about our series to teachers who invited us into their classrooms. Over all the years that went into this project, there are too many people to list separately, but here's a sampling: Thank you to all the teachers and districts who allowed us to visit and model in your classrooms, try our materials, and listen to your insights as we refined our writing instruction. A special thank you to the teachers at Fayette, Logan, Mingo, Pocahontas, Upshur, Wood, Wirt, and Harrison County Schools. We owe special gratitude to French Creek Elementary, Mt. Hope Elementary, and Nutter Fort Elementary teachers. We can't forget the "Writing Teachers Club": Debbie Gaston, Tammy Musil, Judy McGinnis, Jenna Williams, Cheryl Bramble, Karen Vandergrift, Barb Compton, Whitney Fowler, and Jennifer Rome, who spent countless hours learning, questioning, and sharing ideas. "You really need to write a book," you said, and your words have made that happen. You and many others inspired us, including the WC Department of Teaching and Learning (especially Angle, Karen, Lesley, Marcia, Matt, M.C., and Wendy). We can't forget Jean Pearcy, Miles 744, the talented teachers of the West Clermont Schools, the 4 B's (Bailey, Bergen, Blythe, and Brynne), Candy, Mrs. Hendel, the lab rats (Becky, Mary, Mike, Sally, Sharon, and Vera), and the littlest singers at CHPC. Last but not least, a special thank you to Rick and Ro Jensen, Bill McIntyre, and Carolyn Meigs for years of support, and to Dawna Vecchio, Loria Reid, Terry Morrison, Laura Trent, Jeanie Bennett, Millie Shelton, Therese E., and Kathy Snyder for listening, cheering, and celebrating!

Many thanks to administrators who provided opportunities, leadership, and support for teachers as they explored the implementation of writing workshop and applied new teaching strategies: superintendents Beverly Kingery, Susan Collins, director Kay Devono, principals Allen Gorrell, Frank Marino, Joann Gilbert, Pattae Kinney, Jody Decker, Vickie Luchuck, Jody Johnson, and Wilma Dale. We owe many thanks to WVDE Cadre for continuous professional development—you brought us together.

We owe immense gratitude for having been blessed with the company of children who have graced us with their writing, creativity, and wisdom. Thank you to hundreds of children who have shared marvelous writing and insight.

Finally, for never-ending patience, love and support we thank our families: Clint, Luke, and Lindsay; Lanty, Jamey, John, Charlie, Jacki, Jeffrey; and Bill. You all are the best!

About the Authors

Richard Gentry, Ph.D., is nationally recognized for his work in spelling, phase theory, beginning reading and writing, and teaching literacy in elementary school. A former university professor and elementary school teacher, his most recent book is *Raising Confident Readers: How to Teach Your Child to Read and Write—From Baby to Age 7*. Other books include topics such as beginning reading and writing, assessment, and spelling. He also blogs for *Psychology Today* magazine. Richard has spoken at state and national conferences and has provided teachers with inspiring strategies to use in their classroom.

Jan McNeel, M.A.Ed., is a forty-year veteran of education and leader of staff development throughout West Virginia and Maryland. Formerly a Reading First Cadre Member for the West Virginia Department of Education and Title I classroom and Reading Recovery teacher, Jan consults with schools and districts across the state. Jan's studies of literacy acquisition at the Auckland University in New Zealand serve as the foundation of her expertise in reading and writing. Her practical strategies and useful ideas are designed to make reading and writing connections that are teacher-friendly and easy to implement. She has won awards for her excellent work as a master teacher and has presented her work in early literacy at state, regional, and national conferences.

Vickie Wallace-Nesler, M.A.Ed., has been in education for 30 years as an itinerant, Title 1, and regular classroom teacher. Through her current work as a Literacy Coach for grades K–5, conference presenter, and literacy consultant, Vickie brings true insight into the "real world" of educators and their challenges. That experience, along with Master's degrees in both Elementary Education and Reading, National Board certification in Early and Middle Literacy for Reading and Language Arts, and studies at The Teachers College Reading and Writing Project at Columbia University, drive her passion for helping all teachers and students develop a love for learning.

Managing Writer's Workshop

Writer's Workshop begins on the first day of school and is taught every day thereafter. Establishing routines is critical to developing a successful, productive writing time. Therefore, these lessons should be focused on early in the year and revisited them when necessary. Managing Writer's Workshop mini-lessons require time and repetition to familiarize students with the writing workshop. A wide range of topics can be addressed during these mini-lessons. Repeat mini-lessons as needed, especially in regard to *Guidelines for Writer's Workshop* (Lesson 3) and having students share their writing with partners. These lessons will be crucial to having Writer's Workshop run smoothly and successfully for the rest of the year. Ensure students are responding to those lessons in the ways you want them to or spend additional time teaching and modeling. Observe your class to discover the needs of your particular students. Lessons in this section include:

My Writing Folder

Standard

Understands the structure of Writer's Workshop

Materials

- Two-pocket folders
- Green and red dot stickers

Mentor Texts

- *Author: A True Story* by Helen Lester
- *Look at My Book* by Loreen Leedy
- See *Mentor Text List* in Appendix C for other suggestions.

Procedures

Note: Building the writing folder is an ongoing process. As you introduce new tools like sound charts, or *My Editing Tools*, word lists, etc., they are added to student folders. Students also keep their writing in their folders. Writing will be sorted monthly into: take home, keep, or file in portfolios.

Think About Writing

1. Introduce the concept of Writer's Workshop to students. For example, "During this time, we will explore and practice becoming writers. We will meet together, practice writing, and share our writing with each other. This time will be called Writer's Workshop. We will use many of the same tools a real author uses to write. By the end of the year, you will be publishing real books, like alphabet and picture books."
2. Review mentor text if desired, and emphasize the process of writing that an author goes through to develop a book.

Teach

3. Tell students, "Today, I will show you how to use your writing folder to help organize your writing materials." Explain to students that their folders are writing tools and the place they will keep the materials that will help them as they write. Have students place a green dot sticker inside the front cover of their folders. Then, have students place a red dot sticker on the inside of the back of the folder.
4. Explain that the dots will help students separate their work that is still in progress from their finished work. Writing that is finished will be placed into the red dot side. Writing pieces they still need to work on, stay on the green dot side.

My Writing Folder *(cont.)*

Engage

5. Tell students that they will have a chance to talk to partners about writing each day. Have students stand or sit quietly and talk to the person next to them about what they will talk about when they are speaking to each other about their writing.

Apply

6. Ask students to think about how their writing folders will keep them organized.
7. Tell students to draw a picture of themselves and write a story about their picture.

Write/Conference

8. Provide students time to draw and write their stories. Conferencing with students will begin later on, once procedures are firmly in place. As students work, rotate around the room. Help any students who need assistance get settled into the writing time. Then, begin to notice and compliment student writing. Remember to give many praises.

Spotlight Strategy

9. Spotlight great student writing or effort. For example, "Brilliant writing! During this time, I will be spotlighting how you stay focused and use time wisely and your writing expertise. I will be using a flashlight to shine on students who gave it their best." Show the spotlight to everyone to teach procedures.

Share

10. Have students read what they wrote to themselves quietly. Rotate among the students as they whisper.

Homework

Ask students to tell their parents about their writing folders and how they will be used in Writer's Workshop.

Looks Like, Sounds Like, Feels Like

Standard

Understands the structure of Writer's Workshop

Materials

- Chart paper
- Markers
- *Sample Looks Like, Sounds Like, Feels Like Anchor Chart* (page 35; lookssoundsfeelschart.pdf)

Mentor Texts

- *Swimmy* by Leo Lionni
- *How I Spent My Summer Vacation* by Mark Teague
- *Today Was a Terrible Day* by Patricia Reilly Giff
- See *Mentor Text List* in Appendix C for other suggestions.

Procedures

Note: Continue each day to build this chart until you reach your expectations. Revisit the chart each month.

Think About Writing

1. Tell students that in Writer's Workshop, writers spend their time learning how to get their important ideas down on paper. To do this, we need to build a list of helpful expectations so we can work together as a writing community.
2. Review mentor text if desired, and emphasize the need to work together and express ideas through writing.

Teach

3. Tell students, "Today, we will think about what our writing time together should look like." Explain to students that if a visitor walked into the room during Writer's Workshop time the visitor should see students busy drawing, writing, coloring, thinking, or talking to someone about writing.
4. Tell students they will help create an anchor chart to show what Writer's Workshop will look like, sound like, and feel like. Divide the sheet of chart paper into three columns and label the columns *Looks Like*, *Sounds Like*, and *Feels Like*.
5. Draw a picture of two eyes at the top of the first column and list a few items to describe what the classroom should look like when someone walks into the room during Writer's Workshop. Do this as a modeled writing lesson, thinking aloud the reasoning behind your suggestions.

Looks Like, Sounds Like, Feels Like *(cont.)*

Engage

6. Have students turn to someone who is near them and talk about another way Writer's Workshop may look. Add any additional ideas generated from students to the anchor chart. Suggested ideas are provided in the *Sample Looks Like, Sounds Like, Feels Like Anchor Chart* (page 35); however, the chart is most powerful when the majority of ideas are student-generated.
7. Draw a picture of an ear in the next column. Talk with students about what Writer's Workshop will sound like. Repeat steps 5 and 6 to fill in ideas for what Writer's Workshop will sound like. You may wish to allocate one day per column in order to fully develop each concept.
8. Draw a picture of a hand in the last column. Complete the last column on the anchor chart by repeating steps 5 and 6 for what Writer's Workshop will feel like.

Apply

9. Tell students to draw a picture of a special friend or someone they love and write a few details.

Write/Conference

10. Provide time for students to draw and write. Scan your group for potential problems and begin rotating among students with your conferring notebook and begin to notice and compliment your student writers. Remember to give affirmations galore.

Spotlight Strategy

11. Spotlight great student effort. For example, "Stop! Look! Listen! What an amazing picture of a classroom at work in writing. Give yourself a pat on the back. Great self-regulation! You are magnificent at controlling your own behavior."

Share

12. Have students share their writing with someone close by. Ask students to take turns and read their writing. Encourage students to be sure to listen carefully and compliment the writer, "I really like the way you…"

Homework

Ask students to tell their parents what they are doing in Writer's Workshop at school.

Sample Looks Like, Sounds Like, Feels Like Anchor Chart

Our Writer's Workshop...

Looks Like	Sounds Like	Feels Like
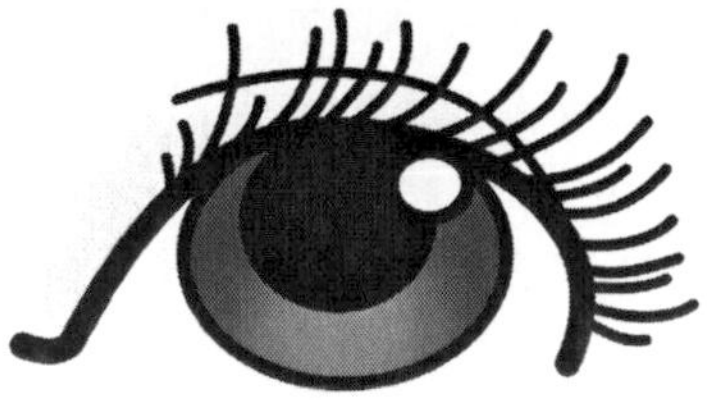	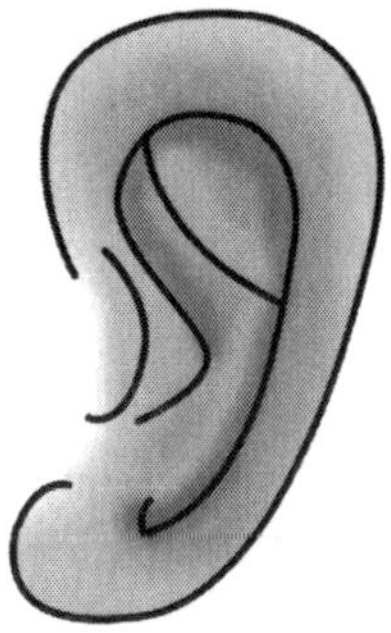	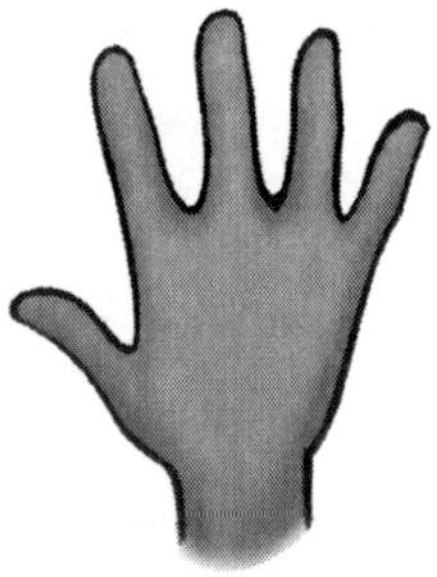
• Pencils, all supplies ready • Journals/folders/notebooks • Crayons/art paper • Word walls • Mentor texts available • Phonics charts/alphabet charts • Labeled items in the room • Author's chair • Partners/small groups • Smiling faces • Writing tool kits • Student engagement • Vocabulary list • Writing prompts • Turn and talk • Productive • Organized • Writing • Busy	• Buzz, hum, beehive • Two-inch voices • Conversation/oral language • Quiet during thinking and teaching phase • "Hum" when sharing w/ partners, triads, quads • Busy • Children making decisions • Learning is happening • Questioning	• Comfortable, natural, happy • Nonthreatening, risk taking • Purposeful • Successful • Confident • Excited • Relaxed • Proud • Comfortable sharing thoughts • "I can" attitude

Guidelines for Writer's Workshop

Standard

Understands the structure of Writer's Workshop

Materials

- *Guidelines for Writer's Workshop* (page 38; guidelineswritersws.pdf)
- Chart paper
- Markers

Mentor Texts

- *I Can Write! A Book by Me, Myself* by Theo LeSieg
- *Howard B. Wigglebottom Learns to Listen* by Howard Binkow
- See *Mentor Text List* in Appendix C for other suggestions.

Procedures

Note: You will need to repeat this lesson until procedure is in place. Assign partners for discussion.

Think About Writing

1. Explain to students that Writer's Workshop follows guidelines and routines in order to create a sense of order and efficiency. In Writer's Workshop, they will learn about the rigor and personal organization it takes to become a good writer.
2. Review a mentor text if desired, and review the need for order and listening skills in a classroom, especially during Writer's Workshop. For example, remind students how Howard learned the importance of listening in *Howard B. Wigglebottom Learns to Listen.*

Teach

3. Tell students, "Today, we will create guidelines for Writer's Workshop. Explain to students that writers follow rules or guidelines during Writer's Workshop, so they make efficient use of the time. Tell students that since the guidelines will make them smart writers, the acronym SMART is used to help them remember the guidelines.
4. Display *Guidelines for Writer's Workshop* (page 38) or create an anchor chart with guidelines for students to follow. Adjust the guidelines as needed to fit the procedures and needs of your class. The guidelines can be written on an anchor chart and posted in the classroom or can be copied and added to the students' writing folders.

Engage

5. Tell students they will work with partners to review the guidelines for Writer's Workshop. Explicitly model for students what they will do and say when they turn to their partners.

Guidelines for Writer's Workshop *(cont.)*

6. Have students turn and talk to partners about the guidelines for Writer's Workshop. Encourage students to use their five fingers, one finger for each letter of the word *SMART* and the anchor chart to guide their discussions. Allow two minutes for students to talk. As they talk, move from group to group and take notes of student responses.
7. Gather students back together, review the guidelines, and share your observations.

Apply

8. Remind students that the guidelines will help us spend our time more efficiently. The expectation for writing in the class is that the guidelines are followed so everyone in the class is able to use the Writer's Workshop time well.
9. Tell students to draw a picture of something that happened at home or school.

Write/Conference

10. Provide students time to draw their pictures. Conferencing with students will begin once procedures are firmly in place. Help any students who need assistance getting settled into the writing time. As students work, rotate around the room. Notice and compliment writing as students work. Remember to give many affirmations to your authors.

Spotlight Strategy

11. Spotlight something you noticed that went well today. For example, "Jesse did something brilliant. He went to his seat and immediately started to work in his writing folder."

Share

12. Have students turn and talk to the person seated nearest them about their pictures, showing the important writing guidelines. Remind students to tell what and why the SMART guidelines for Writer's Workshop will help them become excellent writers. Provide about two minutes for sharing.

Homework

Ask students to take a couple of minutes to think about how knowing what is expected of them will make them more disciplined (self-regulated) writers. Tell students to share their ideas with their parents.

Guidelines for Writer's Workshop

SMART Writers

Speak in two-inch voices.

Move about quietly.

Always work!

Respect others.

Tidy up.

Posture and Pencil Grip

Standard

Understands the structure of Writer's Workshop

Materials

- *Writing Paper* (Appendix D; writingpaper.pdf)
- Pencil

Mentor Texts

- *Library Mouse* by Daniel Kirk
- *Look at My Book* by Loreen Leedy
- See *Mentor Text List* in Appendix C for other suggestions.

Procedures

Note: You will need to repeat this lesson until procedure is in place. Lesson will begin in a group meeting through the modeling phase, and students will move to seats for the important practice of pencil grip and posture.

Think About Writing

1. Remind students about the classroom expectations for Writer's Workshop by reviewing the anchor charts they helped create. Tell students they will continue to practice following the Writer's Workshop guidelines and begin learning about how authors write.
2. Review the mentor text and emphasize the joy of writing.

Teach

3. Tell students, "Today, I will share two important ideas you must understand to be successful writers: pencil grip and posture." Tell students that writers sit with good posture, in an upright position so that oxygen can flow to the brain. Model how to sit up tall with the chair pushed in and both feet on the floor.
4. Explain to students that writers also hold the pencil correctly. Explain that one way to pick up the pencil, so it is held correctly is to *Pinch and Roll* the pencil.
    - Begin with the pencil on the desk so the lead is pointing to them.
    - Pinch the pencil with their thumbs and pointer fingers.
    - Flip the pencil backward so that it is cupped softly between the curve of the thumb and the pointer finger. The pencil should rest gently on the middle finger. (When placed correctly, the pencil will be placed with the thumb on the left of the pencil, the pointer on top of the pencil, and the middle finger gently supporting the pencil.)

Posture and Pencil Grip *(cont.)*

Engage

5. Have students move to their desks to practice pencil grip and posture with their partners. Encourage students to provide support to their partners as they get the feel of proper posture and pencil grip.

Apply

6. Ask students to practice the proper posture and pencil grip as they write. Tell them that this will help as they practice letter formations and begin writing letters, words, sentences, and stories.

Write/Conference

7. Distribute *Writing Paper* (Appendix D). Provide time for students to draw, sketch, or write about a topic of their choice for three to five minutes. As they work, rotate among students and make observations about posture and pencil grip. Keep notes in your conferring notebook and offer lots of praise.

Spotlight Strategy

8. Spotlight great pencil gripping and good posture. For example, "What brilliant writers you are. You have already taken ownership of this important writing time. Just notice how Kim sits with the correct posture." Choose several students to model correct posture and pencil grip. Remember to use this time to celebrate successes.

Share

9. Have students meet with partners to share what they wrote today. Provide approximately two minutes for partners to talk. From teacher observations, choose one or two students who clearly understood the idea and have them share with the whole group.

Homework

Ask students to think about how important it is to use correct posture and pencil grip. Have them tell their parents about this important learning. Tell them to be ready to practice posture and pencil grip tomorrow when they return to workshop time.

Two-Inch Voices

Standard

Understands the structure of Writer's Workshop

Materials

- *Sample Looks Like, Sounds Like, Feels Like Anchor Chart* (page 35)
- Marker
- Ruler

Mentor Texts

- *My Mouth is a Volcano!* Julia Cook
- See *Mentor Text List* in Appendix C for other suggestions.

Procedures

Note: You will need to repeat this lesson until procedure is in place.

Think About Writing

1. Tell students that as we begin to get our Writer's Workshop moving forward, we must actively think about using a noise level that is acceptable during mini-lessons, group writing, conferencing, and sharing.
2. Review a mentor text if desired, and emphasize the need for order and use of appropriate noise level in a classroom.
3. Display and review the *Looks Like, Sounds Like, Feels Like Anchor Chart created using the Sample Looks Like, Sounds Like, Feels Like Anchor Chart* (page 35). Tell students, "Today, you will think about what Writer's Workshop time will sound like." Tell students when we are busy, we sometimes do not know that our noise level might interfere with others' writing or conferencing.

Teach

4. Tell students, "Today, I will teach you about the noise level I expect you to use during our Writer's Workshop time." Explain to students that one way they can monitor their noise level is to use a distance of a two-inch voice. Show students the distance of two inches on a ruler and tell students they should speak so only someone a few inches from their mouth can hear what they are saying.
5. Model a two-inch voice that can be heard only by partners and not by others sitting close by. Turn and have a conversation with a student sitting in the group. Ask questions, such as: "What kind of stories do you like to write? Where do you do your best writing—home or school? What might you write about today?"

Two-Inch Voices *(cont.)*

6. Tell students the voice you just used was the appropriate voice level and that you will be listening for that voice level during Writer's Workshop. Revisit the anchor chart adding student insights into the *Sounds Like* section.

Engage

7. Tell students they will practice using their two-inch voices today. Give students question prompts to engage in partner conversation using two-inch voices such as: What we do during writing time, an interesting piece of writing they are working on, or what they did after school last evening, etc.
8. Provide time for students to talk with their partners. Then gather students back together, and add any additional insights to the *Looks Like, Sounds Like, Feels Like* anchor chart.

Apply

9. Remind students that as they write today, they will use a two-inch voice. This reflects respect for every writer in the room who is trying to concentrate.
10. Tell students they may write or draw about the mentor text or they may use their own ideas.

Write/Conference

11. Provide approximately 10–15 minutes for students to write. As students write, rotate around the room making observations about student noise level. Keep notes in your conferring notebook. Remember to offer students many compliments about work well done.

Spotlight Strategy

12. Spotlight students who used two-inch voices. For example, "Jenny used the exact noise level that we modeled and practiced. Did you notice the *Sounds Like* environment in our writing time today? (*Point to the ear on the chart.*) That is the noise level I will be listening for during our writing time."

Share

13. Have students meet with partners and share what they worked on as writers today for approximately two minutes. As students share, observe to find one or two students who clearly understood the idea and have them share with the whole group.

Homework

Ask students to think about how important it is to show respect for every writer in the room by using a two-inch voice during Writer's Workshop time.

Turn and Talk

Standard

Understands the structure of Writer's Workshop

Materials

- *Sample Looks Like, Sounds Like, Feels Like Anchor Chart* (page 35; lookssoundsfeels.pdf)
- Chart paper
- Markers
- *Sample Partner Conversation Anchor Chart* (page 45; partnerconversation.pdf)

Mentor Texts

- *Listen Buddy!* by Helen Lester
- See *Mentor Text List* in Appendix C for other suggestions.

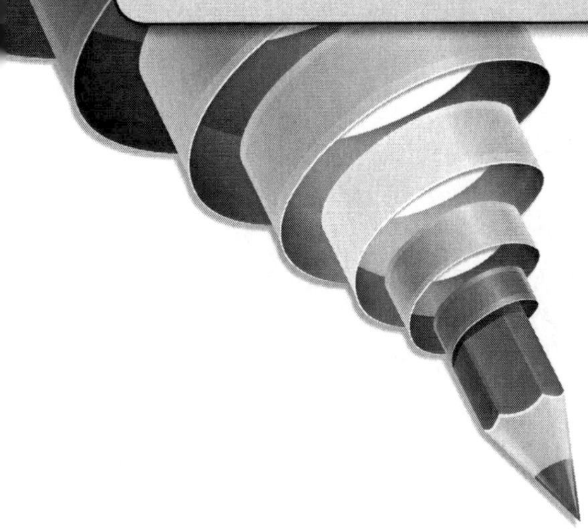

Procedures

Note: Teachers may assign writing partners based on some sort of criteria, such as language acquisition levels, or have students select their own partners. The collective personality of your class should guide your decision. You will need to repeat this lesson until procedure is in place.

Think About Writing

1. Explain to students that we must get solid routines and rituals in Writer's Workshop and schedule them appropriately. It is important that we build into our workshop ways to talk to others about our writing. To do this, we will use a routine called *Turn and Talk*. This discussion strategy will be used throughout our writing time. When we meet with partners, we will talk about writing ideas and skills to become better writers.
2. Review a mentor text if desired, and emphasize the need for order and procedures in a classroom.

Teach

3. Tell students, "Today, we will practice partner conversation." Explain that when you say, "Turn and talk," that is a signal for them to immediately turn to a person who is sitting nearby and quickly follow directions on the discussion topic.
4. Create an anchor chart on chart paper with guidelines for *Turn and Talk*. Gather ideas from students about what they will do during *Turn and Talk*. Use the *Sample Looks Like, Sounds Like, Feels Like Anchor Chart* (page 35) to guide the discussion. Be sure to explicitly talk about and list on the chart what students will do during this time. Post the *Turn and Talk Anchor Chart* you created in the classroom or photocopy the sample for students to place in their writing folders.

Turn and Talk *(cont.)*

5. Model what *Turn and Talk* would look like and sound like. Be sure to emphasize and model an appropriate two-inch voice. Then, provide time for students to practice with each other.
6. Tell students when you say, "Heads-up, Stand-up, Partner-up," it is a signal that you will immediately stand up, join a partner, and make eye contact. Then, follow directions for your discussion topic. Model what *Heads-up, Stand-up, Partner-up* would look like and sound like. Then provide time for students to practice with each other. Praise students for their efforts.
7. Revisit the *Looks Like, Sounds Like, Feels Like Anchor Chart*, adding student insights. (Continue to create this anchor chart using student input and suggestions from the sample chart.)

Engage

8. Tell students you will give them a chance to *Turn and Talk*. Ask partners to discuss how they will be expected to conduct themselves in a *Turn and Talk* or in a *Heads-up, Stand-up, Partner-up* and about the importance of having an opportunity to talk to someone before, during, and after writing.

Apply

9. Tell students that after they write today, they will *Turn and Talk* to partners about what they have written.

Write/Conference

10. Provide time for students to write. Have students work on drafting a new piece or continue with an unfinished writing piece from their folder. As students write, rotate around the room making observations about student noise level. Keep notes in your conferring notebook. Remember to offer students many compliments about work well done.

Spotlight Strategy

11. There is no spotlighting strategy today. Celebrating is done through the actual *Turn and Talk* and *Heads-up, Stand-up, Partner-up*.

Share

12. Gather students together to share their work. Have students *Turn and Talk* to partners. Provide two minutes for students to share their thinking about the value of talking to partners.

Homework

Ask students to think about how *Turn and Talk* and *Heads-up, Stand-up, Partner-up* conversations energize writing ideas. Also, ask them to think about how important it is to show our respect for every writer in the room by using a two-inch voice.

Sample Partner Conversation Anchor Chart

- Find your partner quickly.
- Use a soft, two-inch voice.
- Make eye contact with your partner.

- Stick to the writing topic.
- Ask questions to clarify thinking.
- Make sure each partner has a turn to talk.
- Give a compliment when needed.
- Only "put-ups"—NO "put-downs."

Sharing

Standard

Understands the structure of Writer's Workshop

Materials

- *Sample Looks Like, Sounds Like, Feels Like Anchor Chart* (page 35; lookssoundsfeels.pdf)
- *I Like/I Wonder Cards* (page 48; likewondercards.pdf)

Mentor Texts

- *All for Me and None for All* by Helen Lester
- See *Mentor Text List* in Appendix C for other suggestions.

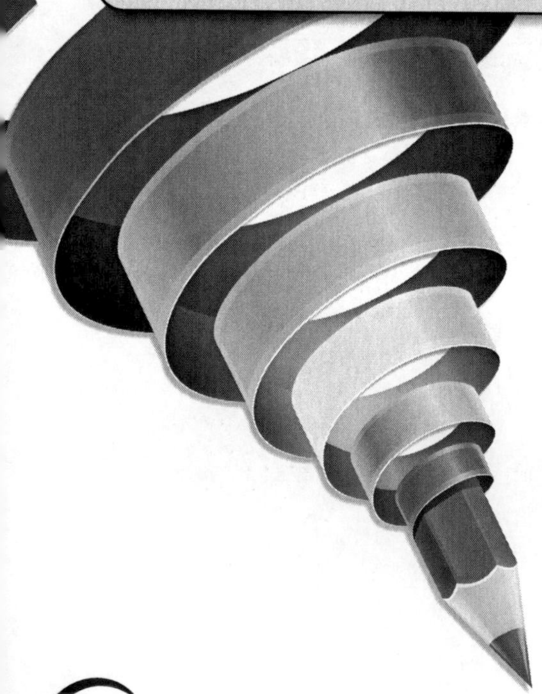

Procedures

Note: Repeat this lesson until the procedure is in place and is automatic. The sharing cards are to be used later in the year as students become familiar with the sharing routine.

Think About Writing

1. Remind students about the classroom expectations for Writer's Workshop by reviewing the *Looks Like, Sounds Like, Feels Like Anchor Chart* they helped create using the *Sample Looks Like, Sounds Like, Feels Like Anchor Chart* (page 35). Tell students that today, they will learn about an important step of Writer's Workshop—sharing. Explain to students that sharing their writing gives them a chance to hear what others are writing and to share their own writing in order to generate ideas.
2. Review a mentor text if desired, and emphasize the need to be respectful to others when sharing.

Teach

3. Tell students, "Today, I will show you how to meet with classmates to share your writing." Have students share for 3–5 minutes at the end of Writer's Workshop. Explain that sometimes sharing will be in a large group and sometimes it will be in smaller groups.
4. Tell students that when they talk with others it is important that everyone work together. One person will share what he or she has written. The other person (or people) must be a good listener and respond to the writing.
5. Explain that responding to writing is important and must be done with care. Display the *I Like/I Wonder Cards* (page 48). Tell students that the words *I like* will remind them to compliment about the person's writing. Model making several compliments. Then, tell students that the words *I wonder* will remind them to ask a question about the person's writing. Model asking several questions.

Sharing *(cont.)*

6. Tell students they will practice forming smaller groups to share. Remind students that the listening partner will practice giving compliments and asking questions. Tell students that when they meet with partners, they should move quickly and form groups of two and begin sharing. Show students how you will count to five and that they should be with a group and sharing by the time you get to five.
7. Model finding a partner and sharing for students. Practice several times until the routine is firmly in place. Provide students with *I Like/I Wonder Cards* to use while they meet with partners and to keep in their writing folders. Tell students that they will also meet in triads(3) and quads (4), and practice these groupings as well.

Engage

8. Ask students to *Heads-up, Stand-up, Partner-up* and talk about what they will do when they share their writing at the end of Writer's Workshop. Praise students for forming groups quickly and sharing their ideas.

Apply

9. Tell students that having conversations with others about their writing is important work. Meeting with a group at the end of writing time allows them to have an audience for all their hard writing work. They should remember to compliment their partner's work.

Write/Conference

10. Provide time for students to write. Have students continue to work from their folders. Students should write every day, even when mini-lessons focus on management.

Spotlight Strategy

11. It will not be necessary to spotlight strategies until the sharing component of the lesson.

Share

12. Tell students they will practice the important procedures for share time. Have students meet in partners, triads (3), and quads (4) for a minute each round. Provide lots of compliments and praise for sharing that is well done.

Homework

Ask students to think about how they met in partners, triads, and quads. Tell students to share with their parents how they will share their writing with classmates and the kind of compliments they might give and receive. Remind them to practice the language of compliments.

I Like/I Wonder Cards

Directions: Create copies of this sheet. Cut out the cards and distribute them to students according to the directions in the lesson.

I like...

I wonder...

I like...

I wonder...

I like...

I wonder...

I like...

I wonder...

Understanding the Writing Process

Standard

Understands the structure of Writer's Workshop

Materials

- *Five-Step Writing Process* (page 51; fivestepprocess.pdf)
- Student writing samples (samples.doc)

Mentor Texts

- *Look at My Book* by Loreen Leedy
- *Chester* by Mélanie Watt
- *Chester's Back* by Mélanie Watt
- See *Mentor Text List* in Appendix C for other suggestions.

Procedures

Note: Students will practice the five steps of the writing process. Students can and will be on different steps of the process at any given time. Not all writing will go through each step. Young writers need many opportunities to prewrite and draft before being asked to revise, edit, and publish. Published pieces should be produced, displayed, and celebrated throughout the year.

Think About Writing

1. Remind students that they have been developing their writing using a variety of ideas. They have also been talking about how authors write.
2. Review a mentor text if desired, and emphasize the author's work on their writing. Tell students that most authors follow a method called the Writing Process.

Teach

3. Tell students, "Today we will explore each step of the Five-Step Writing Process. This will help us become better writers."
4. Display the *Five-Step Writing Process* (page 51) poster. Share writing samples (samples.doc) and each piece in relation to the writing process, noting the purpose of each stage.
    - Prewriting—Gathering and organizing ideas.
    - Drafting—Writing a first draft helps to put ideas on paper so they can be examined more closely.
    - Revising—Reread and check organization, sentences, and word choice to make writing better.
    - Editing—Check writing for capitalization, grammar usage, punctuation, and spelling.
    - Publishing—Make a final copy to share.

Understanding the Writing Process *(cont.)*

Engage

5. Ask students to *Heads-up, Stand-up, Partner-up* and work with their partner to name and describe each of the five steps in the writing process. Encourage students to use the poster to help them remember the steps. Rotate among students and give praises as you listen in on student conversations.

Apply

6. Encourage students to use the *Five-Step Writing Process* as a guide through their writing projects.

Write/Conference

7. Provide time for students to write about a topic of their choice. Observe your class for understanding and then begin to have individual or small group conferences. Keep your conferring notebook ready to make observations.

Spotlight Strategy

8. Spotlight students who are using the steps of writing well. For example, "Wow! You're amazing writers. Notice how Emilio is drafting and Leah is revising. No wasted time! You are right on target."

Share

9. Choose one or two students who clearly understood the idea and have them share their writing and the stage of the writing process with the whole group.

Homework

Ask students to think about how the *Five-Step Writing Process* can help them in their writing. Encourage them to name the steps to their parents.

Five-Step Writing Process

	**Prewriting** ✔ I gather my ideas and organize my thoughts.
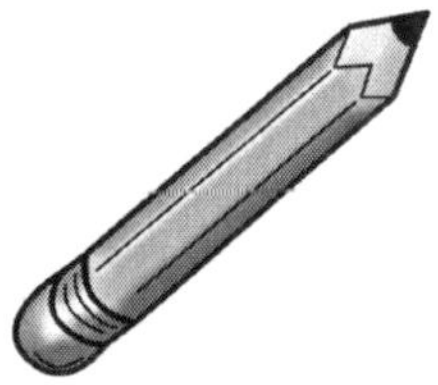	**Drafting** ✔ I write my first thoughts in a logical order with details.
	**Revising** ✔ I reread and check my organization, sentences and my choice of words to make my writing better.
C U P S	**Editing** ✔ I check my writing for capitalization, usage and grammar, punctuation and spelling.
	**Publishing** ✔ I make my final copy to share with others.

Ideas

Thinking, Thinking, Thinking!

Ideas are the heart of writing. The purpose of this section is to help students generate ideas for writing. The lessons assist students to explore the ideas of authors using mentor texts, and discover the unique writing ideas in their own lives. Through class-created anchor charts and individually-created lists, students will collect plenty of ideas, so that when they begin to write they are not at a loss for topics. Students are encouraged to keep their ideas in their writing folders so the ideas are readily at-hand. Lessons in this section include the following:

The *Ida, the Idea Creator* poster (page 54) can be displayed in the room to provide a visual reminder for students that ideas are one of the traits of writing. You may wish to introduce this poster during the first lesson on ideas. Refer to the poster when teaching other lessons on ideas to refresh students' memories and provide them questions to help hone their writing topics.

Ida
Idea Creator

What is my writing about?

- ✔ Did I choose an interesting topic?
- ✔ Did I focus on my idea?
- ✔ Did I include supporting details?
- ✔ Did I stick to my topic?

Ideas Thinking Chart

Standard

Uses prewriting strategies to plan written work

Materials

- Chart paper
- Markers
- *Examples of Brainstorming* (page 57; exbrainstorming.pdf)

Mentor Texts

- *Wallace's Lists* by Barbara Bottner
- *You Have to Write* by Janet S. Wong
- *The Best Story* by Eileen Spinelli
- *Gooney Bird Greene* by Lois Lowry
- See *Mentor Text List* in Appendix C for other suggestions.

Procedures

Note: Repeat this mini-lesson to support students with monthly, theme-related ideas for writing, such as fall, people, space, etc. Charts should be posted to support student needs and create a print-rich environment.

Think About Writing

1. Explain to students that authors have lists of ideas they would like to write about. The ideas can come from almost anywhere. By writing the ideas down on paper, they can be remembered and used to write stories.
2. Review a mentor text, and emphasize that authors have many different ideas that they can choose from when they write.

Teach

3. Tell students, "Today I will show you how to create a list of ideas that can be used when writing." Explain that ideas for writing can come from almost anywhere. Sometimes experiences give us ideas, or even things we see on TV or read in a book. Use *Examples of Brainstorming* (page 57) to help you.
4. Write the title *Brainstorming Bright Ideas for Writing* at the top of a sheet of chart paper. Think aloud as you add bullets and brainstorming ideas to the chart. For example, "Riding a bike. I do a lot of bike riding and have many experiences about riding my bike." Other ideas include: family celebrations, animals, and friends.
5. Demonstrate how to choose a topic from the list and begin writing about the topic. Spend a few minutes thinking aloud, telling and sharing the story, and then begin modeling writing for students.

Ideas Thinking Chart *(cont.)*

Engage

6. Have students *Turn and Talk* to brainstorm ideas with partners. Encourage students to talk across their fingers to generate at least five ideas that can be shared with the class. Provide time for discussion, and then add students' ideas to the chart.

Apply

7. Remind students they will brainstorm ideas and make a list that will help them when they are deciding on a topic for writing.

Write/Conference

8. Provide time for students to write. Remind them to use the idea chart to inspire their writing. Scan the group for any students having difficulty. Then begin to rotate among students and have conversations with small groups of students about their ideas. Use your conferring notebook to keep records of ideas.

Spotlight Strategy

9. Spotlight great student effort. For example, "Excellent work ethic. Sharon went to work right away. Amazing writing work today. You are to be commended."

Share

10. Invite three authors to share their writing in the author's chair. Provide many affirmations.

Homework

Ask students to make a list of five ideas they would like to write about tomorrow. Provide time for students to add their ideas to their lists the following day.

Examples of Brainstorming

Teacher Directions: Build idea anchor charts with students. Generate the list based on their suggestions and your guidance.

General Topics	Ideas for Fall
• riding my bike	• how-to grow a pumpkin
• family celebrations	• trees/leaves
• friends	• making a jack-o-lantern
• cooking	• spiders
• fishing	• trick-or-treating
• pets	• bats
• favorites—food, TV, games	• scary stories/monsters
• insects	• squirrels
• animals—bears, snakes, penguins	• apples
• school	• scarecrows
• birthday	• Thanksgiving dinner
• injuries	• being thankful
• vacations	• visiting relatives
• hobbies—swimming, dancing	• gardens/harvest
• summer	• football
• weekends	• second grade
• going on a hike	• Veteran's Day
• how-to...	• safety on the bus and fire safety
• sports—football, baseball, soccer, cheerleading	• facts about pilgrims/Native Americans

My Ponder Pocket

Standard

Uses prewriting strategies to plan written work

Materials

- *Ponder Pocket* (page 60; ponderpocket.pdf)
- 8.5" × 11" paper cut into fourths
- Sheet protectors (one per student)

Mentor Texts

- *There's a Wocket in My Pocket* by Dr. Seuss
- *Junie B. Jones Has a Peep in Her Pocket* by Barbara Park
- *Rocks in My Pockets* by Marc Harshman
- See *Mentor Text List* in Appendix C for other suggestions.

Procedures

Note: In your explanation, stress the idea of gathering collections to ponder as ideas for topics. Collections are great sources of ideas as possible writing topics. Revisit this lesson many times.

Think About Writing

1. Remind students they have been working on gathering ideas for our writing topics. Explain that authors use many different ways to gather and keep their topics until they want to use them in their writing. For example, "Some authors make lists, others have notebooks of ideas, some have sticky notes. These all become a collection of ideas the author might ponder/think about when developing their writing."
2. Review mentor text if desired, and emphasize the idea of collecting things.

Teach

3. Tell students, "Today I will show you how to collect ideas in a Ponder Pocket."
4. Place a copy of *Ponder Pocket* (page 60) into a sheet protector. Explain to students that the pocket is just like a pocket on jeans, where rocks, feathers, toys, shells, and other treasures can be stored.
5. Model drawing ideas on the blank cards. For example, snakes, insects, rocks, and grasshoppers. Be sure to model all types of topic ideas to reach all students' interests. Think aloud as you record your thoughts on the cards. Model gathering ideas from several places, such as magazines, books, advertisements, TV, etc.
6. Place the cards inside the sheet protector and explain to students that each time an idea is placed in the *Ponder Pocket*, it becomes a personalized connection to their own lives.

My Ponder Pocket *(cont.)*

Engage

7. Have students *Heads-up, Stand-up, Partner-up* and talk with partners about ideas for topics. Provide approximately two minutes. As students talk, rotate around the group and jot down ideas that you hear. At the signal, have students reassemble in the meeting area. Share a couple of ideas that you heard as students conversed.

Apply

8. Provide *Ponder Pocket*, plastic sleeves, and blank cards to students so they can create their own *Ponder Pocket* to gather their ideas. Remind students to place ideas they have for writing in the pocket. Place several blank cards at student writing tables.

Write/Conference

9. Provide time for students to write. Scan the classroom for any confusion and then begin to rotate and help students problem solve. Be a vigilant observer during this time.

Spotlight Strategy

10. Spotlight students who are filling their *Ponder Pockets* with ideas. For example, "I'm noticing that Linda has already sketched and labeled three ideas to drop into her *Ponder Pocket*. Smart writing work! No wasted time!"

Share

11. Have students share the ideas from their *Ponder Pockets* with partners. Provide approximately two minutes for students to share.

Homework

Ask students to work with their families to ponder some ideas that can be added to their *Ponder Pockets*. Have students make a list of five ideas to add to their *Ponder Pockets*.

Ponder Pocket

Teacher Directions: Create copies of this sheet and distribute it to students, according to the directions in the lesson. Students may decorate if desired.

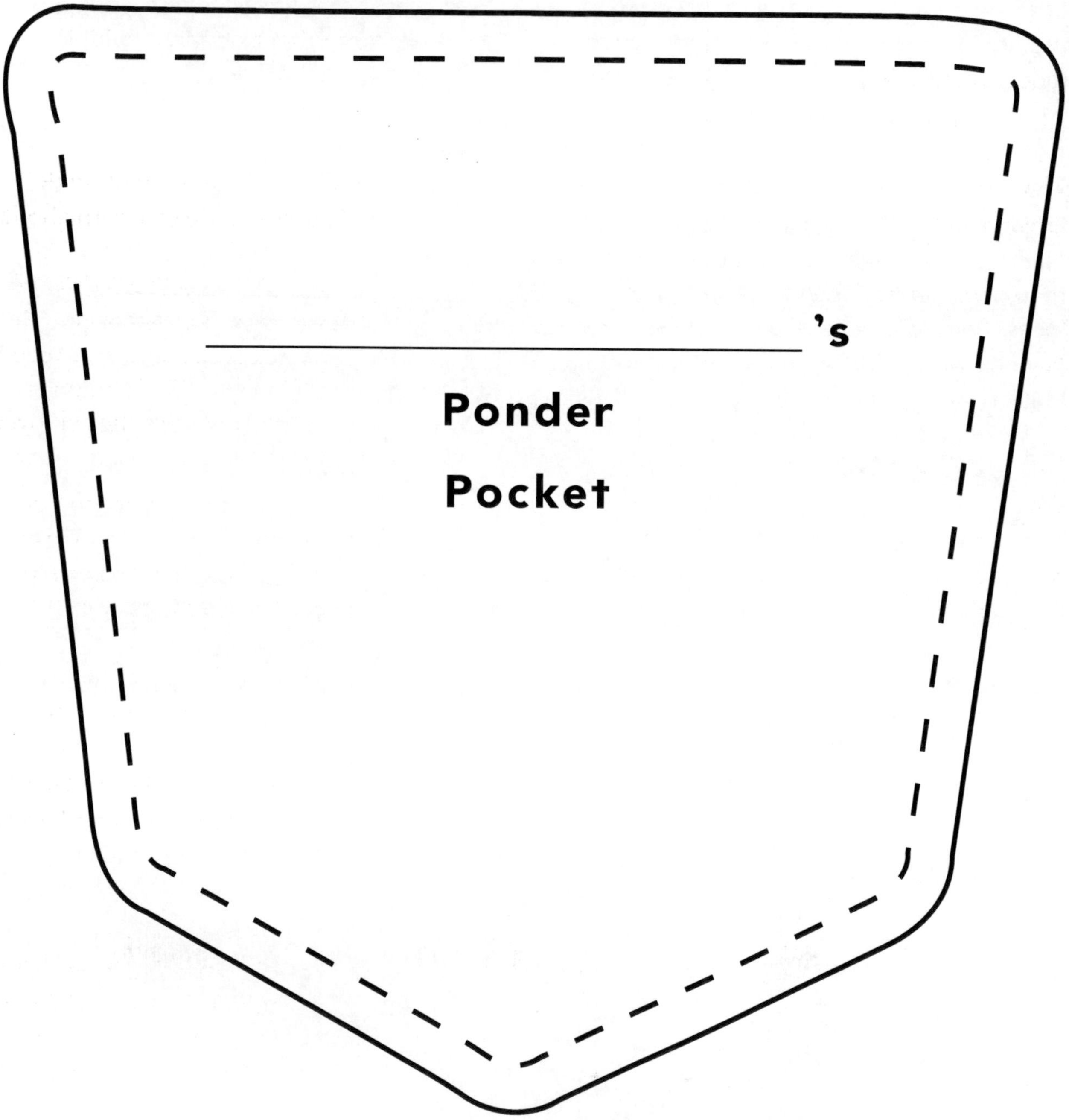

Getting Ideas from Literature

Standard

Uses prewriting strategies to plan written work

Materials

- Chart paper
- Markers
- *Ideas from Literature* (Appendix D, page 258)

Mentor Texts

- *The Gingerbread Man* by Jim Aylesworth
- *Little Red Riding Hood* by James Marshall
- *Pecos Bill* by Steven Kellogg
- *Johnny Appleseed* by Steven Kellogg
- See *Mentor Text List* in Appendix C for other suggestions.

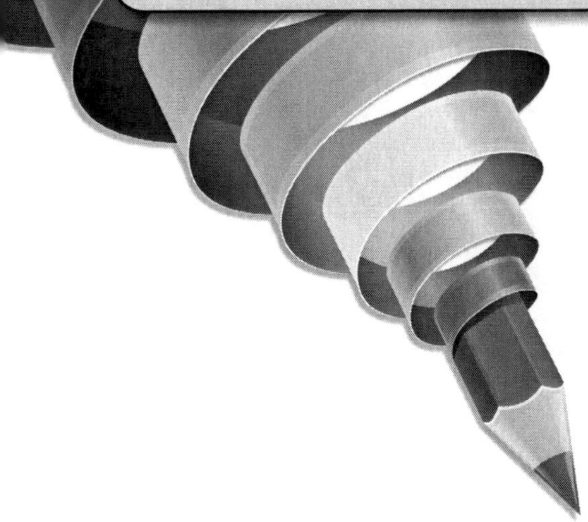

Procedures

Note: This mini-lesson uses *Little Red Riding Hood* for specific examples; however, the idea behind the lesson can be used with numerous texts by connecting the topic or writing craft used by the author. See *Ideas from Literature* list (page 258) for additional book titles and suggested connections. Students enjoy writing like authors. Provide multiple opportunities with rich literature.

Think About Writing

1. Tell students authors often get ideas for writing their own stories by reading literature. We can learn about how to get ideas by looking at what types of things authors write about. For example, in *Little Red Riding Hood*, the author explains how she walks through the forest to take her Grandma a basket of cookies. When she arrives, she is in for a big surprise! Tell students, "Maybe this author got this idea because they enjoyed visiting a grandparent."
2. Review a mentor text if desired, and emphasize that authors get ideas from many different places. We can get ideas from daily life and from stories we know and love and use those as ideas for our own writing.

Teach

3. Tell students, "Today, I will show you how to explore real literature to create ideas for your own stories." Tell students that throughout the year, they will read literature with different characters, settings, and events that they might gather ideas from to craft their own stories.
4. Think aloud about *Little Red Riding Hood* or another piece of literature. For example, "I need to have a clear understanding of the characters and setting. The story takes place in the woods and has Little Red Riding Hood, Grandmother, and a wolf in it." Continue thinking

Getting Ideas from Literature *(cont.)*

aloud. Name the events in the story in the sequence in which they happened. Sketch a story map to demonstrate sequence. Last, check to see how the author ended the story with a wrap-up.

5. Explain to students that you now have an idea you can use to write a story. Model writing the beginning of a story, using a different character name and an idea similar to the literature you are using. For example, change *Little Red Riding Hood* to *Litte Blue Running Boy*.

Engage

6. Have students *Turn and Talk* to share with partners how they might expand on your idea and write a complete story based on the literature. Have them share characters, beginning, middle, end, and setting. Provide approximately three minutes for students to share.

Apply

7. Remind students that writing is all around us, in books on the shelf, on TV, and even on video games. Ideas for writing can be gathered from any of these sources. Provide many simple story books as inspiration.

Write/Conference

8. Provide time for students to write. Have your conferring notebook handy. Move around and question students as they work. Have an authentic conversation about their writing. For example, "How's it going?" "Any problems?" Make observations in your conferring notebook to help you make decisions about your next writing plan.

Spotlight Strategy

9. Spotlight students who have written a story inspired by a book. For example, "Tara has taken an idea from literature and is beginning to expand it into her own story."

Share

10. Have students meet with writing partners and share an idea that can be gathered from literature. Remind students to read and listen with writing in mind. Provide approximately two minutes for students to share.

Homework

Ask students to think about other stories they have heard that could be woven into their own with a twist. Have students write the name of at least one story that they would like to use for an idea. Ask students to write one sentence about their idea for writing based on the story. This sentence can be saved for writing ideas in students' writing folders.

Important People in My Life

Standard

Uses prewriting strategies to plan written work

Materials

- Chart paper
- Markers
- *Important People in My Life* (page 65; importantpeople.pdf)

Mentor Texts

- *My Great-Aunt Arizona* by Gloria Houston
- *Daddy, Daddy, Be There* by Candy Boyd
- *Mr. George Baker* by Amy Hest
- *Dear Annie* by Judith Caseley
- *The Wednesday Surprise* by Eve Bunting
- See *Mentor Text List* in Appendix C for other suggestions.

Procedures

Note: This lesson is especially appropriate to use as an end-of-year Author's Tea or Author's Luncheon activity. Invite family members, neighbors, or other teachers to hear their child's special tribute. Every child needs to be represented by someone. It can serve as both a Mother's Day tribute and/or tie the year together at the end in a special tribute for Father's Day. Students' lists may also include famous/historical figures.

Also, this lesson may be split into two days. On day one, create a whole-class anchor chart and have students create individual charts. Then, on day two, have students elaborate their ideas about one special person. Have students store their ideas in the green dot side of their writing folders.

Think About Writing

1. Ask students to think about the people they see every day at home and at school. Remind students that these people are very special and they can provide wonderful ideas for writing topics.
2. Review a mentor text if desired, and emphasize the special people in our lives who can provide ideas for writing.

Teach

3. Tell students, "Today I will show you how to use the people you have in your lives as a starting point for your stories." Demonstrate how to create a list of important people that can be referenced when students are looking for ideas for writing.
4. Write the title *Important People in My Life* at the top of a sheet of chart paper. Model recording on the list the names or relationships of people who are important to you. As you write each name, think aloud, explaining who the person is and why he or she is important. For example, "I'm going to write *brother* on the list because we share a room. He always looks out for me and helps take care of me."

Important People in My Life *(cont.)*

5. Explain to students they can begin their lists today; however, new people can be added to the list at any time.
6. Model choosing one person from the list and writing about that person. Create several sentences about the person you have selected and include a closing statement. Model writing succinctly, talking through what you write and thinking aloud so students understand your thought process.

Engage

7. Have students *Heads-up, Stand-up, Partner-up* and talk about people they know and care about that they want to remember. Encourage students to use their five fingers to name five important people. Provide approximately two minutes for partners to talk.

Apply

8. Ask students to remember how special people in their lives are important to them as writers. Tell students that those special people become seeds for stories so that they are never without ideas in Writer's Workshop. Tell students they will make their own *Important People In My Life* lists.

Write/Conference

9. Distribute *Important People in My Life* (page 65) to students. Have them write for 10–15 minutes. As students work, rotate around the room having conversations with students about their lists. Remember to prod students to know the "why" and "how" this will help them in writing. Keep notes in your conferring notebook so that you will know whether to revisit this lesson or move ahead. Remember to offer students many compliments about work well done.

Spotlight Strategy

10. Remember to spotlight specific students who thought about a special person and are generating details. Remember to expect students to stick to a focused topic from the beginning. "Special kudos to Yuli for brilliant writing work!"

Share

11. Have students meet with writing partners and share the names of the people on their lists.

Homework

Ask students to tell someone at home about the special people lists we are creating at school. Have students ask their parents for help thinking about other people from their lives they can add to their lists. Ask students to write one sentence about one of the people they would like to write more about. This sentence can be saved for writing ideas in students' writing folders.

Name: ______________________ Date: ______________________

Important People in My Life

Directions: Make a list of the important people that are in your life.

- [ ] ______________________
- [ ] ______________________
- [ ] ______________________
- [ ] ______________________
- [ ] ______________________
- [ ] ______________________
- [ ] ______________________
- [ ] ______________________
- [ ] ______________________
- [ ] ______________________

Important Places

Standard

Uses prewriting strategies to plan written work

Materials

- Chart paper
- Markers
- *Important Places* (page 68; importantplaces.pdf)

Mentor Texts

- *The Relatives Came* by Cynthia Rylant
- See *Mentor Text List* in Appendix C for other suggestions.

Procedures

Note: This lesson may be split into two days. On day one, create a whole-class anchor chart and have students create individual charts. Then, on day two, have students elaborate their ideas about one special place. Students can store their ideas in the green dot side of their writing folders.

Think About Writing

1. Remind students they have been gathering ideas for writing so they always have ideas for when they sit down to write. Review with students the other ways they have gathered ideas for writing.
2. Review a mentor text if desired, and emphasize ways to gather ideas for writing about important places.

Teach

3. Tell students, "Today I will show you how to get inspiration for writing from the places you have visited."
4. Explain to students that a place can be somewhere fun they have visited such as an amusement park or grandma's house. But, it can also be a special place such as their bedrooms or the tree house in their backyards. Ask students to think about their favorite place to be. Allow several students to share their ideas. Tell students these places can become the topics for writing.
5. Write the title *Important Places* at the top of a sheet of chart paper. Write several examples of important places to you. Allow students to add ideas to the list.
6. Select one idea from your *Important Places* list and model how to elaborate on the ideas by thinking of at least three details about the place. Think aloud as you write, so students understand your thought process.

Important Places (cont.)

Engage

7. Have students Turn and Talk to their partners about places they know and may want to use in their writing.

Apply

8. Tell students that they will begin creating their own *Important Places* list today. Explain that it is important to constantly update their lists and add new important places so that their lists of writing ideas are endless.

Write/Conference

9. Distribute *Important Places* (page 68) to students. Have them write for 10–15 minutes. As students work, rotate around the room having conversations with students about their lists. Keep notes in your conferring notebook so that you will know whether to revisit this lesson or move ahead. Remember to offer students many compliments about work well done.

Spotlight Strategy

10. Spotlight wonderful student lists. For example, "You must be so proud of your excellent places." And, "Sanjay quickly sketched an important place and is ready to make a story about that very special place. Superb thinking today!" Spotlight one or two students.

Share

11. Have students meet in triads to share what they accomplished in writing today. Remind students to pay a compliment and ask a question to each person who shares ideas.

Homework

Ask students to think of places that excite or motivate them and make them want to tell someone. Have students write two sentences about one of the places they would like to write more about. These sentences can be saved for writing ideas in students' writing folders.

Name: ______________________ Date: ______________________

Important Places

Directions: Make a list of the places that are important to you.

- ❑ ______________________
- ❑ ______________________
- ❑ ______________________
- ❑ ______________________
- ❑ ______________________
- ❑ ______________________
- ❑ ______________________
- ❑ ______________________
- ❑ ______________________
- ❑ ______________________
- ❑ ______________________
- ❑ ______________________
- ❑ ______________________
- ❑ ______________________
- ❑ ______________________
- ❑ ______________________
- ❑ ______________________
- ❑ ______________________
- ❑ ______________________
- ❑ ______________________

My Heart Treasures

Standard

Uses prewriting strategies to plan written work

Materials

- Chart paper
- Markers
- *My Heart Treasures* (page 71; hearttreasures.pdf)
- a personal treasure (a special memory or object) to share with students

Mentor Texts

- *Treasures of the Heart* by Alice Ann Miller
- *The Memory String* by Eve Bunting
- *Aunt Flossie's Hats* by Elizabeth F. Howard
- *The Treasure* by Uri Shulevitz
- See *Mentor Text List* in Appendix C for other suggestions.

Procedures

Note: Share texts over several days so that students build the idea of treasured objects and memories.

Think About Writing

1. Explain that authors build a host of ideas that can be used to create special stories. Remind students that ideas can come from many different places.
2. Review a mentor text if desired, and emphasize the special things in the book. For example, in her book, *The Memory String*, Eve Bunting talks about a string with a collection of buttons that was a treasure full of special memories for the main character in that story.

Teach

3. Tell students, "Today I will show you how to begin using your own treasures to create ideas for your writing. We will start a class chart of ideas that will prompt us to collect objects that can be used as ideas to write stories."
4. Share a personal treasure (a memory or a special object) with students and explain why the treasure is special to you. Review with students that we collect special treasures throughout our lives, objects or memories that have special meaning.
5. Begin a class chart titled *Our Treasures*. List the treasure you shared with students in step four and add a few more if desired.
6. Demonstrate how to develop a story based on one of the items on the *Our Treasures* chart. As you develop the story, remember to use questions to make your story more interesting. For example, who gave it to you? How is it made? Where or when did you get it? Why is it special?

My Heart Treasures *(cont.)*

Engage

7. Have students *Turn and Talk* to tell partners about treasures they value. Remind students that a treasure can be something very simple as long as it has special meaning and you hold it dear to your heart. Provide approximately three minutes of talk time.

Apply

8. Distribute *My Heart Treasures* (page 71) to students. Remind them that their list of ideas can be endless and can grow each day of their lives.

Write/Conference

9. Provide time for students to write. Have one-on-one conversations with at least 3–5 students. Scaffold their efforts at creating a list and writing stories about a treasured object or memory. Keep records of your observations and remember to give praise and always have a teaching point.

Spotlight Strategy

10. Spotlight excellent student writing. For example, "Brilliant! Amazing! Remarkable! You must be so proud of your excellent writing today. Emma has generated ideas of treasured memories and is off and running with her story."

Share

11. Have students meet with partners to share their writing accomplishments today. Remind students to pay a compliment and give a comment.

Homework

Ask students to look around their houses for treasures and think about how those objects can be shaped into wonderful stories. Encourage students to ask their parents' permission to bring some treasured objects they would like to write about in Writer's Workshop. Have students identify at least two treasures they would like to write more about and write a sentence about each. These sentences can be saved for writing ideas in students' writing folders.

Name: ______________________ Date: ____________________

My Heart Treasures

Directions: Make a list of the treasures that are important to you.

❑ ______________________
❑ ______________________
❑ ______________________
❑ ______________________
❑ ______________________
❑ ______________________
❑ ______________________
❑ ______________________
❑ ______________________
❑ ______________________

❑ ______________________
❑ ______________________
❑ ______________________
❑ ______________________
❑ ______________________
❑ ______________________
❑ ______________________
❑ ______________________
❑ ______________________
❑ ______________________

Amazing Animals

Standard
Uses prewriting strategies to plan written work

Materials
- Chart paper
- Markers
- *Animal Picture Cards* (pages 75–76; animalpiccards.pdf)
- *Those Amazing Animals* (page 74; amazinganimals.pdf)

Mentor Texts
- *The Night I Followed the Dog* by Nina Laden
- *Gregory the Terrible Eater* by Mitchell Sharmat
- *My Puppy is Born* by Joanna Cole
- See *Mentor Text List* in Appendix C for other suggestions.

Procedures
Note: Connect this lesson to informational writing when possible. Use core reading and Common Core State Standards for additional resources.

Think About Writing
1. Remind students they have collected lists of many topics to use as ideas when writing. Explain that one really interesting topic to explore is amazing animals.
2. Review mentor text if desired, and emphasize the animals. Tell students authors can use animals as characters in stories or they can write non-fiction books about animals.

Teach
3. Tell students, "Today I will show you how to gather a list of possible topics on animals and use that list for future writing ideas. Animals are interesting creatures and can be observed in many settings."
4. Create a chart titled *Amazing Animals*. Display the *Animal Picture Cards* (pages 75–76) or other images. Discuss each animal briefly and then add the name of the animal to the chart. Allow students to add other animals of interest to the chart.

Engage
5. Have students *Turn and Talk* to partners about animals that they know about or want to learn about. Remind students to talk until they hear the timer or you signal that time is up.

Amazing Animals *(cont.)*

Apply

6. Distribute *Those Amazing Animals* (page 74) to students. Have them create a list of topics about animals that interest them and use their lists for writing information about animals.

Write/Conference

7. Provide time for students to write their animal lists. Remember to keep records of your students' writing work. Store your records in a folder to show progression of writing behaviors. Keep a checklist of expected writing behaviors and document in your conferring notebook to map out your instructional plans.

Spotlight Strategy

8. Spotlight students working hard on their animal lists. For example, "Wow! Just look at your amazing animal list. You have found the magic key to your writing success. Carlos, you wrote a list and began collecting details."

Share

9. Have students meet with partners to share their animal interests. Ask students to compare their interests to find out if they are the same or different. Remember to ask questions and give a compliment.

Homework

Ask students to look around their neighborhoods, in books, and on TV for animals. Have them ask their parents or other family members about their interest in animals. Ask students to make a list of three animals they would like to write more about and write at least one sentence about each animal. These papers can be saved for writing ideas in students' writing folders.

Name: ____________________ Date: __________

Those Amazing Animals

Directions: Make a list of the ideas that interest you about animals.

Animal Picture Cards

Teacher Directions: Cut out the cards and display for students. Discuss each animal.

Animal Picture Cards *(cont.)*

Things I Know List

Standard
Uses prewriting strategies to plan written work

Materials
- Chart paper
- Markers
- *Things I Know List* (page 79; thingsknowlist.pdf)

Mentor Texts
- *Wallace's List* by Barbara Bottner
- See *Mentor Text List* in Appendix C for other suggestions.

Procedures
Note: Keep the anchor chart you create in this lesson available so that students can view and add their own ideas of expertise. Use the ideas from any author and include ideas for "How to do something." For example, make sandwiches, feed pets, etc. Repeat this lesson periodically.

Think About Writing
1. Remind students of the other lists they have created, and remind them that all the ideas from their lists can be turned into stories. Tell students that one way writers get ideas is from things they know a lot about from their daily lives.
2. Review a mentor text if desired, and emphasize the lists in the book.

Teach
3. Tell students, "Today, I will show you how to create a list about things you know so that you always have an idea that you can weave into a story." Explain that you know there are things the students know lots about or are very good at doing. These ideas can be used as writing topics.
4. Name some things you know students in your class know a lot about. For example, "I know that John knows a lot about dinosaurs. Dinosaurs can be on your list of things you know."
5. Write the title *Things I Know* at the top of a sheet of chart paper. Write several examples of things you are good at doing, for example: doing homework, sharing, and riding a skateboard. Allow students to add their ideas to the list.

Things I Know List *(cont.)*

Engage

6. Have students *Turn and Talk* with partners about ideas they can write on their list of things they know. Encourage them to use their fingers and think of five things about them or their families that could be recorded on the *Things I Know List*. Allow approximately two minutes for partners to talk with each other.

Apply

7. Tell students that they will begin creating their *Things I Know List* today. Explain that it is important to constantly update their lists and add new important experiences so that their lists of writing ideas are endless.

Write/Conference

8. Distribute *Things I Know List* (page 79) to students. Have them write their lists for 10–15 minutes. As students work, rotate around the room having conversations with students about their lists. Ask questions such as: How will creating this list help you with your writing? Keep notes in your conferring notebook. Remember to offer students many compliments about work well done.

Spotlight Strategy

9. Spotlight student writing. For example, "Writers, excellent expert lists! You are amazing writers! Mason has already added several ideas to his growing list." (Read the list.)

10. Have students meet with writing partners to share at least three items from their lists. Remind students to compliment and comment on their partner's lists.

Homework

Ask students to look around their homes for ideas of five other things they are experts on and make a list of these things. Have students add their new lists to their writing folders. They can share their lists during the following day.

Name: ______________________ Date: ______________________

Things I Know List

Directions: Make a list of the things that you know a lot about.

- ❑ ____________________ ❑ ____________________
- ❑ ____________________ ❑ ____________________
- ❑ ____________________ ❑ ____________________
- ❑ ____________________ ❑ ____________________
- ❑ ____________________ ❑ ____________________
- ❑ ____________________ ❑ ____________________
- ❑ ____________________ ❑ ____________________
- ❑ ____________________ ❑ ____________________
- ❑ ____________________ ❑ ____________________
- ❑ ____________________ ❑ ____________________

Sentence Fluency

Getting Started

Sentence fluency helps make writing interesting. It is a trait that allows writers to add a lot of interest to their writing. By changing the sentence length, and where words are placed next to each other in the sentence, writers are able to help guide the reader though their work. Authors with good sentence fluency know the techniques needed to construct sentences that flow and have rhythm. The lessons assist students to explore parts of sentences, ways sentences are built, and ways to expand sentences to develop more interesting ideas. Lessons in this section include the following:

The *Simon, Sentence Builder* poster (page 82) can be displayed in the room to provide a visual reminder for students that sentence fluency is one of the traits of writing. You may wish to introduce this poster during the first lesson on sentence fluency. Then, refer to the poster when teaching other lessons on sentence fluency to refresh students' memories and provide them with questions to help guide them as they create sentences.

Simon Sentence Builder

What kinds of sentences will I use?

- ✔ Did I use long, medium, and short sentences?
- ✔ Did I use statements and questions?
- ✔ Did I use different sentence beginnings?
- ✔ Do my sentences flow smoothly when I read them aloud?

Super Sentence Stems

Standard

Uses strategies to draft and revise written work

Materials

- Chart paper
- Marker
- *Sentence Builders* (page 85; sentencebuilders.pdf)
- *More Sentence Builders* (page 86; moresentencebuilders.pdf)

Mentor Texts

- *The Important Book* by Margaret Wise Brown
- *The Runaway Bunny* by Margaret Wise Brown
- See *Mentor Text List* in Appendix C for other suggestions.

Procedures

Note: Repetitive phrases and sentences support students as they begin to add quantity to their writing.

Think About Writing

1. Explain that sometimes authors, use sentence or phrase patterns to capture their readers attention.
2. Review a mentor text if desired, and emphasize the repetitive phrases. For example, Margaret Wise Brown's *The Runaway Bunny* uses the phrases, "If you …, I will…" Tell students that she also adds interesting details to her phrase patterns.

Teach

3. Tell students, "Today I will show you how to use a sentence stem and link a couple of ideas together." Explain that you will begin with a sentence stem, and then strengthen the sentence so it is more interesting. Show students *Sentence Builders* (page 85) and tell them they will each get a copy to put in their writing folders.
4. Model how to use a sentence stem from *Sentence Builders* to begin a sentence. Write your sentence on a sheet of chart paper. Link a couple of ideas together. For example, *My favorite holiday is Labor Day. It closes the door of summer and opens the door to the beginning of a new school year. Sometimes my family takes a quick weekend getaway, or just uses Monday for last minute shopping. Labor Day is my favorite family holiday.* Remember to think aloud as you add details and a conclusion to your writing.

Super Sentence Stems *(cont.)*

Engage

5. Ask students to *Heads-up, Stand-up, Partner-up* to orally practice using one of the sentence stems with a partner. Encourage students to connect three or more thoughts together. Have them use their fingers to count the ideas. Remind students they should stick to their topic. Encourage them to add phrases that tell where, when, or how. Provide approximately three minutes for partners to practice.

Apply

6. Distribute *More Sentence Builders* (page 86) for students to add to their writing folders. Remind students to refer to the list for sentence ideas, and then make their sentences longer by using details to develop a super sentence.

Write/Conference

7. Provide time for students to write. When students seem to be involved in their writing, begin conferencing with individuals or small groups.

Spotlight Strategy

8. Spotlight sentence stem usage. For example, "Brilliant t writing! Notice how Rachel has used a sentence stem from the chart as an idea and has included three additional details that support it. Great work!"

Share

9. Have two students share their work in the Author's Chair. Remind students to be ready to pay compliments or ask questions.

Homework

Ask students to make a list of three more sentence stems they can use for writing stories and books. For example, I can…, I will…, My mom…, My dad…, Ask students to complete the sentence stems to form three complete sentences. Ask students to save their sentence stems for writing ideas in their writing folders.

Sentence Builders

I like...	My sister...	The boy...
I do not like...	My family...	That girl...
I like to eat...	My family likes to...	I see...
I don't like to eat...	The dog...	I saw...
I am...	A bird...	I went...
I can...	That cat...	I am thankful...
I cannot...	I have...	I know how to...
My friend...	I think...	I like to play...
My mom...	I love...	I go... We go...
My dad...	My favorite ____ is...________	If I were a...
My brother...	because______	Can you...?

Name: ______________________ Date: ________________

More Sentence Builders

I felt happy when...	If I were a mouse...
I felt sad when...	At school I like to...
I was surprised...	If I could have a pet...
I feel silly when...	My best birthday ever was...
I was so scared when...	If I could be invisible, I would...
I get angry when...	A good friend is someone who...
My favorite book is...	If I had a million dollars, I would...
If I were a giant...	If I were an ant...
If I had a magic ring...	If I could break the Guinness Book of Records, it would be for...

Growing Sentences

Standard
Uses strategies to draft and revise written work

Materials
- Rubber band

Mentor Texts
- *Chrysanthemum* by Kevin Henkes
- See *Mentor Text List* in Appendix C for other suggestions.

Procedures

Think About Writing

1. Tell students that one of the greatest tools for learning good writing skills is reading the work of other authors. Explain that we can study and explore how authors use words and sentences that flow together to tell a story.

2. Review a mentor text and emphasize the author's use of different sentence lengths. For example, explain that author Kevin Henkes is a master at sentence writing in his book *Chrysanthemum*. Read several sentences from the book again using the visual model of a stretching rubber band to show sentence length.

Teach

3. Tell students, "Today I will show you how to build your sentence length in oral language as well as written language. We will do *sentence talking*." Explain that partner one will say a sentence and partner two will count the number of words in the sentence. Demonstrate how to use your fingers to count the number of words you say in a sentence. Tell partners the goal is to create sentences that have seven words or more.

4. Model with a student how to be the sentence creator and the sentence counter. Remind them to use their ears to help hear how words are connected to create smooth, fluent sentences.

Engage

5. Ask students to *Heads-up, Stand-up, Partner-up* to practice orally creating sentences with their partners. You may wish to provide some sentence stems, such as: *Today I am…, My mom…, That silly dog…, Last night….*

Growing Sentences *(cont.)*

Apply

6. Tell students that writers think and play with words in sentences. Encourage them to use their ears as tools to hear both long and short sentences in their writing.

Write/Conference

7. Provide time for students to write "growing" sentences Once students are settled, begin conferencing with individuals or small groups of students. Remember to use your conferring notebook to keep notes.

Spotlight Strategy

8. Spotlight student work. For example, "Listen to this marvelous sentence. Hannah used sentences just like Kevin Henkes. Smart writing work!"

Share

9. Move students into triads, and have each student pick out their very best sentence to share. Provide approximately two minutes to share.

Homework

Ask students to teach a sibling, parent, or someone else at home how to be a sentence creator and a sentence counter. Have students create three sentences that have at least seven words. Ask students to keep their sentences as writing ideas in their writing folders.

Parts of a Sentence

Standards

- Uses strategies to draft and revise written work
- Uses complete sentences in written compositions

Materials

- *Parts of a Sentence Picture Cards* (pages 91–93; partssentencepiccards.pdf)

Mentor Texts

- *Bedhead* by Margie Palatini
- See *Mentor Text List* in Appendix C for other suggestions.

Procedures

Note: Read aloud great literature to students so they can hear the rhythm and flow of the language. Use the list of suggested mentor texts in Appendix C or the suggestions in the Common Core State Standards.

Think About Writing

1. Remind students they have been writing words, phrases, and sentences and building their writing stamina. Explain that writers work their sentences and rewrite them to get just the right meaning to express interesting ideas in a clear, logical way.
2. Review a mentor text if desired, and emphasize the author's use of a variety of sentence lengths.

Teach

3. Tell students, "Today I will show you how to create a complete sentence with two parts." Explain that sentences have two basic parts: a subject (the naming part), and a verb (the action part).
4. Display a picture card from the *Parts of a Sentence Picture Cards* (pages 91–93). Model how to name the subject of the picture, for example, *hamster*. Show several other picture cards and model naming the subject of the picture.
5. Next, tell students you will give the verb or action part of the sentence. Display the picture cards again and name an action that can go with the picture. Model creating sentences with the subject and verb. For example, for the word *cried*, create the sentence, *The young boy cried for his mother.* Point out that *cried* was the action part (verb) and *the boy* was the naming part (subject.)

Parts of a Sentence *(cont.)*

Engage

6. Have students *Heads-up, Stand-up, Partner-up* and work with their partner to create sentences with a naming part and an action part. Display pictures and have students practice. Encourage students to keep trying to improve the quality of their sentences by adding different words. Practice creating sentences for approximately three minutes.

Apply

7. Remind students to repeat their sentences in their heads to check for meaning and sentence fluency. Place a packet of picture cards on each table for students to use in writing complete sentences.

Write/Conference

8. Provide time for students to write sentences with naming and action parts. Scan the class for understanding of the sentence strategy; then begin to confer with individual or small groups of students. Remember to keep anecdotal observations to assist in making instructional decisions. If needed, provide intervention to small groups with a reteach.

Spotlight Strategy

9. Spotlight students' sentences. For example, "Amazing sentence work! Listen to the sentence that Luke has created. You are such smart writers."

Share

10. Have students select two of their best sentences to share with a group of four (quads). Provide approximately three minutes for students to share. Remind students to compliment each other.

Homework

Ask students to make a list of three naming words and action words that can be linked together to brighten up their writing work. Have students write three sentences using the naming words and action words they wrote on their lists.

Parts of a Sentence Picture Cards

Teacher Directions: Cut out the cards. Then, practice naming the subjects in the pictures with students.

Parts of a Sentence Picture Cards *(cont.)*

Parts of a Sentence Picture Cards *(cont.)*

What's Missing?

Standards

- Uses strategies to draft and revise written work
- Uses complete sentences in written compositions

Materials

- Charts
- Markers
- *Fragment Cards* (page 96; fragmentcards.pdf)

Mentor Texts

- *Bedhead* by Margie Palatini
- *Whales Passing* by Eve Bunting
- See *Mentor Text List* in Appendix C for other suggestions.

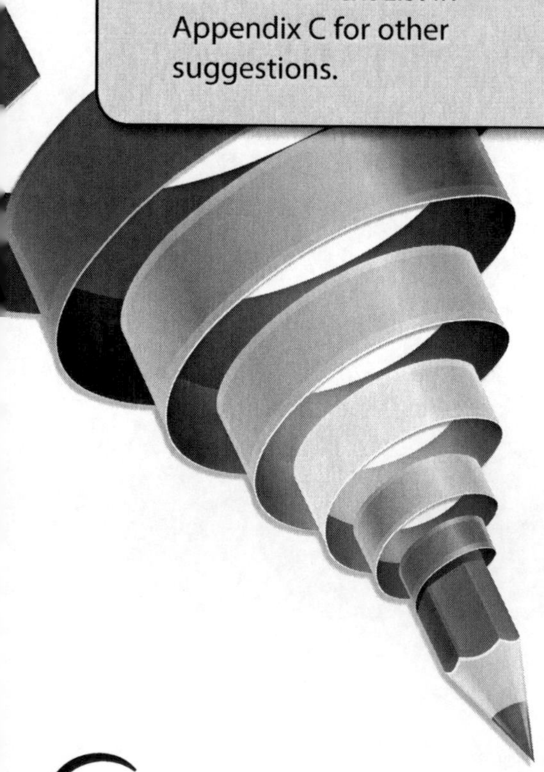

Procedures

Note: You may wish to create your own fragment cards using subjects and predicates from your students' writing. Also, if passing out cards is a management concern, they can also be displayed or projected.

Think About Writing

1. Remind students that they have been working on writing complete sentences. Explain that a sentence is like a giant puzzle. Pieces of the puzzle need to fit together to make a complete thought. A sentence fragment looks like a group of words that make a sentence, but it is not a complete idea. Something is missing. Sometimes the first part or the subject is missing and sometimes the ending part or the predicate (action part) is missing. You have to figure out the missing piece and fit the puzzle together again.
2. Review a mentor text and emphasize the authors' use of complete sentences.

Teach

3. Tell students, "Today I will show you how to add what is missing in a sentence to make a complete thought." Explain that you will read some incomplete sentences, called fragments, and find what is missing.
4. Choose one of the *Fragment Cards* (page 96) and read the words on it to students. Identify what is missing from the card. Model thinking aloud as you figure out what is missing. For example, for the card *the cute little kitten*, tell students you know who is in the sentence—the kitten. The missing part is the action. Write a sentence on chart paper that has the subject and action. For example, *The cute little kitten sat on the windowsill.* Model creating several examples for students.

What's Missing? *(cont.)*

Engage

5. Ask students to *Heads-up, Stand-up, Partner-up* to create sentences from the fragments you tell them. Ask students to identify what part of the puzzle piece is missing and then create a complete sentence. Display or distribute 4–5 *Fragment Cards* to each group and have them practice turning the fragments into complete sentences.

Apply

6. Remind students to be sure each of their sentences has all the pieces of the puzzle, e.g., the subject and the action. Place *Fragment Cards* in baggies on students' desks for practice.

Write/Conference

7. Provide time for students to use *Fragment Cards* to write complete sentences. Then, pull a small group to the writing table and reteach the lesson or perhaps based on your conferring notebook, pull a group in to provide enrichment. Keep notes of your praise and teaching moments. Keep accurate records to plan future instruction.

Spotlight Strategy

8. Spotlight great sentences. For example, "Your sentences are beginning to show great promise. Listen to how Don completed this sentence from a fragment. Excellent thinking!"

Share

9. Have students select two of their best sentences to share with partners. Encourage students to choose sentences that show that they understand when a sentence is a complete thought. Remind students that a sentence must have two parts to complete the puzzle.

Homework

Ask students to write three sentences about today's writing project. Remind students that the goal is to improve sentence sense by adding a missing piece of the sentence puzzle. Challenge students to create super sentences.

Fragment Cards

Teacher Directions: Cut out the cards and distribute them to students. Then, identify what is missing in the sentences with students.

the cute little kitten	ate all the cookies
a squirrel in the tree	picked up the toys
my playful puppy	climbed a tree
two boys	snored loudly
the band	visited the zoo
my best friend	likes to camp

When and Where?

Standards

- Uses strategies to draft and revise written work
- Uses complete sentences in written compositions

Materials

- Chart paper
- Marker

Mentor Texts

- *Owl Moon* by Jane Yolen
- See *Mentor Text* List in Appendix C for other suggestions.

Procedures

Think About Writing

1. Remind students that sentences can be constructed in many different ways, oftentimes using the same words, just in a different order. Explain that many authors have a way with words and the order in which they are put, that make the sentences magical because they are so beautifully written.
2. Review mentor text if desired, and emphasize several interesting sentences the author wrote.

Teach

3. Tell students, "Today I will show you how to add details to your sentences to make them more interesting." Tell students that by answering questions like *when* and *where*, we can add more detail to sentences which makes them more interesting to the reader.
4. Write the word *when* on a sheet of chart paper. Discuss what the word *when* means. Below the word *when*, write the many different times *when* can stand for: 2:00, this morning, last year, tomorrow, on my birthday, when it rains, etc.
5. Tell students you will say a sentence. They should add to the sentence by providing a detail about *when* to the end of the sentence. For example, say the sentence, "I ate strawberries." Students can add the detail, "I ate strawberries this morning." Allow several students to share their ideas of when and record the sentences on the chart paper.

I ate strawberries this morning.

I ate strawberries at 8:00.

I ate strawberries on Tuesday.

I ate strawberries for breakfast.

When and Where? *(cont.)*

6. Create several sentences with only a subject and predicate and have students help add the detail of when. Record all the sentences on the chart paper.
7. Repeat steps 4–6 with the word *where*.

Engage

8. Have students *Heads-up, Stand-up, Partner-up* to brainstorm and create interesting sentences using the words *animal* and *baby*. Allow time for discussion and then share a few with the group.

Apply

9. Remind students that writing sentences using details helps our reader see their stories more clearly. Encourage students to write some sentences using this simple technique.

Write/Conference

10. Provide time for students to write sentences with details. Check for understanding and rotate among students to confer and support. Note observations in your conferring notebook.

Spotlight Strategy

11. Spotlight examples of excellent writing. For example, "Look at all your brilliant sentences! Chani has a sentence that is simply dancing across the page with a subject, a predicate, and a detail. Smart writing work!"

Share

11. Have students share their writing work with a new partner. Provide approximately two minutes for students to share. Then, select a few students who demonstrated skill to share their work with the whole group.

Homework

Ask students to write a sentence with a subject and predicate. Then, ask students to add on to that sentence by explaining when and where in order to create two new sentences.

Rubber Band Sentences

Standards

- Uses strategies to draft and revise written work
- Uses complete sentences in written compositions

Materials

- Rubber band
- 3.5" × 5" index cards
- *Question Cards* (page 101); questioncards.pdf
- Pocket chart

Mentor Texts

- *The Relatives Came* by Cynthia Rylant
- *Bedhead* by Margie Palatini
- See *Mentor Text* List in Appendix C for other suggestions.

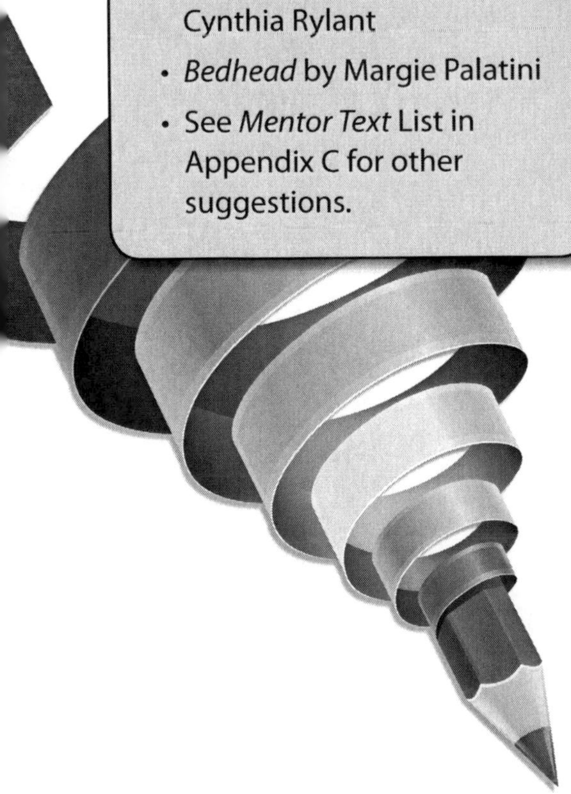

Procedures

Note: Prepare question cards, sentence stems, and responses in advance.

Think About Writing

1. Review with students that writers create interesting stories by using sentences of varying lengths.
2. Review a mentor text, and emphasize the author's use of sentence variation. Select several sentences from the mentor text. Model using a rubber band as you read the sentences. The longer the sentence is, the more you stretch the rubber band. The shorter the sentence, the less you stretch the rubber band.

Teach

3. Tell students, "Today I will show you how to study a sentence, think about what makes a good sentence, and add information so it is more interesting." Explain that when they practice this strategy, their sentence construction will improve.
4. Write a simple sentence on a sheet of chart paper. For example, *The neighbor fished*. Explain that question words can help add details to sentences in order to build more interesting sentences. Place *Question Cards* (page 101) in a pocket chart in the following order: *Who?*, *What?*, *Where?*, and *When*?
5. Ask each question and write a response on an index card and place it beneath the corresponding question word. Encourage students to reread the sentence to see if any additional words are needed to make the sentence complete.

Who?	What?	Where?	When?
The neighbor	fished	at the pond	last night.

Create several sentences using this strategy so students can see sentences expanding in length. Use the rubber band again to illustrate the length of the sentence if desired.

Rubber Band Sentences *(cont.)*

6. Model rearranging the order of the words in the sentence to create sentence variation.

When?	Who?	What?	Where?
Last night,	the neighbor	fished	at the pond.

Engage

7. Provide the following sentence starters for students to choose from: The tiger roared…, The building collapsed…, and The motorcycle roared…. Have *Question Cards* visible to provide student support. Have students *Heads-up, Stand-up, Partner-up* and tell them to select a sentence starter, and use questions to add details to build an interesting sentence with their partner.

Apply

8. Remind students to add details to create interesting sentences for the reader. Encourage students to practice stretching sentences using the given sentence starters, or look in their folder for sentences they can revise by asking questions.

Write/Conference

9. Provide time for students to write. Pull a small group to provide enrichment or guidance as needed. Take notes for planning. Guiding a small group while other children write is the key to classroom growth!

Spotlight Strategy

10. Spotlight super sentence stretching. For example, "Amazing writing work. Just listen to Joe's spectacular sentence. Spotlighting!"

Share

11. Select one or two students to share with the whole group in the author's chair.

Homework

Ask students to go home and select an object, such as a favorite food or toy and write a "rubber band" sentence describing it.

Question Cards

Teacher Directions: Cut out the cards below and use them as directed in the lesson.

Who?

What?

Where?

When?

And Then...

Standards

- Uses strategies to draft and revise written work
- Uses complete sentences in written compositions

Materials

- Highlighting tape
- Chart paper
- Markers

Mentor Texts

- *A Chair for My Mother* by Vera Willams
- See *Mentor Text List* in Appendix C for other suggestions.

Procedures

Note: This mini-lesson may be implemented over several days and revisited each month.

Think About Writing

1. Tell students that authors try to vary their sentences in order to keep the reader interested. If every sentence started the same, the story would be predictable and the reader would get bored easily.
2. Review a mentor text if desired, and emphasize the author's use of interesting sentences.

Teach

3. Tell students, "Today I will show you how to begin your sentences in different ways."
4. Write the following sentences on chart paper:

   A hermit crab has a shell.

   A hermit crab has legs.

   A hermit crab has pinchers.

5. Read the sentences to students and ask them to predict how the next sentence will begin. Discuss with students how using the same sentence structure is predictable. Highlight all of the sentence beginnings to solidify the point.
6. Choose a mentor text and write the first three sentences from the book on chart paper. Discuss the various ways the sentences begin. Ask students to decide if changing the sentence structure adds interest as they read, or not.
7. Tell students they will work with partners to find examples of a variety of sentence beginnings.

And Then... *(cont.)*

Engage

8. Ask students to *Heads-up, Stand-up, Partner-up* and work together to look through some books to find examples of sentence beginning variety. Gather students back together. Provide time for students to share with the whole class what they discovered.

Apply

9. Remind students to be aware of how they begin sentences as they write. Encourage them to concentrate on using a variety of beginnings. Suggest that students pay attention to beginning words they write in sentences.

Write/Conference

10. Provide time for students to write. Encourage students to look back at the beginnings they have already written and change them or begin a new writing with a great beginning. Observe student behaviors. Are they on-task? Then, begin having conversations with students and making astute notes about writing behaviors.

Spotlight Strategy

11. Spotlight excellent editing. For example, "Marcia is checking over her sentence beginnings and is making revisions to improve her story. Great job with this new concept!" Encourage the whole class to celebrate by having them stop what they are doing, stand up, and celebrate by waving their hands over their heads.

Share

12. Ask students to lock eyes with someone with whom they would like to have a conversation. Ask them to partner up and share their collected sentence variety and how they applied this concept in their writing.

Homework

Ask students to explore different types of writing like books, newspapers and magazines, and look for sentence beginnings. Have students write down three interesting sentences they read. Ask students to be ready to share their interesting sentences with the class tomorrow.

Fun with Sentence Variety

Standards

- Uses strategies to draft and revise written work
- Uses complete sentences in written compositions

Materials

- Chart paper
- Markers
- *Fun with Sentence Variety* (page 106; funsentencevariety.pdf)

Mentor Texts

- *The Relatives Came* by Cynthia Rylant
- *Owl Moon* by Jane Yolen
- See *Mentor Text List* in Appendix C for other suggestions.

Procedures

Think About Writing

1. Review with students that they have been working on adding details to their sentences to make them more interesting for their readers.
2. Review a mentor text if desired, and emphasize the author's use of interesting sentences.

Teach

3. Tell students, "Today I will show you a way to add variety to our sentences by adding prepositional phrases and adjectives."
4. Create a four-columned chart on a sheet of chart paper. Name and number the columns as shown below.

1	2	3	4
What is it?	What can it do?	What is it like?	Where/When does the action take place?

5. Model creating sentences by answering the questions in the order of the numbers at the top of the columns. For example:

1—What was it?
car

2—What did it do?
bumped

3—What was it like?
old

4—Where/When did the action take place?
up and over the hills on a snowy day

The old car bumped up and over the hills on a snowy day.

Fun with Sentence Variety *(cont.)*

3-What was it like?	1- What was it?	2-What did it do?	4-Where/ When did it do the action?
old	car	bumped	up and over the hills on a snowy day
The old car bumped up and over the hills on a snowy day.			

This order of the information makes it easy to develop into a complete sentence.

Engage

6. Distribute *Fun with Sentence Variety* (page 106) to students. Have students *Heads-up, Stand-up, Partner-up* and work with partners to brainstorm and create interesting sentences using the numbered columns. Remind students to turn and look and use the chart for practice. Ask students to create a sentence about an animal and another sentence about a baby. Allow time for discussion and then share a few with the group.

Apply

7. Remind students to use sentence fluency, variety, and style to enliven and energize your writing. Using *Fun with Sentence Variety*, encourage them to write sentences in their folders about the other topics they brainstormed in their groups.

Write/Conference

8. Provide time for students to write about other ideas they have brainstormed. Scan your audience for difficulties and then begin to confer. Make observations and remember to compliment and teach.

Spotlight Strategy

9. Spotlight students' sentence variety. For example, "David has a brilliant sentence. Just listen to how his prepositions tell when and where." (Read the sentence.) "Amazing sentence work today. Remember to use this in your writing and always check to see if your sentences give details. Your work ethic is sparkling and shining. Woo, writers, you rock!"

Share

10. Have students meet with partners and share their best sentences. Then have student pairs get together with another pair to make a quad and share again. Remind students to pick out their best sentences. Remember to observe and make anecdotal notes.

Homework

Have students practice creating the sentences with variety by writing three interesting sentences tonight. Encourage students to be ready to share tomorrow in Writer's Workshop.

Fun with Sentence Variety

Directions: Complete the chart below to brainstorm sentence ideas. Write your sentences in the space provided.

3 What is it like?	1 What is it?	2 What can it do?	4 Where/when does it do the action?

My Sentences: ______________________________

____

____

____

Writing Detective: Sentences

Standards

- Uses strategies to draft and revise written work
- Uses complete sentences in written compositions

Materials

- Chart paper
- Markers
- *Writing Detective Sentence Cards* (pages 109–110; detectivecards.pdf)

Mentor Text

- *Owl Moon* by Jane Yolen
- See *Mentor Text List* in Appendix C for other suggestions

Procedures

Note: The process used in this lesson about sentences can be used to add details to a paragraph.

Think About Writing

1. Remind students that authors think about how to form their sentences in order to make their writing interesting to the reader. Authors add details to their writing in order to make it interesting and to help the reader understand their stories better.
2. Review a mentor text if desired, and emphasize the author's use of interesting sentences.

Teach

3. Tell students, "Today I will show you how to use questions to add details to build your sentences." Explain to students that they will be writing detectives to ask questions, such as *Who?*, *What?*, *When?*, *Where?*, and *Why?*
4. Explain to students that as they write sentences, they should keep some questions in mind: *Who?*, *What?*, *When?*, *Where?*, and *Why?* Tell students the more of these questions they are able to answer in a sentence, the more clear the sentence will be.
5. Model how to create a sentence by answering several of the questions.

Who will be in my sentence?	My sister
What will she be doing?	Playing
Where will she do it?	In her room
When did she do it?	This morning

Create a sentence with all the answers to the questions:

My sister was playing in her room this morning.

Writing Detective: Sentences (cont.)

6. Discuss with students how the sentence gives lots of information, so the reader can better understand what has happened.

Engage

7. Ask students to *Heads-up, Stand-up, Partner-up*. Tell students it is their turn to work with partners to be writing detectives. Distribute *Writing Detective Sentence Cards* (pages 109–110). Provide students two or three minutes to orally create sentences that have a subject, predicate, and answer a question from the card. For example: The three-eyed alien landed in the field at midnight. Ask a few partner pairs to share their sentences.

Apply

8. Remind students to give their readers writing details to invite them into their writing. Tell students that the *Writing Detective Sentence Cards* can be a valuable tool as they write. Remind them to keep them in their writing folders so it will be handy while they are writing.

Write/Conference

9. Provide time for students to write. Scan the class for understanding of the sentence strategy. Meet with students having difficulty with sentence structure and use this strategy to support their efforts. You may wish to help struggling students use *Be a Writing Detective* to guide their sentence writing efforts. Record compliments and teaching points in your conferring notebook.

Spotlight Strategy

10. Spotlight by reading a specific students' work. For example, "Listen to the sentence Elian has created being a writing detective. I am so proud of your exceptional work. Spotlight on Elian!"

Share

11. Have students meet with partners to share their work. Encourage students to ask their partners which questions were used to develop the sentences they share.

Homework

Ask students to look around and find ideas for creating great sentences. Have students be writing detectives and write three interesting sentences. Ask students to add their sentences as writing ideas in their writing folders.

Writing Detective Sentence Cards

Teacher Directions: Cut out the cards below on the dotted lines and distribute them to students to help create sentences.

Be a Writing Detective! 	**Be a Writing Detective!** 
Who?	**Who?**
What?	**What?**
When?	**When?**
Where?	**Where?**
Why?	**Why?**

Writing Detective Sentence Cards *(cont.)*

Teacher Directions: Cut out the cards and use as described in lesson.

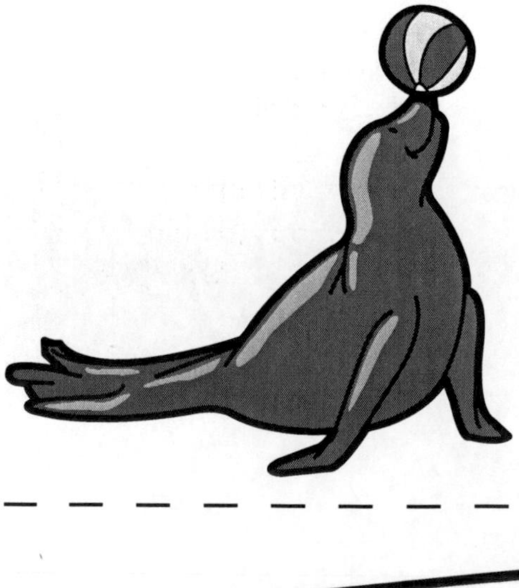

Organization

Linking the Pieces Together

Organization provides the structure of writing. It helps readers make connections from one idea to the next. Organization provides the skeletal support for the overall meaning of writing. The lessons assist students to explore different types of writing and the ways they are organized. Lessons in this section include the following:

The *Owen Organization Conductor* poster (page 112) can be displayed in the room to provide a visual reminder for students that organization is one of the traits of writing. You may wish to introduce this poster during the first lesson on organization. Then, refer to the poster when teaching other lessons on organization to refresh students' memories and provide them questions to help guide them as they work to organize their writing.

Owen Organization Conductor

How do I plan my writing?

- ✔ Did I sequence my thoughts?
- ✔ Did I have a beginning, middle, and end?
- ✔ Did I hook my reader?
- ✔ Did I include transition words?

Poetry—Simple Acrostic

Standards

- Uses strategies to organize written work
- Writes in a variety of forms or genres

Materials

- Chart paper
- Markers

Mentor Texts

- *Animal Acrostics* by David Hummon
- See *Mentor Text List* in Appendix C for other suggestions.

Procedures

Note: You may wish to have the whole class develop an acrostic poem using the same topic. Students may also enjoy working with partners to develop their poetry. Challenge students to add a line or two of alliteration (words with the same beginning sound).

Think About Writing

1. Review with students the traditional direction authors write—from left to right. Explain that some authors like to have fun with the placement of the words in order to provide excitement to the reader.
2. Review a mentor text if desired, and emphasize the author's organization of the text in acrostic poems.

Teach

3. Tell students, "Today I will show you how to create an acrostic poem to entertain your readers."
4. Explain to students that acrostic poems begin with a word or sometimes a phrase. It is usually the topic of the poem and it is written vertically. Model how to create an acrostic poem by writing the word *fish* vertically on a sheet of chart paper.
5. Show students how each letter of the word *fish* becomes the first letter of a word. See the sample below:

Fish

Fin

Icky

Slippery

Hook

Poetry—Simple Acrostic *(cont.)*

6. Model for students how the letters of the word can become the first letter of phrases. For example:

   Birds

   Bugs for breakfast

   Insects for lunch

   Red and brown feathers,

   Dinner is worms,

   Singing all day!

Engage

7. Have students *Heads-up, Stand-up, Partner-up* and work with partners to share their topics and brainstorm some ideas for each letter in the word. Remind students to take turns and give each other ideas.

Apply

8. Remind students that acrostic poems are one way to entertain readers by using wordplay. Ask students to remember to use the example and what they shared with their partners as they go off to write their own acrostic poems.

Write/ Conference

9. Provide time for students to write a simple acrostic poem. Rotate around the room to observe and assist students needing support. Gather a small group to create a group poem, if needed. Use your conferring notebook to note student growth and needs.

Spotlight Strategy

10. Spotlight poetic efforts. For example, "I am so excited to share with you. Catelyn is using very descriptive words to describe her topic. Just like a real poet."

Share

11. Have students meet with partners to share their poetry. Remind students to listen for describing words and to give compliments.

Homework

Ask students to look around at all the fabulous people, places, and things they can use to write an acrostic poem. Have students write an acrostic poem about the word *home* as their homework.

Poetry—Triante

Standards

- Uses strategies to organize written work
- Writes in a variety of forms or genres

Materials

- Chart paper
- Markers
- *Triante Poem Organizer* (page 117; poemorganizer.pdf)
- Chart created in *Ideas Thinking Chart* Lesson (page 55)

Mentor Texts

- Poem collections, such as Shel Silverstein's or Jack Prelutsky's
- CCSS Poetry
- Core Reading Program
- See *Mentor Text List* in Appendix C for other suggestions.

Procedures

Note: Build background for students on this pyramid type of poem by talking with them about objects that also begin with "tri." You could relate the shape of the poem to a triangle, a tricycle, a tripod, etc.

Think About Writing

1. Explain to students they are beginning to understand words and phrases with rhythm, rhyme, and meaning by reading and studying the works of professional authors.
2. Review mentor texts if desired, and emphasize the rhythm and rhyme of the poems.

Teach

3. Tell students, "Today I will show you another fun way to explore, experiment, and play with words. The words used in today's lesson do not rhyme. The words are related to the five senses.
4. Write the following triante pattern on a sheet of chart paper:

   Line 1—Title Word

   Line 2—Smells (2 words)

   Line 3—Touch, Taste (3 words)

   Line 4—Sight (4 words)

   Line 5—Sounds/Actions (5 words)
5. Model how to choose a topic for a poem. The Chart created in the Ideas *Thinking Chart Lesson* (page 55) is *a good place to look for poem ideas*.

Poetry—Triante *(cont.)*

6. Create a triante poem based on the pattern and the topic you have selected. For example:

   Squirrels

   Musky, earthy

   Fuzzy, soft, cuddly

   Grey, fast, fearful, active

   Jumping, climbing, digging, eating, chattering

Engage

7. Have students *Heads-up, Stand-up, Partner-up* and talk to partners about topics that interest them that they may want to use when writing their triante poem. Ask them to name words they may use in their poems. Rotate among students as they share with partners. Listen for good ideas you may want to highlight and use sticky notes to take notes. Provide approximately three minutes for students to talk with each other.

Apply

8. Share something with the class you heard while monitoring to support others who may have struggled. Remind students they may write in any style they wish, but encourage them to try a triante poem.

Write/Conference

9. Provide time for students to write a triante poem or another poem of their choice. Distribute *Triante Poem Organizer* (page 117) to students who may need support with organizing the poem. Work with any students who need reteaching. Remember to keep notes for your next instructional plan. When finished with the small group, rotate among the rest of the class and have individual conferences. Ask questions that teach such as: How did you choose your topic? What problems are you having?

Spotlight Strategy

10. Spotlight the entire group today so that you are building a risk-free environment. Find something positive to say about the group as a whole.

Share

11. Select three students to share in the author's chair. Choose students whose work will echo your lesson.

Homework

Ask students to make a list of the five senses. Have students write six words that relate to each of the senses. Encourage students to have their parents help them think of interesting sense words.

Triante Poem Organizer

Directions: Use the organizer below to write a triante poem.

Topic: ____________

Smell: ____________ Smell: ____________

Touch: ____________ Touch: ____________ Touch: ____________

Sight: ____________ Sight: ____________ Sight: ____________ Sight: ____________

Sounds/ Actions: ____________ Sounds/ Actions: ____________ Sounds/ Actions: ____________ Sounds/ Actions: ____________ Sounds/ Actions: ____________

Making Alphabet Books

Standards

- Uses strategies to organize written work
- Writes in a variety of forms or genres

Materials

- Drawing paper
- Chart paper
- *My Alphabet Book* (abcbook.pdf)

Mentor Texts

- *A My Name is Alice* by Jane Bayer
- *Animal Alphabet* by Bert Kitchen
- See *Mentor Text List* in Appendix C for other suggestions.

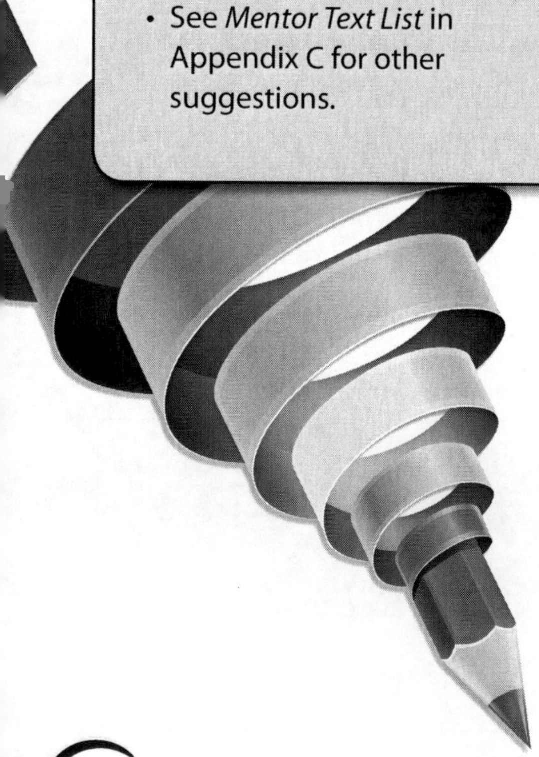

Procedures

Note: This lesson can be used for all levels and with topics in all content areas, for example: weather, space, holidays, or community helpers. You may wish to have your letters already typed on the sheets of paper you distribute, or have students write the letters themselves.

Think About Writing

1. Tell students there are many techniques and activities for creating many different types of text. We have practiced making lists of topics, discovered ways to spin ideas into stories and used "rubber band" writing to make writing fun and energetic. Writers explore and experiment with many ways to write.
2. Review a mentor text if desired, and emphasize the book's organization around the alphabet.

Teach

3. Tell students, "Today I will show you how to build an alphabet book." Remind students there are 26 letters in the alphabet.
4. Review several alphabet books with students. Discuss with students the various ways the alphabet books are laid out, specifically how many letters are on each page or how many letters share a page. Help students identify the text structure of the books. For example, are there pictures with labels? Is there a text pattern? Does the text rhyme?
5. As a class, determine the layout and format of the book you will create. Explain to students that you will create an original alphabet book as a class and decide on a topic, such as *community*, *animals*, *holidays*, etc.

Making Alphabet Books *(cont.)*

6. Choose a letter of the alphabet and model how to write the uppercase and lowercase letter and make illustrations to begin with that letter. Label or write sentences to match your picture(s). Distribute drawing paper and assign each student a letter of the alphabet. Or, have students use My *Alphabet Book* (abcbook.pdf) to create their alphabet books.

Engage

7. Tell students to *Heads-up, Stand-up, Partner-up*. Ask students to think of a picture, word, or sentence that supports the letters they have been assigned. Have students share their ideas with partners.

Apply

8. Tell students that they can create other alphabet books during another Writer's Workshop about topics of their choice. During this Writer's Workshop, they will work on a letter to make a class book about the chosen topic.

Write/Conference

9. Provide time for students to work on their page. Observe your group briefly for any uncertainties and reteach if necessary. When students are engaged, begin to compliment and teach individuals or small groups. Remember to keep records of your observations.

Spotlight Strategy

10. Spotlight alphabet book efforts. For example, "What a brilliant beginning! Each of you is busy with your part of the alphabet book. Nigel is working on the letter *T* and has an excellent drawing. His letters are perfectly formed and he is busy exploring ideas."

Share

11. Have students meet in triads to share their writing. Remind students to give a compliment and a comment. Consider sharing in order of ABCs.

Homework

At home, have students look for things that begin with each letter of the alphabet for ideas of things to draw in their alphabet books. Have them write their ideas down to later add to their books.

My Hand Plan

Standards
- Uses strategies to organize written work
- Writes in a variety of forms or genres

Materials
- Chart paper
- Markers
- *Hand Plan Samples* (pages 122–123; handplansamples.pdf)
- *Topic Ideas* (page 125; topicideas.pdf)
- *My Hand Plan* (page 124; myhandplan.pdf)

Mentor Texts
- *What Do You Do With a Tail Like This?* by Steve Jenkins
- *What Presidents Are Made Of* by Hanoch Piven
- *The Perfect Pet* by Margie Palatini
- *Hey, Little Ant!* by Phillip & Hannah Hoose
- *Snow Day!* by Lester Laminack
- *Animal Alphabet* by Bert Kitchen
- Other CCSS literature for genres of writing
- See *Mentor Text List* in Appendix C for other suggestions.

Procedures
Note: This organizer may be used for all genres and students should develop a complete paragraph by the end of week eighteen. Remember to allow many opportunities for oral rehearsal and student engagement. Each can promote vocabulary, language skills, and increase the volume of writing. You may also use the plan as a story frame planner: pinkie/characters, ring finger/setting, middle finger/problem, pointer/events, thumb/wrap-up and conclusion.

Think About Writing
1. Tell students organization is what helps the reader follow what is happening in a story. Authors must think about how to organize their stories to best be understood. Explain that there are many ways to organize stories.
2. Review a mentor text if desired, and emphasize the author's use of organization and details.

Teach
3. Tell students, "Today I will show you a tool you can use to organize your thinking when you plan your writing."
4. Show students your hand and explain that it can be used to create a *Hand Plan* for organizing your writing. Explain to students the palm represents the topic of the writing. Explain that your pinkie, ring finger, middle finger, and index finger represent the details you want to share about the topic. Finally, the thumb represents the conclusion or wrap-up statement.
5. Have students hold up their hands and review what each finger represents with them.
6. Model for students how to create a *Hand Plan* to organize a story. Create your own or use one of the ideas from the *Hand Plan Samples* (pages 122–123). You may wish to also demonstrate how to trace your hand on a piece of paper and take notes on the drawings of the fingers. Having notes may help some students as they write.

My Hand Plan *(cont.)*

Engage

7. Have students *Heads-up, Stand-up, Partner-up* and work with partners to orally practice their *Hand Plan* for what they will write today. Have them touch their fingers to tell the main idea, details, and wrap up. Suggest topics from *Topic Ideas* (page 125) if students are having a difficult time coming up with their own.
8. Observe as students work. Remember to move around, look around, and listen. Share ideas you heard during partner discussions that provide support for others. Recognize partners for contributions.

Apply

9. Remind students to use their *Hand Plan* as they write today. It will help them to have organized and interesting details they can use when they write.

Write/Conference

10. Provide time for students to write using *My Hand Plan* (page 124). After students are all settled, rotate around the room conferencing with students. Ask questions such as: What are you working on as a writer? What will you do as a writer when finished with your organizer?

Spotlight Strategy

11. Choose one or two students who were very successful with the strategy and have them share their ideas with the class. This reinforces the organization strategy you taught.

Share

12. Have students meet with partners to share how they used their Hand Plan.

Homework

Ask students to look for interesting topics and create a Hand Plan for a story. Have students write one sentence for each of the fingers of their Hand Plan. Have students save their Hand Plans as writing ideas in their writing folders.

Hand Plan Samples

Opinion

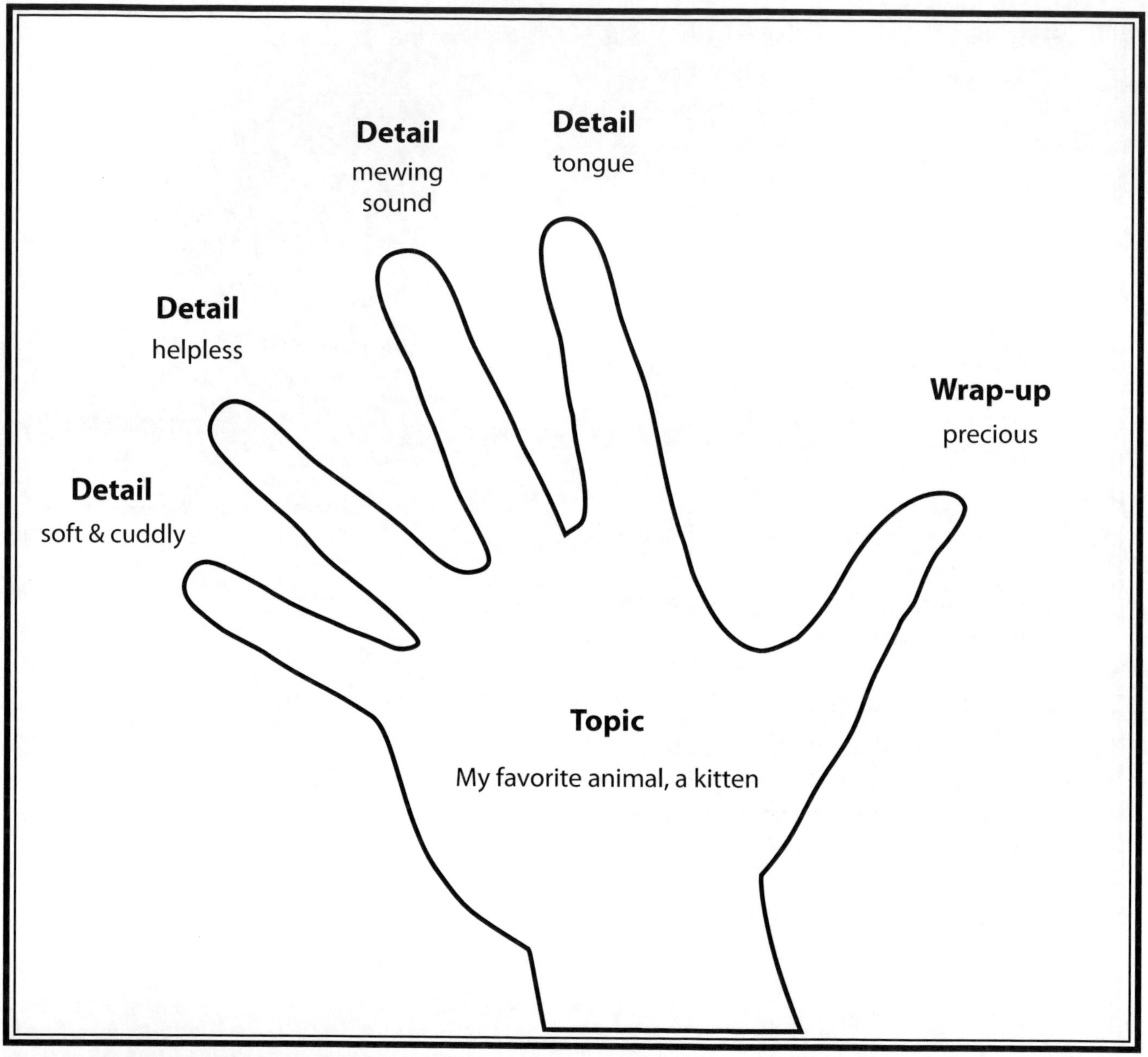

Paragraph:

My favorite animal is a tiny kitten. When you stroke their bodies they are soft and cuddly. As a baby, they are helpless, but affectionate as they grow older. Sometimes they make a mewing sound, just like a baby crying. A kitten's tongue is scratchy and rough. Baby kittens are precious and grow up to make great pets.

Hand Plan Samples *(cont.)*

Narrative

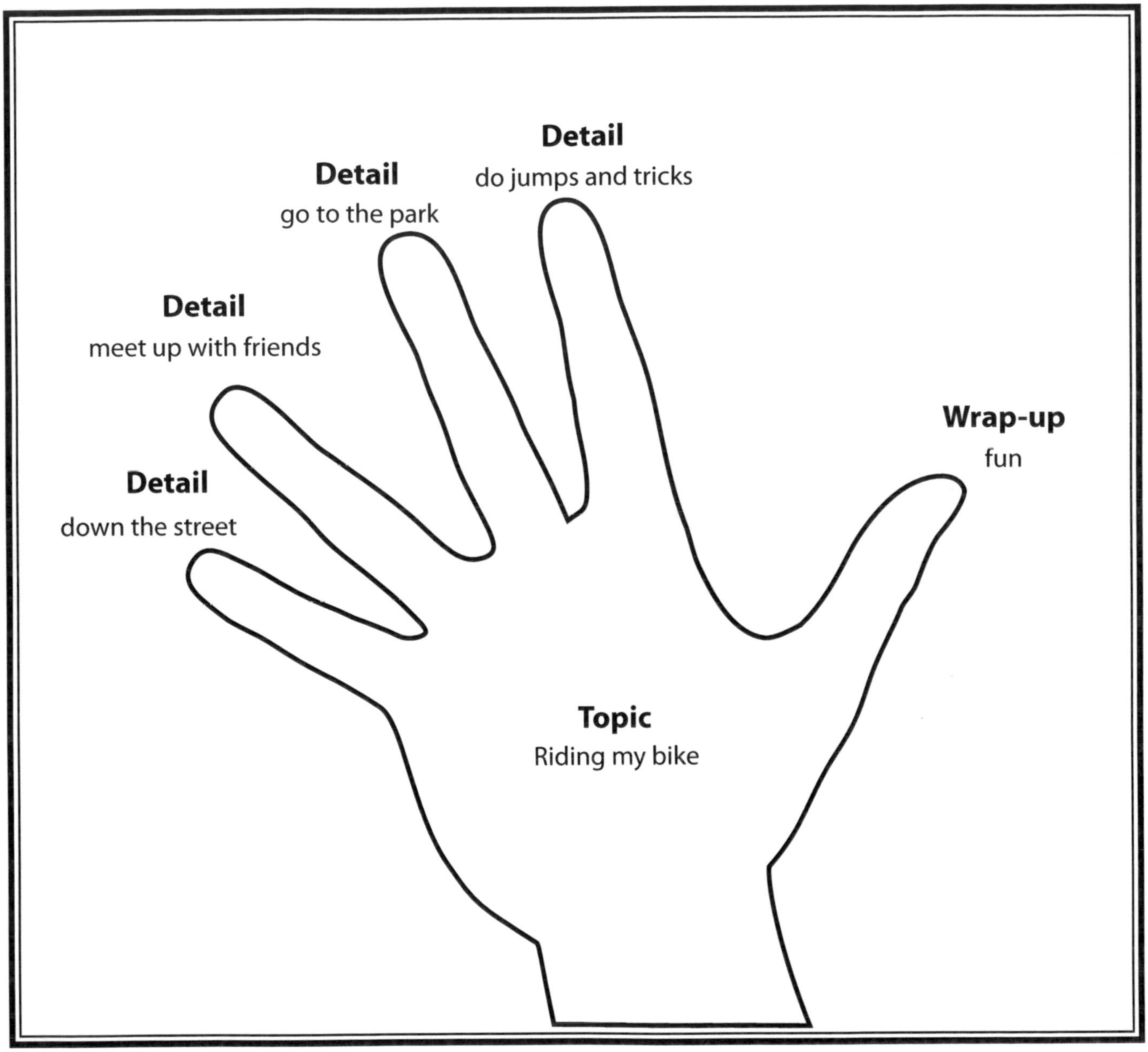

Paragraph:

On warm sunny days, I like to go bike riding. Often I ride down the street by my house and sometimes I meander all around town. During the summer, I often meet up with good friends. Frequently, we ride into the local park that is filled with special bike trails. When we are out of sight, we practice doing special jumps and tricks. Riding bikes keeps me busy and is much more fun than sitting on the couch playing videos.

Name: ______________________ Date: ______________

My Hand Plan

Directions: Use the hand below to help you plan your writing.

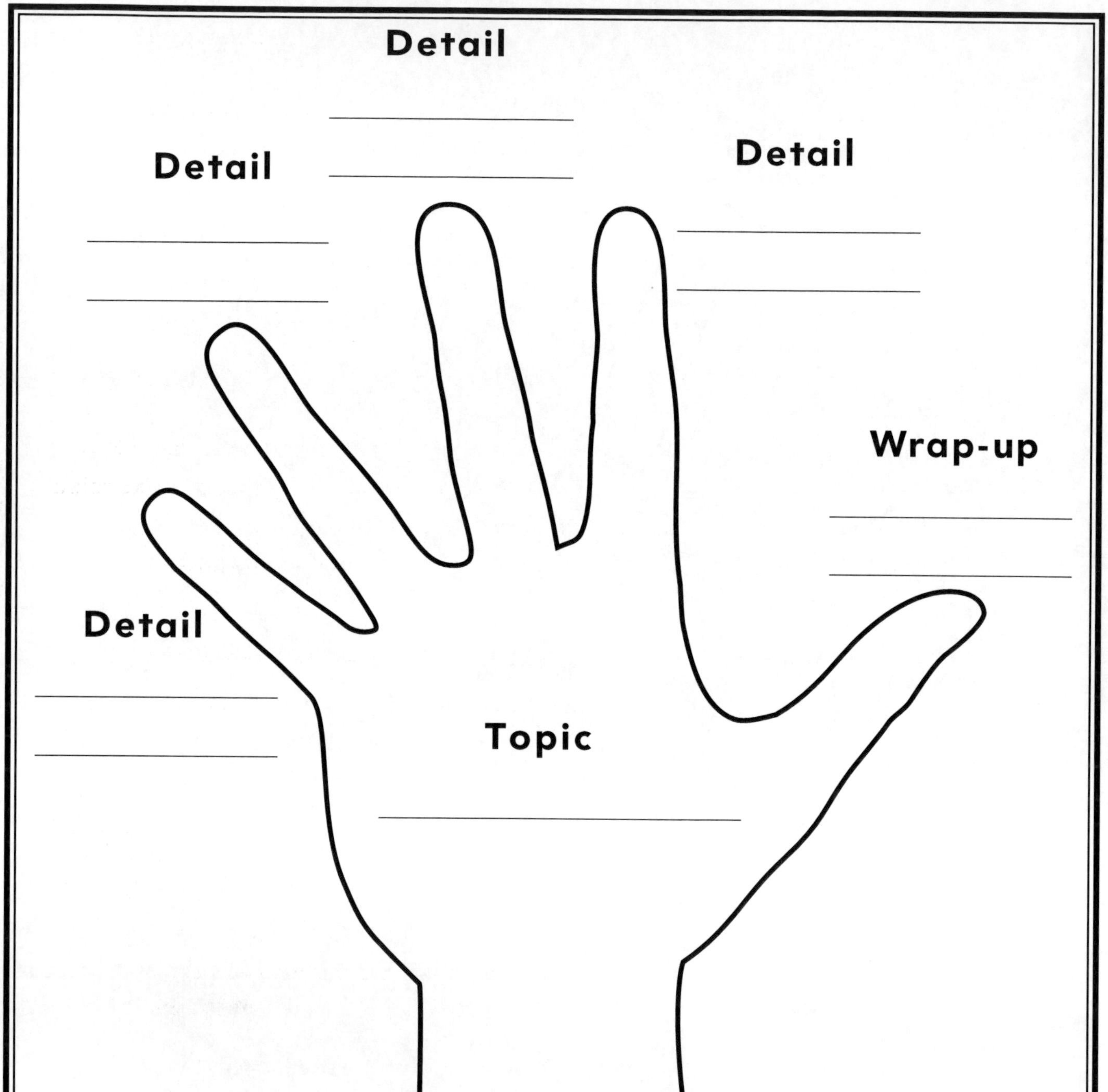

Topic Ideas

Narrative

- Best friends
- Best/worst experience
- Family fun
- Getting along with others
- Helping others
- Making wishes
- Sharing happy times
- Sharing scary times
- Sharing special people
- Sharing special time/trips
- Working together/cooperation

Informative

- Animals and their habitats
- Community helpers
- Other cultures/comparison
- Environment
- Famous/Historical people
- Healthy habits
- Holiday celebrations
- Life Cycles: frogs, chicks, etc.
- Making healthy snacks
- Our nation's symbols
- Plants and Trees
- Safety
- Using manners
- Weather: wind and storms

Opinion

- If I could live anywhere, it would be...
- My favorite family activity
- My favorite holiday
- My favorite season
- My favorite story, character
- Taking care of others
- The best animal for a pet
- The best hobby is...
- The best invention is...
- The best place for a vacation...
- Why eat healthy snacks/exercise
- Why I admire...
- Famous/Historical people
- Why I need a pet
- Why we need a best friend

Now, That's a Story!

Standards

- Uses strategies to organize written work
- Writes in a variety of forms or genres

Materials

- Chart paper
- Markers
- *My Story Mountain* (page 128; mountainstory.pdf)
- *Story Mountain Cards* (pages 129–130; storymountaincards.pdf)

Mentor Texts

- *Goldilocks and the Three Bears* by Jan Brett
- *The Lion and the Mouse* by Jerry Pinkney
- *Amos and Boris* by William Steig
- See *Mentor Text List* in Appendix C for other suggestions.

Procedures

Note: Select your favorite narrative for this mini-lesson to show the story development. Discuss story structure throughout the day during whole- and small-group reading, as well as during read alouds.

Think About Writing

1. Explain to students that writers write many different kinds of stories, essays, and compositions. Tell students that one important part of writing for an author is to organize his or her story.
2. Review a mentor text if desired, and emphasize the structure of the story.

Teach

3. Tell students, "Today I will show you how to organize a story by using an author's secret tool. That tool is called a *Story Mountain*."
4. Display *My Story Mountain* (page 128). Describe and discuss each part of the mountain. Explain how the writer starts at the bottom of the mountain and builds our excitement and curiosity until we reach the problem and then heads back down the mountain as the problem is solved.
5. Draw the shape of a story mountain on chart paper. Retell the story of *The Lion and the Mouse* using the *Story Mountain Cards* (pages 129–130). As you tell the story, tape the appropriate cards on the mountain in the correct place. Review and discuss the structure of the story when you are done retelling the story.

Engage

6. Have students *Heads-up, Stand-up, Partner-up* and work with partners to discuss the story of *The Three Little Pigs*. Ask them to determine each story element using the story mountain. Allow time for discussion and then write the results on a new story mountain as students share their ideas.

Now, That's a Story! *(cont.)*

Apply

7. Remind students to organize their writing in a way that holds the readers' attention and builds an exciting story. Also remind them that stories always include a beginning, middle and end.

Write/Conference

8. Provide time for students to write a story starting with characters and a setting. Observe student behaviors and assist before moving off to confer with individuals or groups. Some students may need additional support to build story structure. Note observations in your conferring notebook.

Spotlight Strategy

9. Spotlight student story building. For example, "Spotlight on Maria! She is building a story and has started with characters and a setting. I can hardly wait to hear about the problem of these characters. Now, that's going to be some story!"

Share

10. Select one or two students to take the author's chair and share their important writing work. Allow others to share as appropriate.

Homework

Ask students to choose their favorite stories. Have students make a list of the story elements. Ask students to be ready to share their findings in Writer's Workshop tomorrow.

Name: ____________________ Date: ____________________

My Story Mountain

Directions: Complete the graphic organizer below to plan your story.

Problem:
What's the trouble?

____

____

Build-Up:
What are your characters doing?

____

____

____

Fix-Up:
How does this problem get solved? Who helps?

____

____

____

Title:

____

Introduction
Characters: Who?
Setting: When/Where?

____

____

Wrap-Up:
What happened at the end of the story?

____

____

Story Mountain Cards

Teacher Directions: Cut out the following cards and use them as directed in the lesson.

The Lion and the Mouse

Story Mountain Cards *(cont.)*

Brilliant Beginnings

Standard

Uses strategies to organize written work

Materials

- Chart paper
- Markers
- *Organization Mentor Texts—Beginnings and Endings* (page 135; organizationbegend.pdf)

Mentor Texts

- *Hello Ocean* by Pam Muñoz Ryan
- *Grandpa's Teeth* by Rod Clement
- *Bedhead* by Margie Palatini
- See *Mentor Text List* in Appendix C for other suggestions.

Procedures

Note: Repeat this mini-lesson using other text to remind students of options for story beginnings. During read-alouds, take time to discuss the beginnings of the different genres. Write those on a chart for student support.

Think About Writing

1. Tell students that when a craftsman is learning a new skill, he or she works with a mentor, someone who is an expert at their craft. After they study with their mentor, they are ready to begin working on their own.
2. Explain that authors read and learn from other authors' stories. We will also explore and examine the writing of authors to help us think, plan, and write our own stories.

Teach

3. Tell students, "Today I will show you how to be an apprentice and examine the work of master authors to learn about how they begin their stories."
4. Explain that many fairy tales begin: *Once upon a time*. But authors begin their stories in many different ways. We can study your favorite authors and start our stories the same ways.
5. Read the openings of several mentor texts. For suggested texts, see *Organization Mentor Texts—Beginnings, and Endings* (page 135). For example, read the opening of *Bedhead* by Margie Palatini. "Shuffle-shlump, shuffle-shlump, shlumped bleary-eyed Oliver out of bed, down the hall, and into the bathroom."
6. Discuss the way the author begins the story. For example, Margie Palatini begins her story with a sound. Create a chart of the various ways author's begin their books. Add to the chart more books and notice other types of openings. Refer to these as "hooks" that grab the reader's attention and leave them wanting more.

Brilliant Beginnings *(cont.)*

7. Model how to begin a new piece of writing similar to the mentor text. For example, based on the opening to *Bedhead*, you might write, "Drip, drop. Drip, drop. Drip, drip, drip. As I ran and looked out the window, I knew the day was ruined."

Engage

8. Have students *Heads-up, Stand-up, Partner-up* and talk with partners to develop a hook or beginning of their own. Allow time for discussion and share some examples.

Apply

9. Remind students that we can study and imitate the work of authors. Challenge students to be on the lookout for brilliant beginnings in the stories and movies they read and watch.

Write/Conference

10. Provide time for students to write stories with a great hook. This may be a more difficult task for some writers. Conference with individuals or pull small groups to check for understanding. Record observations in your log for future planning.

Spotlight Strategy

11. Spotlight brilliant beginnings. For example, "You are filling your page with ideas from the masters. Listen to what Kim has written! You have really grown as writers, and taken a great step forward."

Share

12. Have students share their writing with partners. Ask students to be on the lookout for some brilliant beginnings. Remind students to give a compliment and a suggestion.

Homework

Ask students to find two of their favorite books at home and to read how the stories begin. Have students write the first three sentences of each story. Have students compare the beginnings of their stories the next day.

Excellent Endings

Standard

Uses strategies to organize written work

Materials

- Chart paper
- Markers
- Mentor text
- *Organization Mentor Texts—Beginnings and Endings* (page 135; organizationbegend.pdf)

Mentor Texts

- *A Bad Case of Stripes* by David Shannon
- *The Relatives Came* by Cynthia Rylant
- See *Mentor Text List* in Appendix C for other suggestions.

Procedures

Note: Repeat this mini-lesson using mentor text to provide students with other options for story endings. During read-alouds, take time to discuss the endings of the different genres. Write those on a chart for student support.

Think About Writing

1. Review with students what they have been working on, including brilliant beginnings to hook their readers. Explain that authors plan the order of their stories very carefully.
2. Tell students that another important area to examine is the way authors end their writing. The ending of your writing should wrap up the story and give the reader something to think about.

Teach

3. Tell students, "Today I will show you a strategy that authors use to develop their story endings that you might like to try in your own writing."
4. Explain to students that a circular ending is one way authors end stories. It is a way to tie the beginning and the ending together. Review a mentor text with a circular ending with students and discuss the circular ending. For suggested texts, see *Organization Mentor Texts—Beginnings and Endings* (page 135) For example, *A Bad Case of Stripes* by David Shannon begins with the sentence, "Camilla Cream loved lima beans." It ends with the sentence, "She ate all the lima beans she wanted and never had a touch of the stripes again." Discuss with students how the beginning and ending relate to each other.
5. Review other mentor texts and discuss the way the stories end. Begin a chart, and add various ways authors end their stories to the chart as you read other stories.

Excellent Endings *(cont.)*

Engage

6. Have students Turn and Talk with partners about how they might use a circular ending in one of their writing pieces.

Apply

7. Remind students that we can study and imitate the work of our favorite authors. Encourage students to be on the lookout for excellent endings in the stories and movies they read and watch.

Write/Conference

8. Provide time for students to write. Rotate and conference with individual students or pull small groups to check for understanding. Record observations in your log for future planning.

Spotlight Strategy

9. Spotlight excellent endings. For example, "Alex is working on making connections to his beginning and developing an excellent ending. I am impressed!" Be sure to recognize student efforts with praise.

Share

10. Select two or three students who have explored circular endings to sit in the author's chair to share their writing with the class. Encourage students to compliment and ask questions.

Homework

Have students look at the endings of two of their favorite books at home. Ask students to copy the last three sentences of each book on paper. Have students share the endings they copied the next day in Writer's Workshop.

Organization Mentor Texts—Beginnings and Endings

Mentor Texts to Explore Brilliant Beginnings

- *Bedhead* by Margie Palatini (Sound)
- *Click, Clack, Moo* by Doreen Cronin (Sound)
- *Hello Ocean* by Pam Muñoz Ryan (Senses)
- *Grandpa's Teeth* by Rod Clement (Dialogue/Problem)
- *The Day Jimmy's Boa Ate the Wash* by Trinka Hakes Noble (Flashback)
- *Alexander and the Terrible, Horrible, No Good, Very Bad Day* by Judith Viorst (Action)
- *I Love Guinea Pigs* by Dick King-Smith (Interesting fact/silly)
- *Chrysanthemum* by Kevin Henkes (Character)
- *My Mama Had a Dancing Heart* by Libba Gray (Thought)
- *When I was Young in the Mountains* by Cynthia Rylant (Thoughts)
- *Charlotte's Web* by E. B. White (Question)
- *Hey, Little Ant* by Phillip and Hannah Hoose (Question)
- *Aunt Flossie's Hats* by Elizabeth Howard (Setting)

Mentor Texts to Explore Excellent Endings

- *My Great-Aunt Arizona* by Gloria Houston (Emotion)
- *Night Tree* by Eve Bunting (Emotion/Circular)
- *Hello Ocean* by Pam Muñoz Ryan (Emotions/Circular)
- *Owl Moon* by Jane Yolen (Senses)
- *Grandpa's Teeth* by Rod Clement (Surprise ending)
- *The Wednesday Surprise* by Eve Bunting (Surprise ending)
- *Chester's Way* by Kevin Henkes (Circular)
- *A Bad Case of Stripes* by David Shannon (Circular)
- *The Relatives Came* by Cynthia Rylant (Circular)
- *If You Give a Mouse a Cookie* by Laura Joffe Numeroff (Circular)
- *Shortcut* by Donald Crews (Lesson Learned)
- *Stellaluna* by Janell Cannon (Lesson Learned)

Telling, Sketching, and Writing Narrative Text

Standards

- Uses strategies to organize written work
- Writes in a variety of forms or genres

Materials

- *Sample Narratives* (page 138; samplenarratives.pdf)
- *Beginning, Middle, and End* (page 139; begmidend.pdf)
- *Beginning, Middle and End Writing Paper* (page 140; begmidendpaper.pdf) *(optional)*
- Markers or crayons

Mentor Text

- *The Wednesday Surprise* by Eve Bunting
- *Shortcut* by Donald Crews
- *My Lucky Day* by Keiko Kasza
- See *Mentor Text List* in Appendix C for other suggestions.

Procedures

Note: This lesson on developing a beginning, middle, and end can be repeated and adapted to topics from your read-aloud literature, Core Reading Program, or titles from the Common Core State Standards reading list. Initially, narrative writing may begin with a few sequenced events. Encourage writers to develop beginning, middle, and end paragraphs with topic sentences and specific, interesting details to support. Show students how even informative and opinion writing have a beginning, middle, and end structure.

Think About Writing

1. Explain that authors use interesting sentences and words in their writing. Authors use a brilliant beginning, a logical order to relate events, add details for a mighty middle, and develop an excellent ending.
2. Review a mentor text if desired, and emphasize the author's organization of the story.

Teach

3. Tell students, "Today I will show you how to write a short story about a special time in your life." Explain that they can start gathering ideas for personal narratives by making lists of experiences, like happy times, scary times, etc. Consider showing *Sample Narratives* (page 138) for added examples.
4. Fold a piece of paper in thirds so when it is opened there are three parts. Explain that each section of the paper will be for each section of the story (beginning, middle, and end) and label the sections accordingly. If desired, you can use the *Beginning, Middle, and End* (page 139) story organizer instead.
5. Touch each section of the paper and orally tell each part of the story. Then draw a quick picture in each section to visually show the story. Label the pictures. Each label becomes a specific detail in the writing.
6. Retell the story from beginning to end listening for the logical sequence of the events.

Telling, Sketching, and Writing Narrative Text *(cont.)*

Engage

7. Distribute *Beginning, Middle, and End*. Have students *Heads-up, Stand-up, Partner-up* and work with partners for several minutes. Partner one will touch each box and tell a story using a sequence that makes sense. Partner two will do the same. Observe, encourage, and guide students as needed. Move around and note attempts to share with the group.

Apply

8. Remind students to have a logical sequence to their story writing. Encourage them to use their ears and listen to the flow of stories from many authors.

Write/Conference

9. Provide time for students to write. They can use their *Beginning, Middle and End* in their writing. Keep yourself free to rotate through the classroom on this lesson. Be available to encourage and provide support. Students may use the *Beginning, Middle, and End Writing Paper* (page 140), if desired. Use additional paper if necessary.

Spotlight Strategy

10. Spotlight students who have a clear understanding of sketching a beginning, middle, and end in a logical sequence and spotlight.

Share

11. Have students share their beginning, middle, and end sketches with partners. Remind students to touch, tell and provide compliments and suggestions.

Homework

Ask students to think about their experiences and memories that can be woven into stories. Have students ask their parents to share some special times they remember. Ask students to identify one special time and write three sentences about the event.

Sample Narratives

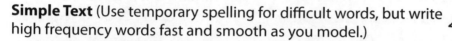

Simple Text (Use temporary spelling for difficult words, but write high frequency words fast and smooth as you model.)

My daughter, Jacalyn Ann, had a pair of hamsters in a cage. One summer day, both hamsters escaped and decided to reside in the kitchen behind the refrigerator. They chewed through the ice maker tubes and water line. It took us forever to catch them, and the damage from their escape was very expensive. That was a terrible week for our family.

Simple Text with Time Cue Words

My daughter, Jacalyn Ann had a pair of hamsters. One day they jumped out of their cage. Next, they hid behind the refrigerator. Then, we caught them and put them back into their cage. It was a great Hamster Rescue!

Enriched Text (This is more complex text that needs to be modeled over several days.)

My daughter, Jacalyn Ann, had a pair of mischievous hamsters. One lovely summer day, we heard something behind the refrigerator. "Oh, no" my daughter yelled! The cover is missing from my hamster cage!"

Days went by, as we frantically tried to nab the quick little creatures. We tried to entice them into a bag with food. A plastic bowl with sunflower seeds was placed beside the refrigerator. Scritch! Scratch! They continued to gnaw away at the back of the refrigerator. Gone was our ice maker tube! Gone was our water line. We were heartbroken and frustrated.

After a few days, Jacalyn came up with a plan. She placed the hamster cage beside the refrigerator, loaded it with tasty food and left it for the night. The next morning, as we tiptoed into the kitchen, the hamsters were curled up in their tissue nest, happy to be back in their private home. That's how the Great Hamster Escape became the Rescue of a Lifetime.

Name: ________________________ Date: ____________________

Beginning, Middle, and End

Directions: Tell a story using the boxes below and touch each box in order as you tell it. Make sure that your story has a beginning, middle, and end. Then, draw a picture that tells your story in each box.

Beginning

Middle

End

Name: ______________________ Date: ________________

Beginning, Middle, and End Writing Paper

Directions: Write your story on the lines below. Make sure to have a hook, beginning, middle, and an end.

Hook:
Beginning:

Middle:

End:

Writing a Letter

Standards

- Uses strategies to organize written work
- Writes in a variety of forms or genres

Materials

- Chart paper
- Markers
- *Letter Samples* (page 144; lettersamples.pdf)
- *My Friendly Letter* (page 143; myfriendlyletter.pdf)

Mentor Text

- *Dear Mr. Blueberry* by Simon James
- *A Letter to Amy* by Ezra Jack Keats
- *Dear Annie* by Judith Caseley
- *Dear Bear* by Joanna Harrison
- See *Mentor Text List* in Appendix C for other suggestions.

Procedures

Note: You may wish to read a variety of texts prior to writing to build understanding. Revisit this mini-lesson to write to grandparents, sports figures, school personnel, friends, literature characters.

Think About Writing

1. Tell students that books are a great place to get ideas for writing. By looking at how authors have organized their books, we can get ideas for different ways we can organize our writing.
2. Review mentor texts if desired, emphasizing the author's organization of the book into letters or notes.

Teach

3. Tell students, "Today I will show you how to write a simple letter to your family or friends." Share samples of letters, cards, thank you notes, and postcards.
4. Explain to students that letters are organized in a different way than many of the stories they have been writing. Letters follow a special format. Explain that a letter has five basic parts:

   Heading: The heading is located in the upper right-hand corner. It also includes the date.

   Greeting: The greeting usually begins with *Dear*, then the person's name. Always use a comma.

   Body: This is the message of your letter or note, or what you want to say to your reader.

   Closing: Tells the reader you are finishing your thoughts.

   Signature: You sign your name directly below the closing.

Writing a Letter *(cont.)*

5. Demonstrate the organization of a letter by modeling how to write a letter on a sheet of chart paper. Discuss and label each of the sections of the letter as you write them. Use *Letter Samples* (page 144) as needed.

Engage

6. Have students *Turn and Talk* to partners and use their five fingers to review the letter parts with their partners.
7. Ask students to think about a letter they would like to write. Have them talk with partners about what they will include in their letters. Ask each of the following questions: To whom would you send a letter? What date will you put on your letter? What greeting will you use? What might you say in your message? How will you close your letter? Give students time to share in-between questions.

Apply

8. Tell students that one way to communicate is to use notes and letters. Remind students they may want to write thank-you notes for gifts received, invitations, and letters. Ask students to think about their partner discussions while they are writing their note or letter.

Write/Conference

9. Distribute *My Friendly Letter* (page 143). Provide time for students to write. This will be a new format for many students. Be ready to problem solve for anyone who may be confused. Keep your conferencing notebook handy for observations.

Spotlight Strategy

10. Gather students back together to spotlight student work. For example, "James got right to work and has accomplished so much writing in such a short amount of time. James, please share your letter with our group! Remarkable writing work!"

Share

11. Have students meet with partners to share their notes or letters. Select one or two students to share in the author's chair. This is a new genre and having students correctly model the format is a powerful teaching tool for the other students.

Homework

Ask students to think about other special people with whom they might communicate. Have students bring the addresses of two people for whom they would like to write a letter.

Name: ______________________ Date: ______________________

My Friendly Letter

Directions: Write a friendly letter in the space below.

Date:

____

Dear ______________________,

____

____

____

____

____

____

Sincerely,

____

Letter Samples

Sample Friendly Letter

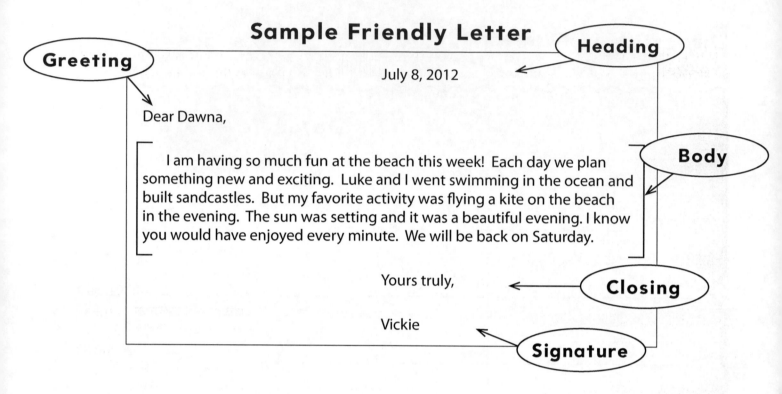

Greeting

Heading

July 8, 2012

Dear Dawna,

Body

I am having so much fun at the beach this week! Each day we plan something new and exciting. Luke and I went swimming in the ocean and built sandcastles. But my favorite activity was flying a kite on the beach in the evening. The sun was setting and it was a beautiful evening. I know you would have enjoyed every minute. We will be back on Saturday.

Yours truly,

Closing

Vickie

Signature

Sample Thank You Note

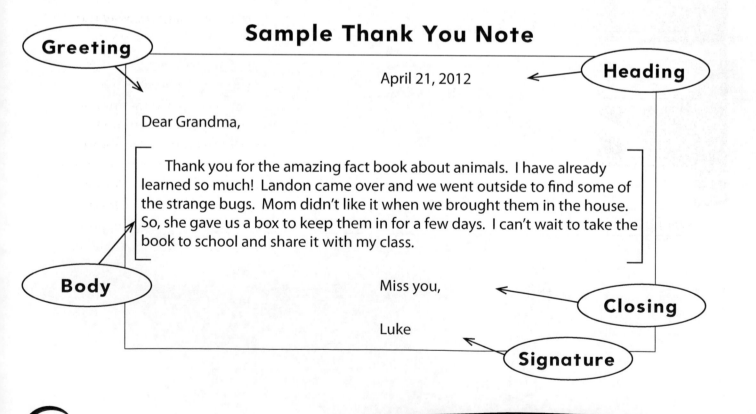

Greeting

Heading

April 21, 2012

Dear Grandma,

Thank you for the amazing fact book about animals. I have already learned so much! Landon came over and we went outside to find some of the strange bugs. Mom didn't like it when we brought them in the house. So, she gave us a box to keep them in for a few days. I can't wait to take the book to school and share it with my class.

Body

Miss you,

Closing

Luke

Signature

Addressing an Envelope

Standards

- Uses strategies to organize written work
- Writes in a variety of forms or genres

Materials

- Chart paper
- Markers
- Envelopes

Mentor Texts

- *With Love, Little Red Hen* by Alma Flor Ada
- See *Mentor Text List* in Appendix C for other suggestions.

Procedures

Note: Inexpensive envelopes can be purchased at discount stores, or consider asking parents for donations of envelopes.

Think About Writing

1. Review the letter-writing format in *Writing a Letter* (page 141).
2. Review mentor texts if desired, and emphasize the addresses on the envelopes.

Teach

3. Tell students, "Today I will show you how to address an envelope in which you can place your letters to mail." Explain to students that letters are usually written because they are going to be mailed. The mail carrier knows where to deliver the mail because there is a format for addressing an envelope.
4. Show students an envelope. Show them the way the letter fits in the envelope, and how to properly seal it.
5. Model for students how to address the envelope. In the upper left-hand corner of the envelope, place your name and address. Halfway down in the middle of the envelope and slightly to the left side, write the complete name and address of the person to whom you are writing. Separate the name of the city from the state with a comma and make the state a two-letter abbreviation; both letters should be capitals. Draw a picture of an envelope on a sheet of chart paper and label the parts of the address. Display the chart paper in the room for students to view.

Addressing an Envelope *(cont.)*

Engage

6. Ask students to *Turn and Talk* with partners about the procedures for addressing an envelope. Encourage them to clear up any confusion before they head off to work.

Apply

7. Remind students that sending letters is an excellent way to use their writing skills and share their thoughts with others. Letter writing and envelope addressing are life skills that they will use regularly as they move through school and through life.

Write/Conference

8. Distribute envelopes to students. Address them using the chart paper as a reference. Monitor addressing to ensure proper placement of text. Remember to compliment, praise, and teach.

Spotlight Strategy

9. Spotlight envelopes addressed well. For example, "Please turn and look at the beautiful envelope addressed by Annika. When I finish showing Annika's envelope, please give her a round of applause with your finger and thumb."

Share

10. Have students meet with partners to share the envelopes they created today. Remind students to provide lots of compliments to their partners.

Homework

Ask students to talk with their families about letter writing. Have them ask if their parents address envelopes to pay bills, to write to family members, or to stay in touch with a friend? Have students ask their parents if they can help address the envelopes.

Informative: My 1-2-3 Report

Standards

- Uses strategies to organize written work
- Writes in a variety of forms or genres

Materials

- *My Report Planner: 1-2-3* (page 150; reportplanner123.pdf)
- *Informative Report Sample* (page 149; informreportsample.pdf)

Mentor Texts

- Select nonfiction titles based on your theme.
- Gail Gibbons, Jim Arnosky, and Wendy Pfeffer are a few of the many recognized authors of nonfiction for young children
- *National Geographic Kids* and *Eye Wonder*: DK Publishing are also excellent resources for young researchers
- See *Mentor Text List* in Appendix C for other suggestions.

Procedures

Note: This mini-lesson is designed to move through the Five-Step Writing Process and will take several days. Immerse students in informational texts and provide access to texts for researching topics.

Think About Writing

1. Remind students that they have read, studied, and written many different writing genres. Explain that today, they will explore another form of informational writing, a report. Authors write reports to give facts and details about a topic that is of interest to them. Scientists, journalists, and even police officers write reports to give facts and information to their readers.
2. Review a mentor text if desired, and emphasize the way the author presents information.

Teach

3. Tell students, "Today we will begin developing informational reports. We will work each day, using the five steps of the writing process, to create reports.
4. Display *My Report Planner: 1-2-3* (page 150). Think aloud as you determine a subject you wish to write about. Write the topic in the first box, for example, penguins. Also consider using the *Informative Report Sample* (page 149) for an extra example.
5. Remind students that we write reports to tell others what we know and to learn more about a topic. Model thinking aloud as you consider and record two questions you have about penguins, for example: Where do penguins live? How do they stay warm?
6. Record six things you know about penguins in order to complete *My Report Planner*. Be sure to model or show examples of each step and allow students time for discussion and sharing daily.

Informative: My 1-2-3 Report *(cont.)*

Engage

7. Have students think about what topics they will write about. Ask them to think about what they already know and what they wonder about the topic. Have students *Heads-up, Stand-up, Partner-up* and share their ideas with partners. Provide approximately two minutes for students to share. Observe students and share your observations with the class.

Apply

8. Review with students that writing reports is one way we can share information and details about topics that interest us.

Write/Conference

9. Provide time for students to write an informative report. They can use *My Report Planner 1-2-3* to help plan their writing. Meet with students individually or in small groups that demonstrate the need for additional support. Guide them through making decisions about their writing topics.

Spotlight Strategy

10. Spotlight good writing organization. For example, "Extraordinary planning today. Let's stop for just a moment and notice how Gennivieve is writing a superb informative text. What a great example for all of us. Fabulous Facts!"

Share

11. Have students meet with partners to share their writing progress. Remind them to listen carefully, compliment, and ask any questions they may have about their partner's writing.

Homework

Ask students to begin to research and ask their families questions about the topics they have chosen for writing. Remind students they can continue working on their projects tomorrow in Writer's Workshop.

Informative Report Sample

1—**My topic** is Emperor penguins.	
2—My first question is... Where do Emperor penguins live?	**2—My second question is...** How do they stay warm?
3—I learned... • need to live near the water • live in the Antarctic really cold. 140 degrees below zero	**3—I learned...** • they huddle together • they have fat and feathers • they rub oil to be waterproof

Note:

- Write a first draft using the above information or your own topic. Be sure to include an Introduction, body, and conclusion. Then you will give students time to research and record their information.
- Next, revise by adding details, sentences or better word choice, e.g., fat/blubber – add "down" feather.
- Focus attention next on editing for capitalization, grammar, punctuation, and spelling.
- Students may choose to add other informational text features, such as: illustrations, labels, captions, bold font, etc.
- Create class or individual books/reports for writing display. Celebrate accomplishments.

Name: ______________________ Date: ________________

My Report Planner: 1-2-3

Directions: Complete the graphic organizer below to plan your report.

1—My topic is...	
2—My first question is...	2—My second question is...
3—I know...	3—I know...
3—I know...	3—I know...
3—I know...	3—I know...

I Know How To . . .

Standards

- Uses strategies to organize written work
- Writes in a variety of forms or genres

Materials

- Chart paper
- Markers
- *How-to Planner* (page 153; howtoplanner.pdf)
- 3" × 5" index cards
- Milk
- Cup
- Chocolate syrup
- Spoon

Mentor Text

- *Look at My Book: How Kids Can Write and Illustrate* by Loreen Leedy
- *How to Make a Bird Feeder* by Liyala Tuckfield
- Samples of game instructions
- Recipe books

Procedures

Note: Be sure to share many examples of how-to books prior to modeling this genre. Allow adequate time to model, explore topic choices, plan, draft, and write. This is a fun piece to publish for a class book titled, *We Know How To…*

Think About Writing

1. Review with students all the different ways they have learned to organize writing. Tell students that today, they will take a closer look at another way to organize their ideas.

Teach

2. Tell students, "Today I will show you how to write directions for making chocolate milk." Explain that when they write how-to stories, they are telling the reader how to do something.
3. Write the words: *first, then, next,* and *last* on index cards. Remind students that when providing directions, it is helpful to include words that show the sequence of events. These words help the reader understand the order in which things happen.
4. Model making chocolate milk. After modeling each step, move to the chart paper and complete the planner with simple illustrations, words, and phrases for that step. Repeat for each step.

   First, I need to get my supplies (milk, chocolate syrup, cup, and spoon).

   Then, I pour some milk into the cup.

   Next, I pour some chocolate syrup into the milk.

   Last, I stir with the spoon and enjoy my delicious snack!

5. Build a class idea chart of *Things We Know How to Do.* Review sequence words and their use. Give partners time to discuss and plan their individual topics before moving on to the planner.

I Know How To . . . *(cont.)*

Engage

6. Ask students to *Turn and Talk* to partners to repeat the directions on how to make chocolate milk. Have students use four fingers with the order words to help organize their thoughts: *first, then, next,* and *last*. Explain that they will write about their topic in the same way using the sequence words.

Apply

7. Remind students to explore the newly introduced genre of how-to in their writing. Have students choose a how-to idea from the anchor chart of ideas.

Write/Conference

8. Distribute the *How-to Planner* (page 153). Provide time for students to write. Remember to take the time to really listen to your students. Confirm what they have already done accurately, and make suggestions for new thinking. Remember to write down your thoughts in your conferring notebook.

Spotlight Strategy

9. Call attention to one or two students who have grasped writing a how-to piece and spotlight their work.

Share

10. Have students meet in triads. Have them take turns sharing their how-to writing. Encourage students to listen carefully to their partners and see if the directions are clear. Remind students to compliment and question each other.

Homework

Ask students to think of other ideas for how-to books. Remind students they are all experts at something.

Name: ______________________ Date: ______________

How-to Planner ______________________

Directions: Draw a picture and write each step of your How-to story in the boxes. Then write your How-to story on the lines provided.

First, ______________	Next, ______________
Then, ______________	Last, ______________

Word Choice

Showing Your Story

A writer's use of rich, descriptive words can visually show the reader a mental image. By studying word choice, students will learn how to use vivid, colorful, and dynamic words to enrich their writing and make it as precise as possible. The use of amazing words is encouraged; however, everyday words used correctly are also celebrated. These lessons assist students in exploring different types of words and the ways they can be used to create interest in writing pieces. Lessons in this section include the following:

The *Wally, Word Choice Detective* poster (page 156) can be displayed in the room to provide a visual reminder for students that word choice is one of the traits of writing. You may wish to introduce this poster during the first lesson on word choice. Then, refer to the poster when teaching other lessons on word choice to refresh students' memories and provide them with questions to guide them as they make choices for words they use in their writing.

Wally Word Choice Detective

What words will paint a picture for my reader?

- ✔ Did I use some *amazing* words?
- ✔ Did I use sensory words?
- ✔ Did I use action words?
- ✔ Did I use a variety of words?

Using High Frequency Words

Standard

Uses conventions of spelling in written compositions

Materials

- Chart paper
- Marker
- *Learn a Word Chart* (page 159; learnwordchart.pdf)
- *High Frequency Word List* (page 160; highfreqwordlist.pdf)

Mentor Texts

- Use rhymes and text that have focus words
- See *Mentor Text List* in Appendix C for other suggestions.

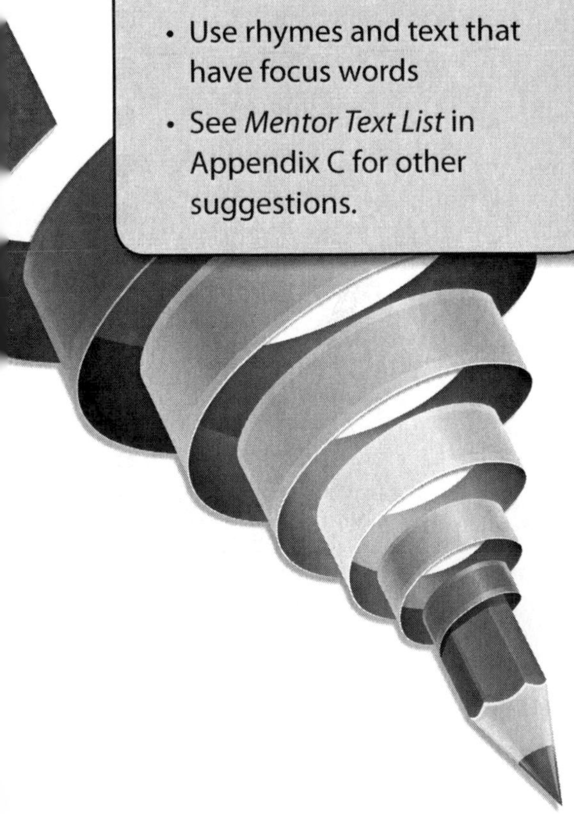

Procedures

Think About Writing

1. Tell students that authors can write more smoothly if they know how to spell many words. Of course authors do not know how to spell all the words; however, the more they can learn to spell, the easier it will be to get their ideas down on paper.
2. Review a mentor text if desired, and emphasize the author's use of word choice.

Teach

3. Tell students, "Today I will teach you a strategy to build a core of words that you can write quickly and smoothly." Show students the *Learn a Word Chart* (page 159) to provide visual support to the steps you will teach students so they can learn the word.
4. Choose a word from the *High Frequency Word List* (page 160). Write the word on a sheet of chart paper. Complete each of the steps below with the word.
   - Say, "Ready, See it!" Point to the left of the word, students should look at the word and think it in their heads. Provide a few seconds for students to look at the word.
   - Say, "Say It!" Slide your finger under the word as students say the word.
   - Say, "Spell It!" Tap your finger under each letter. As you tap each letter, students should say the letter name, so they spell the word.
   - Say, "Write it!" Have students pretend one hand is paper and the index finger of the other hand is a pencil. Students write the word on their hands three times quickly and smoothly. Move around and observe, providing corrective feedback to any student making incorrect letter strokes.

Using High Frequency Words *(cont.)*

- Say, "Check it!" Find the word on the chart paper and check the spelling.

Practice additional words until students are familiar with the procedure.

Engage

5. Have students *Heads-up, Stand-up, Partner-up* and practice *See it! Say it! Spell it! Write it! Check it!* with partners. Remind students that it helps us become better spellers for writing. Provide students additional words to practice. Monitor partners and provide support when needed.

Apply

6. Remind students good writers write with automaticity, quickly and smoothly. This activity will help make their writing easier and make them a better speller for writing projects. Tell students when they have finished their word practice, they can choose an idea and begin writing.

Write/Conference

7. Provide time for students to write about a topic of their choice. Scan the room to be sure students understand. Then rotate among students and support their efforts with questions and comments.

Spotlight Strategy

8. Spotlight students who are using the word chart. For example, "What a genius! Alexis is using the word chart and is practicing *See it! Say it! Spell it! Write it! Check it!* Good writers use all the tools around them to help them write words."

Share

9. Have students meet with partners. Ask them to show their partners some words they can write fast and smooth. Have students practice those words together.

Homework

Ask students to think about how letters, sounds, words, and language surrounds them. Encourage them to grow their word knowledge by finding words in newspapers and magazines and be ready to share their thinking tomorrow in Writer's Workshop.

Learn a Word Chart

See it!	
Say it!	
Spell it!	
Write it!	
Check it!	

High Frequency Word List

Words I Use in My Writing							
A a	**B b**	**C c**	**D d**	**E e**	**F f**	**G g**	**H h**
a about after again all always am an and another any are around as ask at away	be because bed best big boy brother but by	cat	dad day did didn't do dog don't down	each eat even every everyone	family father favorite find first fly football for found friend from fun funny	game get girl give giving go going good	had has have he help her here him his home homework house how
I i	**J j**	**K k**	**L l**	**M m**	**N n**	**O o**	**P p**
I if in into is it it's	jump just	kids know	let like little live long look lot love	made make man many may me mom money more must mother much must my	name never new next nice night no not now	of off old on once only open or other our out over	people play please pretty put
Q q-R r	**S s**	**T t**		**U u-V v**	**W w**		**Xx-Yy-Zz**
quiet quit quail ran really ride right room round run	said saw say school see she sister so some something sometimes soon started stop	take teacher team tell thank that that's the them then there they	thing things think this thought time to told too took try	under up us very	walk wanted was way we well went were what when where who why	will with work world would	years yes you your

—adapted from Teaching Kids to Spell, Gentry (1993) and Teaching Primary Reading, Dolch (1941)

Using Our Senses

Standards

- Uses descriptive words to convey basic ideas
- Uses writing and other methods to describe familiar persons, places, objects, or experiences

Materials

- 8.5" × 11" paper
- Objects for demonstration, such as fruit, vegetables, sand, cookies, rocks, seashells, etc.
- *Using Our Senses* (page 164; usingsenses.pdf)
- *Using Our Senses Sample* (page 163; usingsensessample.pdf)

Mentor Text

- *Hello Ocean* by Pam Muñoz Ryan
- *The Magic School Bus Explores the Senses* by Janna Cole
- See *Mentor Text List* in Appendix C for other suggestions.

Procedures

Note: Give partners a bag with an item inside. Have students complete the activity without drawing the picture or saying the name of the object. Then have students switch bags with another partner pair, and they draw what they think was described by the first team.

Think About Writing

1. Tell students authors often use their senses when writing. Using the five senses is a great way to make writing come alive.
2. Review a mentor text if desired, and emphasize the author's use of sensory words.

Teach

3. Tell students, "Today I will show you how to create "Show Me" sentences to help readers see a picture of your writing. You can help the reader "paint a picture" in their mind with your words."
4. Fold a sheet of paper in half and then in half again so when you open it there are four sections. Display an object that you will describe.
5. Sketch a picture of the object and write the name in the first box. Use the *Using Our Senses Sample* (page 163) as an example.
6. Label the second box: *Using My Senses*. Use all five senses to describe the object. Think aloud and ask questions as you model this for students. For example, "What do I see?"

Using Our Senses *(cont.)*

7. Combine the last two sections of the paper to make one large section. Model how to create a simple story using the sensory words from box two. For example, if an orange is the object being described, the paragraph may sound like the following:

   I can hardly wait to eat this orange. Its shape is as round as a soccer ball. I think it might be cold because it has goose bumps. When you take a bite from a ripe orange like this one, the pulp is so juicy it drips down your chin. Mmm! It tastes so sweet! Do you want a bite?

   Explicitly show students how you included the sensory words in the sentences. See *Using Our Senses Sample* (page 163) for an example.

Engage

8. Have students *Heads-up, Stand-up, Partner-up* and work with partners to practice thinking of sensory words for another object. Remind students to take turns.

Apply

9. Remind students to use their senses to create interesting sentences.

Write/Conference

10. Provide time for students to write. Distribute *Using Our Senses* (page 164) to help organize student writing. As you conference with students, be explicit in what you are teaching the writer. Remember to keep clear notes on your observations to be used for planning future writing instruction.

Spotlight Strategy

11. Gather students together to spotlight student work. For example, "Wow! You continually amaze me. Just listen to Eric's sensory sentences."

Share

12. Have students reread what they wrote today and identify their best sentences. Provide approximately one minute. Then have students meet with triads to share their best sentences.

Homework

Ask students to notice words and sentences that call out to them as being exceptional and sensory. Encourage them to remember those words so they can make sensory sentences tomorrow.

Using Our Senses Sample

Observing:	Using My Senses:
 Orange	round sweet orange sticky juicy goose bumps pulp ripe bumpy

My Story:
I can hardly wait to eat this orange. Its shape is as round as a soccer ball. I think it might be cold because it has goose bumps. When you take a bite from a ripe orange like this one, the pulp is so juicy it drips down your chin. Mmm! It tastes so sweet! Do you want a bite?

Using Our Senses

Directions: Complete the graphic organizer below to write a story using sensory details.

Observing:	Using My Senses:

My Story:

More Action Words

Standards

- Uses descriptive words to convey basic ideas
- Uses verbs in written compositions

Materials

- Chart paper
- Markers
- *Action Words Sample* (page 167; actionwordssample.pdf)

Mentor Text

- *The Great Fuzz Frenzy* by Susan Crummel and Janet Stevens
- *The Rain Stomper* by Addie Boswell
- *Rattlesnake Dance* by Jim Arnofsky
- See *Mentor Text List* in Appendix C for other suggestions.

Procedure

Note: A fun activity is to take action photos of students in the classroom and on the playground. Print the photos and use them to create an action book. For example: Callie climbs on the jungle gym. Allow students to use the book as a writing resource.

Think About Writing

1. Tell students that writers build sentences with a naming part and an action part. Writers use a variety of words to show their readers exactly what their characters are doing in their stories.
2. Review a mentor text, if desired and emphasize the action words in the story. For example, ask students to listen for the action words author Janet Stevens uses in *The Great Fuzz Frenzy.* Some interesting words include: swirled, twirled, pulled, plucked, puffed, stretched, and tugged. Use the *Action Words Sample* (page 167) as necessary.

Teach

3. Tell students, "Today I will show you how to think about actions that can help your reader know more about your story."
4. Create an anchor chart titled *Animals Can*. Write the word *run* on the chart. Tell students the word *run* is an action word; it is something an animal can do. Suggest several other words to add to the chart.
5. Have students think of other actions an animal can do. Add these words to the chart. Review with students that the words on the chart are all words they can use when writing stories that will help their reader understand their ideas clearly.

More Action Words *(cont.)*

6. Create a story on chart paper about something animals can do using many of the action words from the anchor chart. Either model your thought process as you create the story or have students help write the story.

Engage

7. Have students *Turn and Talk* to partners to think of some of the action words they will use in their writing. Encourage them to think of their own or to use the anchor chart as a resource.

Apply

8. Remind students to use action words that help readers know more about what is going on in the stories that they write. Encourage them to use the action words from the anchor chart in their writings today.

Write/Conference

9. Provide time for students to write using action words. Remember to scan your class for understanding and then begin individual conferences. Ask questions such as, "What are you working on as a writer today?" and "Can you use an action word to tell more about what your animal is doing?"

Spotlight Strategy

10. Spotlight students using action words in their writing. For example, "David is using some outstanding action words in his writing. You're incredible! Good writers use action words to show their readers what is happening in their stories."

Share

11. Have students meet with partners to share their stories. Encourage students to listen for the action words in their partner's writing.

Homework

Ask students to listen for action words they can use in writing. Have students remember to add them to their writing folders or the anchor chart tomorrow in Writer's Workshop.

Action Words Sample

Animals Can...		
• bark	• jump	• scamper
• beg	• lick	• soar
• burrow	• play	• sprint
• buzz	• prowl	• sleep
• dig	• play	• slither
• eat	• prowl	• waddle
• fetch	• roar	• walk
• gallop	• roll over	• whine
• growl	• run	

Word Power

Standards

- Uses descriptive words to convey basic ideas
- Uses writing and other methods to describe familiar persons, places, objects, or experiences

Materials

- Vocabulary notebook—made by student or furnished by teacher

Mentor Text

- *Fancy Nancy's Favorite Fancy Words* by Jane O'Connor
- *Word Wizard* by Cathryn Falwell
- *Pete the Cat: I Love My White Shoes* by Eric Litwin
- See *Mentor Text List* in Appendix C for other suggestions.

Procedures

Note: Do this as a daily exercise just before writing, and vocabulary is sure to increase.

Think About Writing

1. Tell students, "When we speak, we use a lot of words in a short amount of time. When we write, we can only produce a short amount of words in that same amount of time." Explain that authors use many tools when writing to help express what they want to say.
2. Review mentor text if desired, and emphasize the author's use of strong words.

Teach

3. Tell students, "Today I will show you how to make a vocabulary notebook to grow your word power."
4. Explain to students that each day, just before beginning Writer's Workshop, they will add new words to a vocabulary notebook. The words they add to the notebook are strong words that can be included in their writing to help the reader better visualize what is being read.
5. Provide students with a notebook. Explain that they will then snap, clap, stomp, and cheer the new words so the words get stored in their heads. Then they will draw a picture to match the words. Tell students each day they will add two to three words to the notebook.
6. Select a word from a mentor text or other source. Model for students in your own notebook how you want them to write it in theirs. After each step, model it in your own notebook. Have students add the words to their notebooks. Provide a child-friendly definition of the word. Snap, clap, stomp, and cheer the words. Have students add the definition and draw a picture as a visual reminder of the word.

Word Power *(cont.)*

7. Continually add new words to students' vocabulary notebooks so the number of strong words they have grows. Encourage students to use words from their notebooks in writing.

Engage

8. Select one or two other words from mentor texts or other sources and have students add those words to their notebooks.

Apply

9. Remind students to be aware of word knowledge. Encourage them to be champion word wizards.

Write/Conference

10. Provide time for students to write about a topic of their choice. Do not plan to conference today. Provide support for students who are still adding pictures to their notebooks.

Spotlight Strategy

11. Spotlight student work. For example, "You really rock! Now that you know how to write words in your notebook, you can begin keeping record of great words without my help."

Share

12. Have students work with partners to share the words they wrote in their notebooks.

Homework

Ask students to be word magicians at home tonight. Encourage students to notice all of the words that are around them. Encourage them to write them in their notebooks during the next Writer's Workshop.

A Rainbow of Words

Standards

- Uses descriptive words to convey basic ideas
- Uses writing and other methods to describe familiar persons, places, objects, or experiences

Materials

- Paint chips or large box of crayons
- *A Rainbow of Writing Words* (page 172; rainbowwriting.pdf)

Mentor Texts

- *Color Dance* by Ann Jonas
- *Color Me A Rhyme* by Jane Yolen
- *Pete the Cat: I Love My White Shoes* by Eric Litwin
- See *Mentor Text List* in Appendix C for other suggestions.

Procedures

Note: This mini-lesson may be adapted to explore additional descriptive word charts, for example: size words, seasonal words, birthday words, emotion words, etc.

Think About Writing

1. Explain to students that authors add energy and excitement to their writing by carefully choosing words and constructing sentences to create stories. Authors use just the right words so the reader can see the story in their mind.
2. Review a mentor text if desired, and emphasize the color words. For example, "You have been using colors in your stories…but wait until you hear the colors used by Jane Yolen. They are not found in your ordinary crayon box!"

Teach

3. Tell students, "Today I will show you how to go beyond using basic colors and begin using vibrant, exciting color words in your writing."
4. Draw a rainbow and label it with the basic colors. Discuss the basic colors with students.
5. Return to the rainbow drawing and add other colors you recall from the mentor text that represents a shade of one of the basic colors, for example: chartreuse, emerald, pickle green, orchid, lavender, plum, and tickle me pink. Explain how these words are all shades of basic colors and so much more descriptive for the reader.
6. Model writing a sentence using a basic color word and revising to a more vivid color word.

A Rainbow of Words *(cont.)*

Engage

7. Provide students with crayons or paint chips. Have students *Heads-up, Stand-up, Partner-up* and work with partners to decide which basic color it best matches. Then have students think of a more descriptive word that tells about the shade of that color. Have students exchange crayons or paint chips with each other and repeat the activity.

Apply

8. Distribute *A Rainbow of Writing Words* (page 172) to students. Have them work in small groups to think of and list some vivid, interesting color words to include on the page. Provide resources for students to gather color names, such as a large box of crayons.

Write/Conference

9. Provide time for students to write. Have them use *A Rainbow of Writing Words* to create their writing. Scan the class for student engagement and work ethic. Observe, confer, and notice.

Spotlight Strategy

10. Spotlight students using a rainbow of color words in their writing. For example, "Writers, perfect thinking and planning. Listen to John's colorful words."

Share

11. Have students, *Heads-up, Stand-up, Partner-up* to share their finest examples. Remind students to give compliments.

Homework

Ask students to look around their homes at all the amazing colors they see. These colors can be added to their writing folder and can be used in their writing. Encourage students to come tomorrow ready to share their discoveries!

A Rainbow of Writing Words

Directions: Write as many color words as you can to describe the colors in the spaces provided.

Red
Orange
Yellow
Green
Blue
Purple
Other Colorful Words

Sounds All Around from A to Z

Standard

Uses descriptive words to convey basic ideas

Materials

- *Teacher Resources for Onomatopoeia* (pages 181–182; teacheronomatopoeia.pdf) *(optional)*
- *Onomatopoeia Dictionary* (pages 175–180; onomatopoeiadic.pdf)

Mentor Texts

- *Bear Snores On* by Karma Wilson
- *Andrew's Loose Tooth and Mortimer* by Robert Munsch
- *The Snowy Day* by Ezra Jack Keats
- See *Mentor Text List* in Appendix C for other suggestions.

Procedures

Note: You may wish to create the booklet on one day and revisit on the next day to share additional text and encourage writers to use the words in their own writing.

Think About Writing

1. Explain to students that authors carefully choose the words to their stories to give the reader a good picture of what is happening in the story. Sometimes, the words even help the reader hear what is happening in the story.
2. Review a mentor text if desired, and emphasize the author's use of sound words.

Teach

3. Tell students, "Today I will show you how to use *onomatopoeia* in your writing." Explain that *onomatopoeia* is a writing tool authors use to include words that sound like the action they are describing, for example, animal noises like: *meow* or *woof* or noise words like: *plop* and *bang*. These are the sounds all around us that we hear every day.
4. Write the word *Onomatopoeia* on a sheet of chart paper. Think aloud as you recall and record any sound words from the mentor text on the chart.

Engage

5. Ask students to think of other onomatopoeia. Provide time for them to *Turn and Talk* to partners. Add any words they think of to the list. Refer to the *Teacher Resources for Onomatopoeia* (pages 181–182) for extra examples.
6. Tell students more words can be added to the anchor chart throughout the year as they encounter them in their reading, writing and listening.

Sounds All Around from A to Z *(cont.)*

Apply

7. Remind students to use words that help their readers hear what is happening in their writing, just like the mentor text author. Distribute the *Onomatopoeia Dictionary* (pages 175–180) to students. Ask them to work with partners to assemble the pages and discuss other words to add to the dictionary. Have students store the dictionary in their writing folders to use as a resource when they are writing. Tell students they can add new words from the anchor chart they may want to include in their own writing.

Write/Conference

8. Provide time for students to write new words in their onomatopeia dictionary. Monitor, support, and provide positive feedback as you rotate among students to confer.

Spotlight Strategy

9. Spotlight students that are working together efficiently and with strong work ethic.

Share

10. Have the partners who worked together to create the dictionary meet up with another group of partners to create quads. Ask students to share their dictionaries and discuss the onomatopoeia words they included and how they plan to use them in writing.

Homework

Ask students to listen for sound words all around them this evening. Encourage students to remember the words so they can be added to their dictionaries or the anchor chart tomorrow.

Onomatopoeia Dictionary

Teacher Directions: Cut out the pages below. Staple them in ABC order. Have students add new words to their dictionaries as they learn them.

My Onomatopoeia Dictionary

Sounds All Around from A to Z

Name ______________________

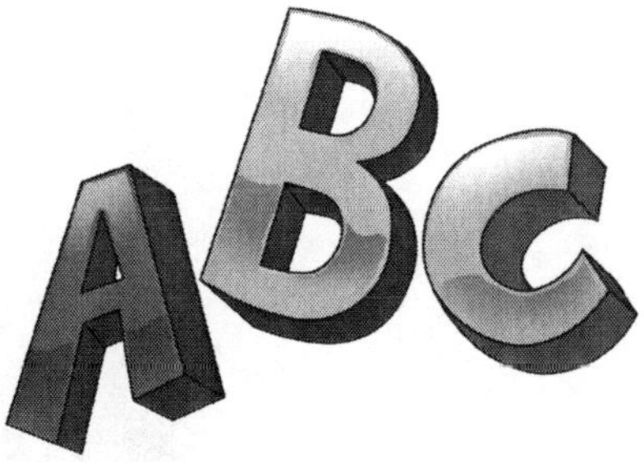

A is for achoo

B is for beep

C is for crunch

Onomatopoeia Dictionary *(cont.)*

D is for ding	**E** is for eek
F is for fizz	**G** is for gasp

Onomatopoeia Dictionary *(cont.)*

H is for hum	**I** is for itch
J is for jangle	**K** is for knock-knock

Onomatopoeia Dictionary *(cont.)*

L is for
la

M is for
mumble

N is for
neigh

O is for
ouch

Onomatopoeia Dictionary *(cont.)*

P is for puff	**Q** is for quack
R is for rumble	**S** is for splash

Onomatopoeia Dictionary *(cont.)*

T is for tick tock	**U** and **V** are for ugh and vroom
W is for wham	**Y** and **Z** are for yikes and zonk

Teacher Resources for Onomatopoeia

A	C	E	I	P	S	U
achoo	chatter	eeek	icky	phew	screech	ugh
ahem	cheep		itch	ping	shuffle	
	chirp	**F**		plop	shush	**V**
B	chomp	fizz	**J**	plunk	sizzle	vroom
baa	choo, choo	flick	jangle	poof	slam	
bah	clang	flutter	jingle	pop	slap	**W**
bam	clank			puff	slash	whack
bang	clap	**G**	**K**	purr	slurp	wham
bash	clatter	gasp	knock-knock		smack	whip
bawl	click	giggle		**Q**	snap	whisper
beep	clink	growl	**L**	quack	sniff	whizz
belch	cluck	gr-r-r-r	la		snip	whoop
blare	clunk	grunt		**R**	snort	whoosh
blurt	coo	gurgle	**M**	Rat-a-tat-tat	splash	woof
boing	crack		meow	rattle	squelch	whirl
boink	crackle	**H**	moo	rev	squish	
bong	crunch	hack	mumble	ring	stomp	
bonk	cuckoo	hiccup	murmur	roar	swirl	**X**
boo		hiss		rumble	swish	
boom	**D**	honk	**N**	rustle	swoosh	
bow-wow	ding	hoot	neigh			**Y**
bubble	drip	howl			**T**	yo yo
bump	drop	huh	**O**		thud	
buzz		hum	oink		thump	
			ouch		tick-tock	**Z**
			ow		tinkle	zap
					tsk	zing
					twang	zip
					tweet	zoom
					twirl	

Teacher Resources for Onomatopoeia *(cont.)*

Game—What's That Sound?

Provide students with a sound and have students name the source. For example, say, "Moo," and students should respond, "Cow." The game can also be played by having the teacher name the source and students name the sound. Examples include: cat, duck, dog, sheep, snake, train, balloon, ocean, door, wind, storm, fireworks, phone, etc.

Additional Mentor Text Containing Onomatopoeia

- *Achoo! Bang! Crash!* by Ross McDonald
- *Night in the Country* by Cynthia Rylant
- *Zoom Broom* by Margie Palatinni
- *How I Became a Pirate* by Melinda Long
- *Click Clack Moo* and *Giggle Giggle Quack* by Doreen Cronin
- *Little Old Lady Who Wasn't Afraid of Anything* by Linda Williams
- *Little Mouse, Big Red Strawberry, and The Big Hungry Bear* by Audrey Wood

Awesome Adjectives

Standards

- Uses descriptive words to convey basic ideas
- Uses adjectives in written compositions

Materials

- *Wally, Word Choice Detective* (page 156; wally.pdf)
- Chart paper
- Marker
- Sticky notes or word cards

Mentor Texts

- *The Big Yawn* by Kevin Faulkner
- *That's My Dog* by Rick Walton
- See *Mentor Text List* in Appendix C for other suggestions.

Procedures

Note: You may wish to compile noun and adjective anchor charts from mentor texts you have read. For example: In *The Big Yawn*, the noun *mouth* and the adjectives *scaly*, *gigantic*, *toothy*, and *tremendous* could be added to the anchor chart.

Think About Writing

1. Review with students that the words an author chooses help bring a story to life. They add excitement and make the reader want to continue to read.
2. Review a mentor text if desired, and emphasize the mental images that the author creates using words.

Teach

3. Tell students, "Today I will show you how to use words that add more details to your sentences so the reader can get a better picture of what you are writing." Explain that describing words can add more interest.
4. Ask students to help make a list of nouns, for example: *house*, *bike*, and *man*. Write the words on a sheet of chart paper. Leave room in front of each word to add an adjective; for example, ________ *bike*.
5. Choose one of the words. Have students close their eyes and create a picture of the word in their heads. describe the word in more detail. Ask students to change the pictures they have in their heads based on the words you use. For example, for the word *man*, first describe the man as a *young man*. Then describe him as a *bald man*. Finally, describe him as a *funny man*. Discuss with students how their pictures of the man changed.
6. Make a list on the chart paper of the different describing words you used. Tell students these describing words are called adjectives. Explain that adjectives tell more about or describe nouns.

Awesome Adjectives *(cont.)*

7. Emphasize with students that the more descriptive they can be in telling about the nouns in their stories, the better the reader will be able to picture what they have written. Remind them to refer to the *Wally the Word Choice Detective* poster (page 156) displayed in the room from previous lessons.

Engage

8. Have students work *Heads-up, Stand-up, Partner-up* and work with partners to think of adjectives to tell about the other nouns on the chart paper.

9. Ask students to create sentences using the adjectives and nouns. As students are talking, move around the group to listen to and take notes on students' sentences. Have several pairs of students share their sentences with the whole group.

Apply

10. Remind students to think about how the words they choose create a mental image for the reader. Encourage students to use adjectives to add details in their writing.

Write/Conference

11. Provide time for students to write using adjectives to add details. After you have scanned for potential confusion, rotate among students and confer with individuals or small groups. It is important to pull in at-risk groups once your students are focused and sustained. Use your conferring notebook to keep observations.

Spotlight Strategy

12. Spotlight student work. For example, "Now you've got it! Listen to the extraordinary adjectives used by Shani. You're making it all happen."

Share

13. Have students meet in triads. Then, choose three students to share their work with the whole group. Remember to give a compliment and a comment.

Homework

Ask students to notice adjectives in books and on TV. Ask students to make a list to use during Writer's Workshop tomorrow.

Sparkling Synonym Stars

Standards

- Uses descriptive words to convey basic ideas
- Uses writing and other methods to describe familiar persons, places, objects, or experiences

Materials

- Chart paper
- Markers
- *Sparkling Synonym Star* (page 187; synonymstar.pdf)

Mentor Texts

- *Thesaurus Rex* by Laya Steinberg
- *If You Were a Synonym* by Michael Dahl
- *Max's Words* by Kate Banks
- See *Mentor Text List* in Appendix C for other suggestions.

Procedures

Note: Revisit this mini-lesson and add stars as overused words are encountered in student writing. Display the *Sparkling Synonym Stars* (page 187) for student support.

Think About Writing

1. Tell students they have been doing a great job growing as writers, developing their writing ideas, and creating super sentences that are interesting for readers. Explain that it is also important for writers to select just the right words to show their reader a mental image of their stories.
2. Review a mentor text if desired, and emphasize the author's use of interesting words. For example, in *Thesaurus Rex*, he was stretching. That is another way to say he was reaching or extending.

Teach

3. Tell students, "Today I will show you how to create even more interesting stories by using synonyms." Explain that a synonym is a word that means almost the same as another word, it is similar.
4. Draw a large star on a sheet of chart paper. Tell students the star can be turned into a *Sparkling Synonym Star* by adding words with similar meanings to the word in the middle. Write the word *nice* in the middle of the star. On each point, add a word with a similar meaning, thinking aloud as you share why you have selected that word, for example: *kind, polite, pleasing, friendly, cheery.*
5. Model completing another *Sparkling Synonym Star* for the word *look*. Use *gaze, peer, stare, glance, and peek.*

Sparkling Synonym Stars (cont.)

Engage

6. Ask students to *Heads-up, Stand-up, Partner-up*. Name other words and then provide students time to work with their partners to name synonyms. Suggested words include: *big*, *fast*, and *neat*.

Apply

7. Remind students to use a variety of words to express their thoughts in their writing. Encourage students to begin a new writing project or select a writing sample from their folders to revise by adding some synonyms.

Write/Conference

8. Provide time for students to write using synonyms. Remind students to reread their writing piece at least three times. Check your conferring notebook to make certain you are visiting all students. Take notes on possible spotlighting targets as you move around. Give individual praise.

Spotlight Strategy

9. Spotlight sparkling student synonym stars. For example, "Tamika has used a sparkling synonym in her writing. That's remarkable work!"

Share

10. Have students meet with partners to share how they used synonyms in their writing today. Remind students to give compliments!

Homework

Ask students to listen for words that sizzle, sparkle, and dazzle. Encourage them to be ready to return to writing tomorrow and share their findings.

Name: ______________________ Date: ______________

Sparkling Synonym Star

Directions: Write a word in the middle of the star. Record a synonym for your chosen word at each point of the star.

Transition Words

Standard

Uses descriptive words to convey basic ideas

Materials

- *Transition Words Cards* (page 190; transitioncards.pdf)
- *Sequencing Picture Cards* (pages 191–192; sequencingpiccards.pdf)

Mentor Texts

- *How Groundhog's Garden Grew* by Lynne Cherry
- *A Story for Bear* by Dennis Haseley
- Fairy tales
- See *Mentor Text List* in Appendix C for other suggestions.

Procedures

Note: A set of transition words and two sets of sequencing picture cards are provided with this lesson. Choose one to use with the lesson. Review the concept of sequencing and transition words as needed. Note transition words as you read them in other mentor texts throughout the year. Create a transition words anchor chart that can be added to as you encounter them.

Think About Writing

1. Tell students that authors often use words to help the reader understand the flow and organization of the story. The words are carefully chosen and placed so the story has a logical sequence.
2. Review a mentor text if desired, and emphasize the transition words the author uses.

Teach

3. Tell students, "Today I will show you how to use writing signals to sequence and focus your ideas for your reader."
4. Review the *Transition Words Cards* (page 190). Discuss the order of the words. Explain that the words *next* and *then* can be used interchangeably.
5. Use the *Sequencing Picture Cards* (page 191) to retell the story of *Goldilocks and the Three Bears*. Connect the transition words to the pictures, and retell the story as you really emphasize the transition words.

Engage

6. Display the *Sequencing Picture Cards* for a seed's growth (page 192). Have students *Heads-up, Stand-up, Partner-up* and work with partners to use transition words to retell the event. Allow time for partners to practice.
7. Gather students back together and have one or two groups share the sequence out loud.

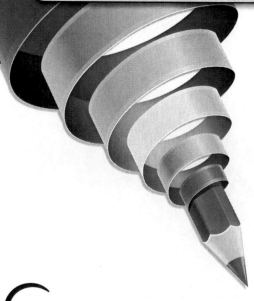

Transition Words *(cont.)*

Apply

8. Remind students to use transition words in their writing where it is appropriate to help the reader understand the sequence of their stories.

Write/Conference

9. Provide time for students to write using transition words. As you are working with students, keep in mind that it takes time and practice for students to effectively use transition words. You may attend to a small group or individually confer. Remember to jot down your observations.

Spotlight Strategy

10. Spotlight great transitioning work. For example, "Tatiana is signaling to her reader that she is moving into a new thought!"

Share

11. Have students meet in triads to share their writing. Ask students to share any transition words they used in their writing. Provide approximately two minutes.

Homework

Ask students to tell their families about something they did today such as jump rope, eat dinner, or ride their bikes. Encourage students to tell about the event using transition words.

Transition Words Cards

Teacher Directions: Cut out the cards below and use them as directed in the lesson.

First	**Then**
Next	**Finally**

Sequencing Picture Cards

Teacher Directions: Cut out the cards below and use them as directed in the lesson.

Sequencing Picture Cards *(cont.)*

seed

sprout

plant

flower

Lucky Me Similes

Standards

- Uses descriptive words to convey basic ideas
- Uses writing and other methods to describe familiar persons, places, objects, or experiences

Materials

- Chart paper
- Markers
- *Simile Cards* (page 195; similecards.pdf)

Mentor Texts

- *Quick as a Cricket* by Audrey Wood
- *Swimmy* by Leo Leonni
- *Umbrella* by Taro Yashima
- *Owl Moon* by Jane Yolen
- See *Mentor Text List* in Appendix C for other suggestions.

Procedures

Note: Select a seasonal object such as a snowflake, leaf, shamrock, flower, caterpillar, etc. Draw a picture of the object in the center and add similes that describe it around the object.

Think About Writing

1. Tell students that authors use strong word choice to create images in readers' minds If the author creates images, the reader feels like they are a part of the story.
2. Review a mentor text if desired, and emphasize the author's use of strong word choices and similes. For example, the opening of *Owl Moon* Jane Yolen, compares trees to statues. "The trees stood as still as giant statues." In the same story, she compares voices to the quietness of a dream. "And when their voices faded away it was as quiet as a dream.'"

Teach

3. Tell students, "Today I will show you how to make comparisons in your writing to help the reader create images in their mind."
4. Explain that a *simile* is a comparison of two unlike things that always contains the words *like* or *as*. Similes are used in poetry, music, nursery rhymes, and in stories. Tell students that we often use similes in our everyday language. For example, "The biscuits were as hard as rocks." Biscuits are being compared to rocks.
5. Write the following sentence on chart paper: *Luke came home from school as hungry as a bear*. Explicitly model what is being compared in this sentence. Tell students that bears are large, hungry animals and when Luke came home, he was also very hungry. So, the writer compared Luke to a bear because they are both hungry. Repeat modeling several other similes, as needed.

Lucky Me Similes *(cont.)*

Engage

6. Ask students to *Heads-up, Stand-up, Partner-up*. Display or distribute *Simile Cards* (page 195). Have students talk with their partners to determine the meaning of the simile and then build a sentence showing a comparison. Have students practice with several similes, as time allows or as needed.

Apply

7. Remind students to create interesting, spectacular sentences using similes. Provide *Simile Cards* for each table or display where visible to everyone.

Write/Conference

8. Provide time for students to work. Scan for work ethic and focus. Begin to rotate and have focused conversations with students. Make wise observations so that you can design future lesson ideas.

Spotlight Strategy

9. Spotlight student simile work. For example, "Stupendous similes. I'm so lucky to read your first attempt. Just listen to Justine and Martin's similes!"

Share

10. Have several students take the author's chair to share their similes.

Homework

Ask students to look at objects around their houses and try to create similes. For example, "My dog is as...," or, "My house is as...," or, "The sky is as...."

Simile Cards

Teacher Directions: Create copies of the cards below. Distribute the cards as directed in the lesson.

as slow as a turtle	as fat as a pig
as easy as ABC	as wise as an owl
as sweet as candy	as white as snow
works like a dog	sleeps like a log
eats like a bird	sings like an angel
strong as a bull	fast as the wind

Voice

Expressing Yourself

Voice is what makes writing come alive. It is the personality of the writer coming through in the writing. Although sometimes difficult to teach, it is recognizable in writing through the personal tone and feeling of the writing piece. This section contains background on recognizing voice along with student samples. In addition, lessons focus on how students can connect with their readers to compel them to continue reading. Lessons in this section include the following:

- Lesson 1: More Than Happy, Sad, and Mad (page 199)
- Lesson 2: Voice Times Two (page 202)

The *Val and Van Voice* poster (page 198) can be displayed in the room to provide a visual reminder for students that voice is one of the traits of writing. You may wish to introduce this poster during the first lesson on voice. Then, refer to the poster when teaching other lessons on voice to refresh students' memories and provide them with questions to help guide them as they make an effort to show voice in their writing.

Val and Van Voice

What is the purpose of my writing?

- ✔ Did I write to an audience?
- ✔ Did I share my feelings?
- ✔ Did I make my reader smile, cry, think?
- ✔ Does my writing sound like me?

More Than Happy, Sad, and Mad

Standard
Writes expressive compositions (uses an individual, authentic voice)

Materials
- Chart paper
- Markers
- *My Feelings* (page 201; myfeelings.pdf)

Mentor Texts
- *Feelings* by Aliki
- *Today I Feel Silly* by Jamie Lee Curtis
- See *Mentor Text List* in Appendix C for other suggestions.

Procedure
Note: This mini-lesson may be revisited by adding additional feeling words to the anchor chart for writing support.

Think About Writing
1. Tell students that authors carefully choose their words to help the reader understand how the characters in their stories feel. Explain to students that when the reader can really feel the situation the author has done a great job of using what we call voice. Voice is what makes us really care about the story. Voice can often be attributed to feelings described in a story.
2. Review a mentor text if desired, and emphasize the author's use of voice. Discuss the feelings related to the character.

Teach
3. Tell students, "Today I will show you how to explore using your feelings to tell stories more clearly."
4. Explain to students they will play a guessing game. You will make faces and they will guess how you are feeling. Make faces to show the following feelings: happy, sad, and mad. Create a three-columned anchor chart. Write each of the feelings students guessed at the top of the anchor chart.
5. Tell students that those words show feelings; however, there are more descriptive words that can show the same feelings. Ask students to list other words that also describe each of the feelings. You may need to provide hints to help guide students towards the feeling words. Some suggested words are listed below.

happy	**sad**	**mad**
tickled	down	furious
joyful	unhappy	angry
delighted	dreary	outraged

More Than Happy, Sad, and Mad *(cont.)*

6. Explain to students when they show emotions in their writing, it will help the reader connect with their stories better. Encourage students to continue to add to the anchor chart as they find words in reading or in life.

Engage

7. Have partners *Heads-up, Stand-up, Partner-up* and work together to identify the feeling they will describe in their writing today. Distribute *My Feelings* (page 201). Encourage partners to ask each other what made them feel that way. Allow time for discussion.

Apply

8. Remind students that there are many feelings they can use in their writing. Encourage students to use the anchor chart to find words that tell more than *happy*, *sad*, and *mad*.

Write/Conference

9. Provide time for students to write a story about a feeling. Scan for and resolve any confusion. Confer with students individually or in small groups. Make observations in your conferring notebook.

Spotlight Strategy

10. Spotlight student work writing about emotions. For example, "Jesus made decisions quickly and is using details to show his emotion. Amazing writing work today. You are to be commended."

Share

11. Have students come to the author's chair and share their writing. Remember to provide lots of affirmation.

Homework

Ask students to listen for voice in stories they hear from books or on TV. Remind them that voice is the magic that makes us laugh, shiver, or even cry.

Name: ______________________ Date: ________________

My Feelings

Directions: Complete the sentences below to tell about a feeling you have had. Then draw a picture of your story.

On ______________________,

(day of the week)

____

____

____

____

____

I was ______________________.

(feeling word)

Voice Times Two

Standard

Writes expressive compositions (uses an individual, authentic voice)

Materials

- Chart paper
- Markers

Mentor Texts

- *Once Upon a Cool Motorcycle Dude* by Kevin O'Malley
- *Hey, Little Ant* by Phillip & Hannah Hoose
- See *Mentor Text List* in Appendix C for other suggestions.

Procedure

Note: This mini-lesson lends itself to two-voice poetry and is a fun author's tea activity or class book.

Think About Writing

1. Remind students that great authors have voice in their writing. It is what makes the stories more memorable to the readers. Voice is created when the author chooses just the right words to make you feel just like the characters in the story.
2. Review a mentor text if desired, and emphasize the author's use of voice. Have students listen for the way the author uses characters, their feelings, and the illustrations to show voice.

Teach

3. Tell students, "Today I will show you how to use voice in your writing to show your reader what your characters are thinking and feeling."
4. Demonstrate for students how to show voice for two different characters. Make a two-column chart with two different characters at the top. For example, you may wish to show a voice for a parent who wants his or her child to help with some chores around the house and a child who does not want to. Develop a few ideas for the characters. For example:

Child	Parent
It is hard work. I want to play. Can't someone else do it? It's not my turn..	You are part of the family. Everyone helps. You will learn responsibility. The trash is overflowing.

Voice Times Two *(cont.)*

5. Fold a sheet of paper in half. On one half write a brief story from the child's perspective. On the other half, write a brief story from the parent's perspective. Extend the lesson by sketching illustrations and adding speech bubbles for each of the characters.
6. Model this lesson with several other character pairs, for example: pigs/wolf, goldilocks/bears, boy/girl, boy/ant, flower/bee, mouse/rat, and Washington/Lincoln.

Engage

7. Have students *Turn and Talk* with partners to discuss characters they may use in their writing. Allow time for discussion. Then have students share their ideas to the whole group. List students' ideas on chart paper for them to reference as they write.

Apply

8. Remind students that they can give their stories voice by showing their character's feelings, emotions, and attitudes both in their word choice and illustrations.

Write/Conference

9. Provide time for students to write their stories. Scan for and resolve any confusion. Confer with students individually or small group, making observations in your conferring notebook.

Spotlight Strategy

10. Spotlight use of voice in student writing. For example, "Listen to the way Makala has added voice to her writing. I know right away her character is angry. Outstanding writing work!"

Share

11. Have students meet with partners to share their writing. Ask partners to listen carefully to see if they can tell what the character is feeling.

Homework

Have students write down a title of a book at home of which they enjoy the voice the author uses. Tell them to be prepared to share the title and how the author's voice makes them feel.

Conventions

Checking Your Writing

Writing that does not follow standard conventions is difficult to read. The use of correct capitalization, punctuation, spelling, and grammar is what makes writing consistent and easy to read. Students need to have reasonable control over the conventions of writing. This section provides lessons that guide students as they internalize conventions, helping them check their work after they have written a piece. Lessons in this section include the following:

The *Callie Super Conventions Checker* poster (page 206) can be displayed in the room to provide a visual reminder for students that conventions is one of the traits of writing. You may wish to introduce this poster during the first lesson on conventions. Then, refer to the poster when teaching other lessons on conventions to refresh students' memories and provide them questions to help guide them as they make an effort to use correct conventions in their writing.

Callie Super Conventions Checker

How do I edit my paper?

- ✔ Did I check my capitalization?
- ✔ Did I check my punctuation?
- ✔ Did I check my spelling?
- ✔ Did I use good spacing?
- ✔ Did I read over my story?

Using Our Sound Charts

Standard

Uses conventions of spelling in written compositions

Materials

- *Sound Chart Word List* (page 209; soundchartlist.pdf)
- *Alphabet Chart* (page 210; alphabetchart.pdf)
- *Short Vowel Chart* (page 211; shortvowelchart.pdf)
- *Long Vowel Chart* (page 212; longvowelchart.pdf)
- *Digraphs and Consonant Blends Chart* (pages 213–214; blendschart.pdf)
- *Vowel Team Chart* (pages 215–216; vowelteamchart.pdf)

Mentor Texts

- *Look at My Book* by Loreen Leedy
- See *Mentor Text List* in Appendix C for other suggestions.

Procedures

Note: Introduce the charts in this lesson on separate days or all on the same day, depending on the needs and abilities of your students.

Think About Writing

1. Tell students that authors keep resources and tools at their fingertips when writing. Explain that many writers use computers, a thesaurus, they sketch, and even make notes on napkins, and scraps of paper.
2. Review a mentor text if desired, and emphasize the author's use of conventions.

Teach

3. Tell students, "Today we will look at sound charts to determine how they might support us in writing."
4. Show students each resource. Describe the purpose of the chart and model how to use it to spell several words.
   - *Alphabet Chart* (page 210)—Explain that if students are unsure of a sound in a word, they can locate the picture that matches the needed sound.
   - *Short and Long Vowel Charts* (pages 211–212)—Tell students this chart can help when trying to find the short or long vowel sound needed when writing the vowel in a word.
   - *Digraphs and Consonant Blends Charts* (pages 213–214)—This chart can be used for the beginning, middle, or ending of a word. Some words begin with a blend or digraph; some blends/digraphs can be in the middle, and some at the end.
   - *Vowel Team Chart* (pages 215–216)—This can be used to determine the vowels that work together to make a vowel sound.

Using Our Sound Charts *(cont.)*

Engage

5. Provide partners with the chart or charts. Explain that they will play a search and find game. Name a word from the *Sound Chart Word List* (page 209) and have students work with partners to find the picture with the sound that matches.

Apply

6. Remind students to use sound charts to write words correctly.

Write/Conference

7. Provide time for students to write using the sound chart to spell. You may work with a small group, or rotate and conference independently.

Spotlight Strategy

8. Spotlight student use of the sound chart while spelling. For example, "As I moved around today, I noticed that Shania used sound charts effectively. Smart work!"

Share

9. Have students meet with partners to share how they used one of the charts to spell words.

Homework

Ask students to be aware of the sounds they hear as they watch TV, talk to their parents, or read a book at bedtime. Encourage students to be aware of their sound charts and how smart writers use tools for effective writing.

Sound Chart Word List

ABC Chart/ Beginning	SHORT Vowels	LONG Vowels	Blends /Digraphs	Vowel Teams
fish	mat	cake	brass	hoe
pack	chip	poke	trunk	meat
teeth	ant	hike	cripple	spray
win	rock	rope	plate	rain
goat	cub	rule	whisper	moon
rabbit	run	ice cream	chime	lawyer
alligator	pen	Abe	brush	shower
monkey	got	cute	drag	enjoy
doughnut	jump	game	slid	farmer

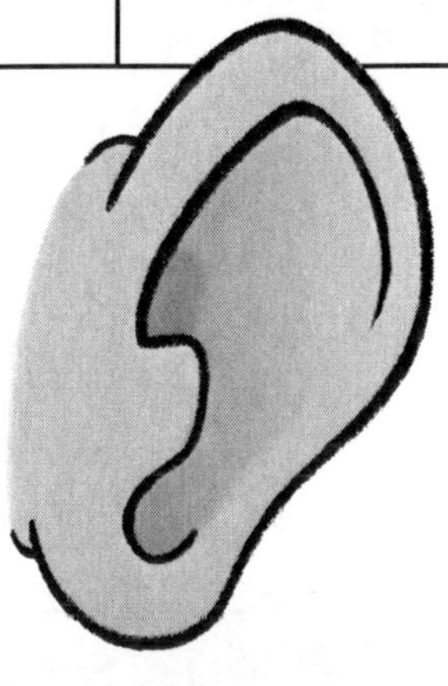

Alphabet Chart

A a  ant	B b  baseball	C c  car	D d  dragon	E e 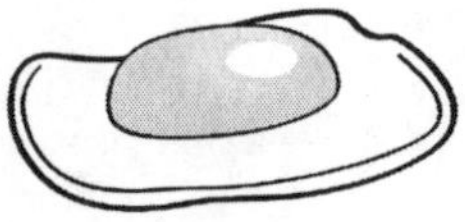 egg
F f  fan	G g  globe	H h  helicopter	I i  igloo	J j  jam
K k  key	L l 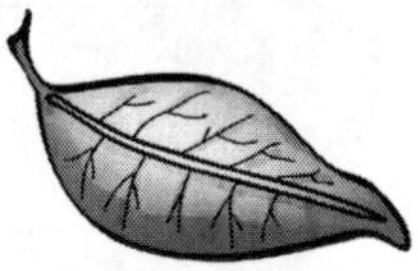 leaf	M m  mail	N n  nest	O o  owl
P p  pizza	Q q  quilt	R r  ring	S s  seal	T t  train
U u  umbrella	V v  vest	W w  watch	X x 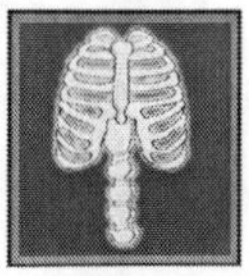 X-ray	Y y Z z 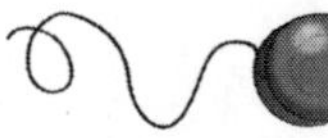 yo-yo  zebra

Short Vowel Chart

Short Vowels				
a	e	i	o	u
 alligator	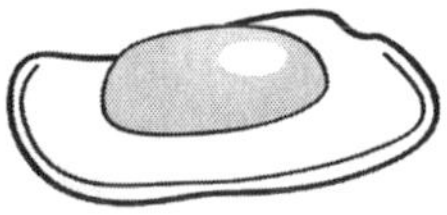 egg	 igloo	 ox	 umbrella
 bat	 bell	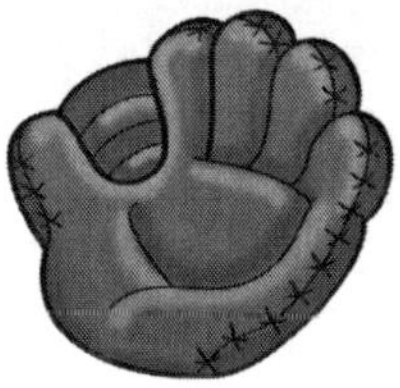 mit	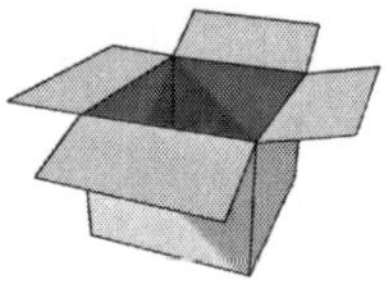 box	 duck

Long Vowel Chart

Long Vowels				
a	e	i	o	u
 apron	 eagle	 ice cream	 oatmeal	 uniform
 baby	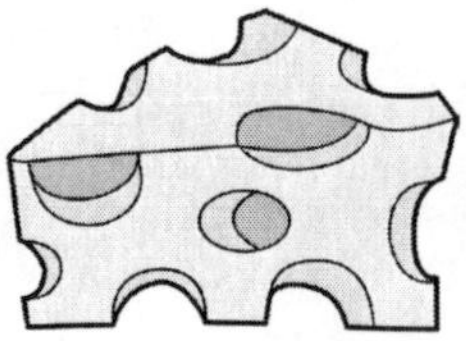 cheese	 spider	 boat	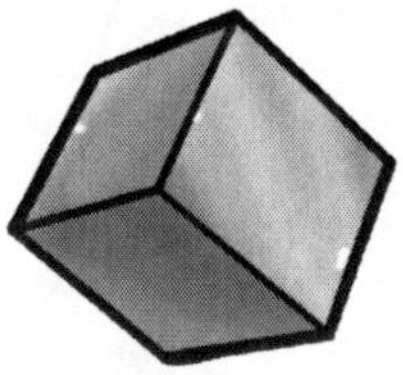 cube

Digraphs and Consonant Blends Chart

sh  shoes	**ch**  chain	**th** 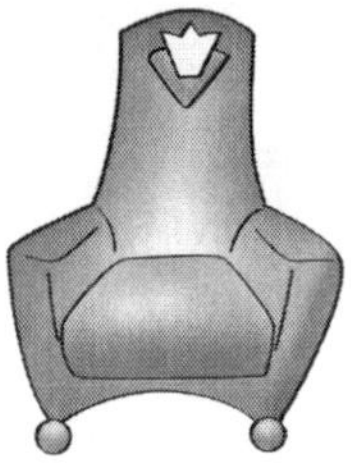 throne	**wh**  wheel	**bl** 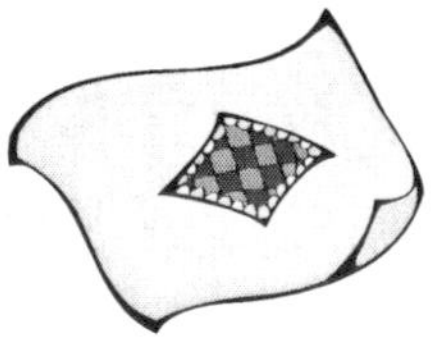 blanket
cl  clock	**fl**  fly	**gl**  globe	**pl**  plane	**sl**  sled
br  broom	**cr**  crab	**dr**  dragonfly	**fr**  fruit	**gr** 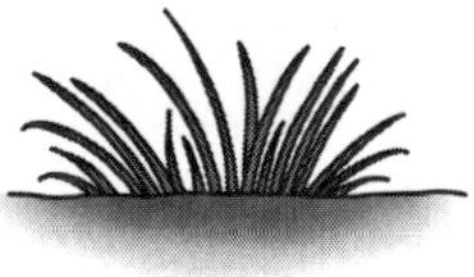 grass

Digraphs and Consonant Blends Chart *(cont.)*

pr	tr	sm	sn	sp
		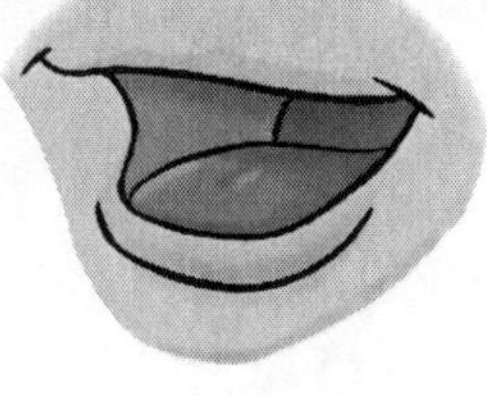		
pretzel	train	smile	snow	spaghetti
st	sw	tw	sc	sk

star	sweater	twelve	scarf	skunk

Vowel Team Chart

CVCe	CVCe	CVCe	CVCe	ai
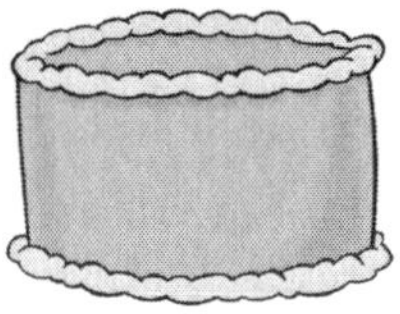				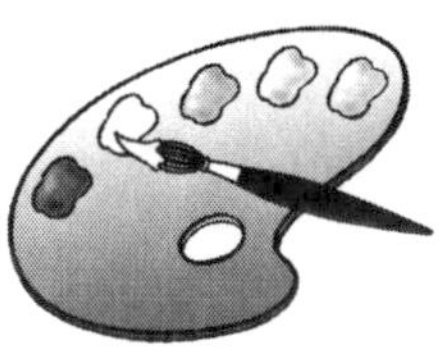
cake	bike	rope	mule	paint
ay	ea	ee	oa	oe
				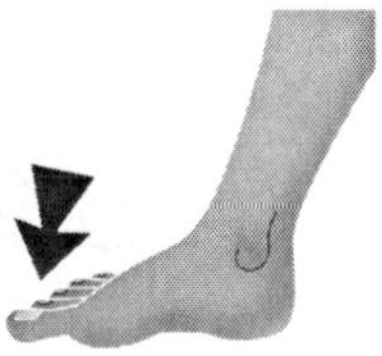
hay	leaf	bee	goat	toe
ie	ue	au	aw	ew

tie	glue	sauce	hawk	stew

Vowel Team Chart *(cont.)*

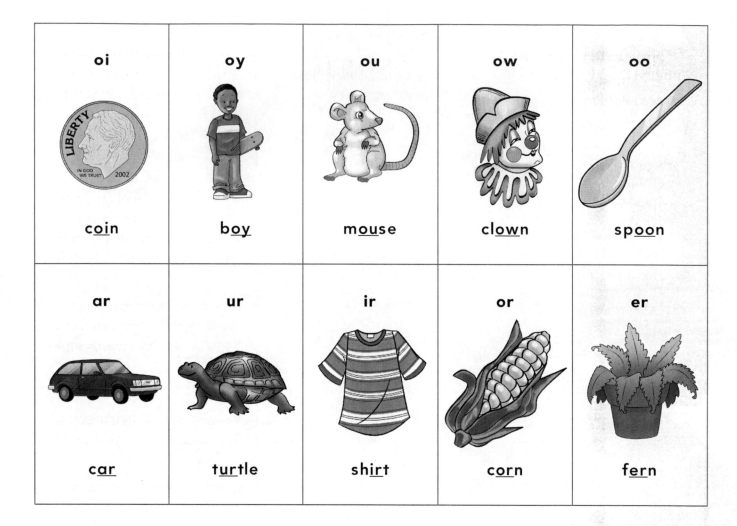

oi	oy	ou	ow	oo
				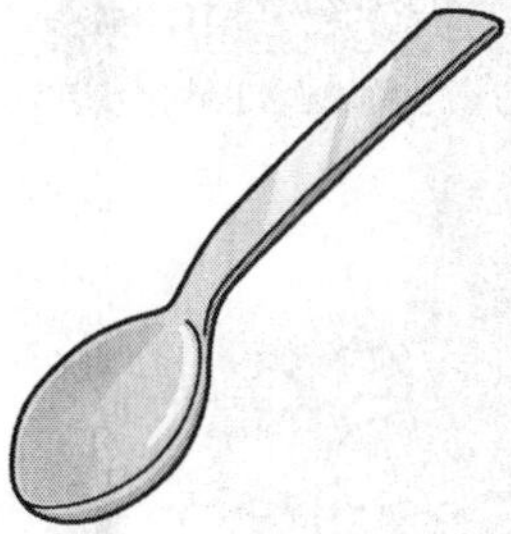
coin	boy	mouse	clown	spoon
ar	ur	ir	or	er

car	turtle	shirt	corn	fern

Count and Spell

Standard

Uses conventions of spelling in written compositions

Materials

- *Sound Box Word List* (page 219; soundboxwordlist.pdf)

Mentor Texts

- *The Great Fuzz Frenzy* by Susan Stevens Crummel
- See *Mentor Text List* in Appendix C for other suggestions.

Procedures

Note: The goal for students is automaticity with two to five phonemes. Providing support early builds a strong sound/symbol match to problem solve difficult words. Start simple and move to complex.

Think About Writing

1. Tell students that authors have to have the words spelled correctly in their books or the readers may not understand what has been written. Authors know how to spell many words quickly and that helps them concentrate on what they want to write rather than how to spell each word.
2. Tell students that using sound boxes will give them more confidence. Explain that they will learn to separate words into sounds to problem solve tricky words rapidly.

Teach

3. Tell students, "Today I will show you how to use sound boxes to help you quickly sound out words you are not sure how to spell."
4. Say a word for students, for example *am*. Show students how to segment the word by saying one sound at a time. As you say each sound, hold up a finger. For example when saying the word *am*, hold up your index finger when saying /a/ and your middle finger when saying /m/. Since two fingers are up, there are two sounds in the word.
5. Draw two short horizontal lines on a sheet of chart paper and segment the word again. This time as you say each sound, write the corresponding letter. For example, for /a/, write the letter *a* on the first horizontal line. Say the sound /m/ and write the letter *m* on the second horizontal line.

Count and Spell *(cont.)*

Engage

6. Practice this activity using shorter words with students. As students become proficient with shorter words, move on to longer words. Use the *Sound Box Word List* (page 219) for ideas.

Apply

7. Encourage students to use the Count and Spell strategy as they attempt to spell words as they are writing their stories.

Write/Conference

8. Provide time for students to write while paying attention to good spelling. Then, rotate around the room to confer with students and make observations.

Spotlight Strategy

9. Notice someone using the strategy and have them share quickly with the whole group to spotlight.

Share

10. Have students turn and talk to partners to share several words they tried to write using the *Count and Spell* strategy. Provide approximately two minutes for sharing.

Homework

Ask students to practice spelling words by using the *Count and Spell* strategy. Have students explain the strategy to their parents so they will know how to support and practice with the students.

Sound Box Word List

2 Phonemes	3 Phonemes	4 Phonemes	5 Phonemes
am	bed	best	blend
at	beg	black	cradle
boo	big	brown	crunch
bow	boat	bump	grand
day	bus	clap	plant
egg	cub	crab	pleased
go	cup	dress	plump
if	fall	dump	scrape
is	hop	fast	scream
it	house	glad	slept
me	job	grape	spend
my	man	green	splash
see	mouth	left	spread
shoe	over	milk	spring
shy	play	skate	stamp
so	push	stop	stand
toe	shop	swim	stripe
up	sun	think	strong
we	tell	truck	trust
zoo	web	wind	twist

Capital Rap

Standards

- Uses strategies to edit and publish written work
- Uses conventions of capitalization in written compositions

Materials

- Capital Rap (page 222; capitalrap.pdf)
- Chart paper
- Markers

Mentor Texts

- *One Monday Morning* by Uri Shulevitz
- *I Like Myself!* by Karen Beaumont
- See *Mentor Text List* in Appendix C for other suggestions.

Procedures

Note: Teach this lesson over several days and revisit regularly until students have perfected the skill of capitalization. You may wish to introduce one section of the *Capital Rap* (page 222) and focus on those specific concepts before moving onto the next section.

Think About Writing

1. Explain to students that authors need to use punctuation correctly so that the reader understands the message.
2. Review a mentor text if desired, and emphasize the author's use of capitalization. For example, in *I Like Myself,* author Karen Beaumont is like a busy bee. She flies around on almost every page using the word I to begin many sentences. Every sentence in her book begins with a capital letter. In *One Monday Morning*, Uri Shulevitz uses days of the week to sequence his story. Remind students that they should try to emulate the authors they love as they work on writing projects.

Teach

3. Tell students, "Today I will show you how to use a rap to remember capitalization."
4. Teach students the *Capital Rap*.
    - Use a soft voice and snap fingers to the beat, "I am important, so are you, the beginning of a sentence is important, too."
    - Have students join in as you point to the words in the rap and repeat several times.
    - Write the example sentences on chart paper and emphasize the capitalization rule as you correct the sentences with students.

Capital Rap *(cont.)*

Richard and i are friends. (capitalize *I*)

mrs. Gaston is our teacher. (capitalize a person's name)

we like to write and read stories. (capitalize the first letter of a sentence)

5. Remind students they can use the *Capital Rap* to fix up their writing so it is correct.

Engage

6. Have students *Heads-up, Stand-up, Partner-up* and work with partners to repeat the *Capital Rap* using a soft voice and a snapping finger. Then have partners explain to each other in their own words exactly what the rap is reminding them to do. Encourage students to take turns. Provide approximately two minutes of talk time.

Apply

7. Remind students to use the conventions of print—capitalization, punctuation, and spelling—to make their messages clear for the reader. Encourage students to work on a piece of writing from their folders or begin a new piece as they work today.

Write/Conference

8. Provide time for students to write or edit a previous piece. Remember, the orchestration of your classroom environment can only be successful if you have planned well. Conferencing is the result of your observation of student writing behaviors. Be ready to jot down what you notice to plan your next instruction.

Spotlight Strategy

9. Spotlight student use of the *Capital Rap*. For example, "You are all doing such important work. Anyone have a spotlight they would like to share? Remarkable remembering of the *Capital Rap*."

Share

10. Have students meet with partners to share the work they did today. Ask students to look for correct capitalization in their partners' work.

Homework

Ask students to share the *Capital Rap* with their parents. Have them practice the rap at home this evening and encourage them to have their parents join in the fun.

Capital Rap

Teacher Directions: Teach students to sing the rap in a soft voice as they snap to the beat. Review the examples of capitalization as you teach each section of *Capital Rap*.

Rap	Examples
Capital Rap, Capital Rap *I* am important so are you, the beginning of a sentence is important, too. Capital Rap, Capital Rap	Capitalize the word ***I.*** Richard and I are friends. Capitalize a person's name. Mrs. Gaston is our teacher. Capitalize the first letter in a sentence. We like to write and read stories.
Capital Rap, Capital Rap Days of the week and months of the year, cities and states, need capitals; it's clear! Capital Rap, Capital Rap	Capitalize the days of the week. Today is Saturday! Capitalize the months of the year. My birthday is in April. Capitalize the names of cities and states. I live in Chicago, Illinois.
Capital Rap, Capital Rap Titles of a book, movie or TV, a special place or holiday, need capitals, you see! Capital Rap, Capital Rap	Capitalize the important words in a title. I read "The Princess and the Pea." Capitalize the names of special places. My family went to Disneyland. Capitalize names of holidays. We have a picnic on the Fourth of July.

Rockin' Editors

Standards

- Uses strategies to edit and publish written work
- Uses conventions of capitalization in written compositions
- Uses conventions of punctuation in written compositions

Materials

- *Rockin' Editors* (page 225; rockineditors.pdf)
- Chart paper
- Markers
- Sticky notes

Mentor Texts

- *Are You My Mother*? by P. D. Eastman
- See *Mentor Text List* in Appendix C for other suggestions.

Procedures

Note: Revisit this mini-lesson for additional practice in conventions for editing, such as commas and quotation marks.

Think About Writing

1. Explain to students that authors develop interesting sentences in their writing. Readers must have a strategy to understand when one sentence ends and another begins. Good writers know to begin their sentences with a capital letter and end their thoughts with an ending punctuation mark.
2. Review mentor text if desired, and emphasize how the author uses punctuation to clarify and add energy to his or her writing.

Teach

3. Tell students, "Today, we will practice movement to remember writing conventions."
4. Write the following sentences on a sheet of chart paper:
    - the deer ran into the forest
    - is it looking for food
    - i am going to follow it said sam
    - crunch went my feet in the snow
5. Place the strips in a pocket chart and read the sentences without any stopping. Discuss the difficulty with understanding the message.
6. Tell students using correct conventions, such as commas, quotation marks, and capital letters, helps the reader understand the meaning of a sentence. Model using your body as you say the first sentence to help students remember conventions:

Rockin' Editors *(cont.)*

- Stand tall with arms together overhead and say the first word in the sentence. (The) Tell students this represents a capital letter.
- Continue saying the rest of the sentence. (deer ran into the forest).
- Signify the period at the end of the sentence by grinding your right foot into the ground. (.)

7. Add sticky notes to the sentence written on the chart paper to correct it.
8. Continue modeling the remainder of the sentences using body movements to represent conventions. Use *Rockin' Editors* (page 225) for body movements that correspond to each convention.

Engage

9. Have students *Heads-up, Stand-up, Partner-up* and work with partners to practice body motions to show conventions. Have students practice using the sentences on the chart paper. Allow approximately two minutes for student practice. Rove, comment, take notes, and encourage students as they practice. Gather students back together, and highlight and compliment partners using appropriate behaviors and demonstrating lesson focus.

Apply

10. Remind students they should use conventions to help the reader understand the message. Remind students to always check this in their writing!

Write/Conference

11. Provide time for students to write about a topic of their choice. Observe students to check for understanding. Initiate individual or small group conferences. Take notes in your conferring notebook.

Spotlight Strategy

12. Spotlight student editing. For example, "Amee did what good writers do! She used excellent examples of conventions!"

Share

13. Have students meet with partners to share how they included capitals and punctuation in their writing.

Homework

Ask students to notice conventions in the books they read tonight.

Rockin' Editors

Capital: Stand tall arms/hands together overhead

Period: Right foot grinds into floor

Question: Shrug shoulders with hands up

Exclamation: Right arm straight up, down, punch

Comma: Right hand karate chop- gently

Quotation Mark: Bent elbows, slant left, wiggle hands, slant right, wiggle hands

My Editing Tools

Standard
Uses strategies to edit and publish written work

Materials
- Chart paper
- Markers
- *My Editing Tools* (page 228; myeditingtools.pdf)
- Sentences with errors

Mentor Texts
- *Punk-tuation Celebration* by Pam Hall
- See *Mentor Text List* in Appendix C for other suggestions.

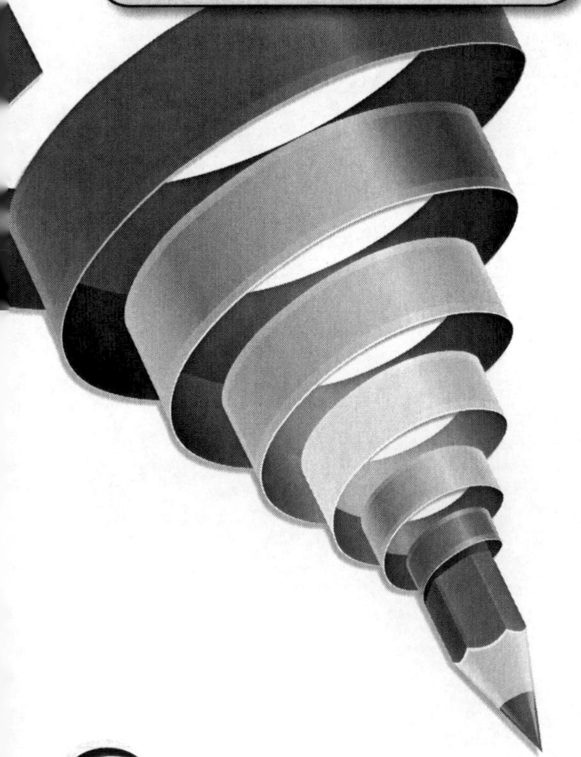

Procedure
Note: You may divide this lesson into four components: capitalization, punctuation, spelling, and inserting/deleting. This mini-lesson can be revisited again and again.

Think About Writing
1. Tell students that authors want to make sure their work is written correctly so it can be easily understood. They check their work carefully and have editors check their work carefully so there are no mistakes.
2. Review a mentor text if desired, and emphasize the author's use of conventions to impact the message.

Teach
3. Tell students, "Today I will show you how to use an editing checklist to check and fix your writing."
4. Show students how to use the checklist to review their work. Demonstrate how to use the editing marks to make corrections. Create an anchor chart to display in the classroom so the editing marks are easily visible.
   - **Capitalization**—Review with students what types of words should be capitalized. Write a sentence on the board such as: sally went to kansas On tuesday. Review with students the words in the sentence that need to be capitalized and why. Demonstrate how to use a triple underline under the letter that needs to be capitalized and a slash to to show words that need to be made lowercase.
   - **Punctuation**—Have students name the three ending punctuation marks used in sentences. Write each on the board or chart paper. Demonstrate how to draw a circle around the ending marks and tell students the circle reminds them that the ending mark was missing and to add it in the writing. Write some sample sentences with missing ending punctuation on chart paper. Model how to add the ending punctuation.

My Editing Tools *(cont.)*

- **Spelling**—Review with students how to review their writing for words that do not look right. Remind students how to count and spell words they are not sure about. Write some sample sentences with misspelled words on the chart paper and model how to fix the spelling of several words.
- **Inserting/Taking Out**—Demonstrate the use of these editing marks for deleting words or inserting missing words.

Engage

5. Tell students, "Writers, Heads-up, Stand-up, Partner-up to practice a few sentences together. With your partner look at the following sentences. What do you notice about capitalization/punctuation/spelling? Where will you place the editing marks? Be ready to share your observations." Share pre-prepared sentences one at a time allowing time for partner discussion. Remember to focus on one component until students become familiar with editing marks.

Apply

6. Provide students with *My Editing Tools* (page 228) to keep in their writing folders. Ask students to choose a piece from their writing folders they will check.

Write/Conference

7. Have students work with partners to edit the writing samples they chose. Remind students to use *My Editing Tools* for marks they can make to fix their writing. No conferencing today. Rotate around the room to provide praise, support, and guidance.

Spotlight Strategy

8. Spotlight great writing. For example, "What clever writers! Christian is just focusing on periods. Pretty soon he'll be an expert and he can move onto the next editing mark!"

Share

9. Have students meet with different partners to share how they improved their writing. Provide approximately two minutes.

Homework

Ask students to notice conversations they hear on TV or between family members. Ask them to think about the punctuation that might be used to write what they have heard.

My Editing Tools

Editor's Marks	Meaning	Example
≡	Capitalize	david gobbled up the grapes. (≡ under d)
/	Make lower case	My mother hugged Me when I Came Home. (/ through C and H)
(.) (?) (!)	Add ending punctuation	The clouds danced in the sky (.)
(sp)	Spelling mistake	sp (laffed) at the story.
^	Insert/Add	The dog barked all night. ^ annoying
~~that~~	Delete/Take out	It was the first ~~only~~ time I went to the zoo.

Proper Punctuation

Standards

- Uses strategies to edit and publish written work
- Uses conventions of punctuation in written compositions

Materials

- Chart paper
- Markers

Mentor Texts

- *Bedhead* by Margie Palatini
- *Punctuation Takes a Vacation* by Robin Pulver
- *Punk-tuation Celebration* by Pamela Hall
- See *Mentor Text List* in Appendix C for other suggestions.

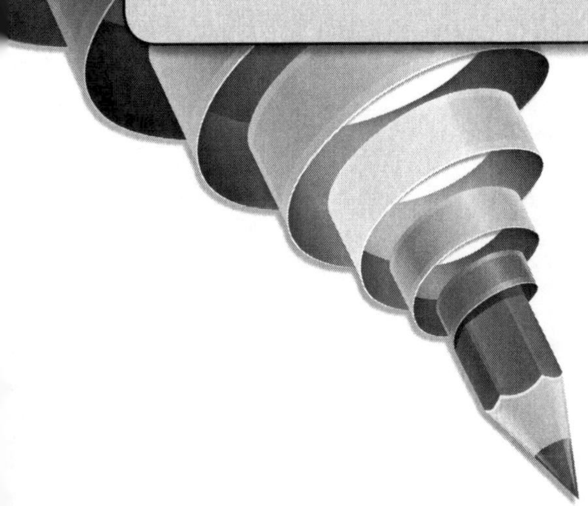

Procedure

Note: Revisit this lesson to emphasize types of punctuation.

Think About Writing

1. Tell students that authors use resources to improve their writing and record their thinking in a way that looks right, sounds right, and makes sense.
2. Review a mentor text if desired, and emphasize the author's use of punctuation. Ask students to imagine the chaos in reading and writing stories and books without punctuation.

Teach

3. Tell students, "Today I will show you how proper punctuation will improve your writing. We will look at examples of literature that offer strategies for improving the rhythm and flow of sentences."
4. Review the following punctuation by writing the sentences without the punctuation on a sheet of chart paper. Think aloud as you determine the proper punctuation for each sentence. You may want to refer back to the movement in *Rockin' Editors* mini-lesson (page 223).

   - Ending Punctuation—ends the sentence

     We played outside on the playground.
     (telling, period)

     How did you climb that fence?
     (question, question mark)

     Wow, a tire swing is really cool!
     (exclamatory, exclamation mark)

Proper Punctuation *(cont.)*

- Quotation Marks—shows when someone is speaking

  Use a quotation from any piece of literature. For example, in *Bedhead* by Margie Palatini, Oliver, the main character has many conversations with other characters in the story.

  "Been there, done that." moaned Oliver.

- Commas—keeps words from running together and tells the reader to pause

  For dinner, I had pizza, salad, soda, and a slice of pie for dessert.

Engage

5. Have students *Heads-up, Stand-up, Partner-up* and work with partners to tell how punctuation builds meaningful sentences. How might you use them in writing? Ask students to name punctuation they will use in their writing. Provide approximately two to three minutes for discussion.

Apply

6. Remind students to reread work in their writing folder, journals, or a piece of writing to check for punctuation.

Write/Conference

7. Provide time for students to review their writing. Conference with 3–4 students about only punctuation. As you look over their work, remember to have only one teaching point and be certain that you start your conference with praise.

Spotlight Strategy

8. Spotlight proper punctuation in students' work. For example, "You are so smart to use your resources to help you with your work. Kara and her partner are becoming very familiar with punctuation and are polishing up their work."

Share

9. Have students meet with partners to share what they have accomplished. Then select two or three students who have clearly understood this lesson and can provide an important model for others. Have those students take the author's chair.

Homework

Ask students to notice punctuation in writing at home. Encourage them to have their parents help them find punctuation. Tell students to be ready to share their observations tomorrow!

Editing with CUPS

Standard

Uses strategies to edit and publish written work

Materials

- Writing sample
- *CUPS* (page 233; cups.pdf)
- Colored pens or pencils
- Markers
- Chart paper

Mentor Texts

- *Punk-tuation Celebration* by Pamela Hall
- *Punctuation Takes a Vacation* by Robin Pulver
- See *Mentor Text List* in Appendix C for other suggestions.

Procedures

Note: Add *CUPS* to student folders for future support during writing.

Think About Writing

1. Tell students that authors check their work to make sure it is easy for the reader to understand. This means making sure words are spelled correctly and sentences make sense.
2. Review a mentor text if desired, and emphasize the use of conventions in the book.

Teach

3. Tell students, "Today I will show you how to ask questions to improve your writing by checking for capitalization, grammar usage, punctuation, and spelling."
4. Write the letters *C-U-P-S* vertically down the side of a sheet of chart paper. Explain to students that these letters will remind them how to check their writing. Write notes of the kinds of questions students should ask when thinking about that letter. See *CUPS* (page 233) for additional ideas.
    - **C**—Capitalization
    - **U**—Usage
    - **P**—Punctuation
    - **S**—Spelling
5. Display a piece of student writing. Show students how to use CUPS to check the writing. Write the letters C-U-P-S vertically on the side or bottom of the paper.

Editing with CUPS *(cont.)*

6. Model how to use each letter to remind you to check for each item *CUPS* stands for. Think aloud as you do this. For example, "*C* reminds me to check for capitalization. I use my green pencil to put three lines under any letter that needs to be capitalized, and I put a check mark beside the *C* when I am finished." Continue modeling how to check for usage, punctuation, and spelling. Use different colored pencils for each.

Engage

7. Ask students to *Heads-up, Stand-up, Partner-up*. Have students tell partners what CUPS stands for and how they will use it to check their writing.

Apply

8. Ask students to reread their writing and check for *CUPS*: capitalization, usage of grammar, punctuation, and spelling. Remind students that checking their papers with *CUPS*, and making corrections, will help their readers enjoy the writing.
9. Have students select a writing sample from their folders, reread carefully, write **CUPS** down the side, and carefully edit their papers.

Write/Conference

10. Provide time for students to review their writing using *CUPS*. Gather a small group to support through the editing process. Then, move around and check in with the other students.

Spotlight Strategy

11. Spotlight student work. For example, "Writers, you rock! Notice what I observed! Tina, Sheldon, and Jose are independently working to edit and improve their papers."

Share

12. Have students meet with someone to share their CUPS work. Remind students to provide a compliment and ask a question.

Homework

Ask students to be convention checkers at home tonight. Have them look around their houses for evidence of conventions: capitalization, usage, punctuation, or spelling. Encourage students to be ready to share when Writer's Workshop begins tomorrow.

CUPS

CUPS your paper!

C—Capitalization

Are the ***first words*** in each sentence, proper ***names***, ***titles***, and the names of ***days*** and ***months*** capitalized? Remember ***I***!

U—Usage and Grammar

Does your writing sound right? Check for ***correct*** word choice and complete sentences.

P—Punctuation

Is the punctuation correct? Check for **periods** (.), ***question marks*** (?) or ***exclamation points*** (!), ***commas*** (,) and ***quotation marks*** (" ").

S—Spelling

Are all the words ***spelled correctly***?

Use your resources like word walls, word lists, and a dictionary.

Essential Materials

Create a toolkit of items you can carry around with you as you conference with students. The toolkit can be a shoebox, a plastic tote, or anything you are comfortable carrying around from student to student. Any supplies that will help make your conference run smoothly are appropriate to put in the tote. Suggested items are listed below:

- Teacher Conferring Notebook
- Mentor text used for daily writing lesson (changes regularly)
- Highlighters or highlighting tape (to draw attention to words)
- Scissors, glue, tape, or a small stapler for revision, cutting, pasting, and moving around
- Sticky notes for making suggestions
- Colored pens for editing (green, red, blue, black)
    - Green—capitalization
    - Red—ending punctuation
    - Blue—spelling
    - Black—inserting
- Rubberband for stretching sentences
- Whiteboard or magnetic board with markers for modeling
- Magnetic chips or large colored buttons
- 1 package of correction tape or correction fluid
- Assorted paper

Conferring Notebook
Getting to the Core of Writing

Mini-Lesson Log

Date	Mini-Lesson Instructional Focus

Conference Log

P: Praise—What strategies did I notice the child using independently?

TP: Teaching Point—What teaching point will move this child forward in his or her development as a writer?

Name: Date: P: TP:	Name: Date: P: TP:	Name: Date: P: TP:	Name: Date: P: TP:
Name: Date: P: TP:	Name: Date: P: TP:	Name: Date: P: TP:	Name: Date: P: TP:
Name: Date: P: TP:	Name: Date: P: TP:	Name: Date: P: TP:	Name: Date: P: TP:

Conference Countdown

10 **Conversation**—The conversation should feel like a friendly chat with the student doing the most talking. Keep in mind, the person doing the most talking is doing the most learning.

9 **It's about the WRITER, not the Writing**—Teach the strategy that will support the writer after he or she is finished with this particular piece of writing. For example, do not just spell a word for a child, but teach him or her to segment the sounds to spell many words.

8 **Focus on the Content**—You are not there to simply fix up the conventions of a writing piece. When possible, have the student read the piece aloud before you even look at it and focus purely on the content. It's a challenge!

7 **Observe, Praise, Guide, Connect**—Establish a routine to become effective and efficient.

6 **Begin with Praise!**—Everyone likes a compliment. Beginning with a compliment gives students a sense of joy and pride in their work as well as recognizes developing writing skills.

5 **Talk Like a Writer to a Writer**—Use the language and vocabulary of a writer and respect the student's developmental level of writing.

4 **Connect or not to Connect?**—When conferring, only make connections to your daily mini-lesson when appropriate for the student's piece of writing.

3 **Record and Reflect**—Use your Conferring Notebook to monitor the progress of writing in your classroom and individual students. The information is valuable in defining your focus for writing instruction.

2 **Variety**—Incorporate a variety of activities that meet the multiple learning modalities of your students, like varying your conferring group sizes and using manipulatives.

1 **Be There!**—Your face and eyes tell it all. Let students know you truly care about the writing they are sharing with you.

Conferring Step-by-Step

The four phases of a conference structure are:

1. Observe
2. Praise
3. Guide
4. Connect

Observe—Use observation as a chance to build your background knowledge of the writer. During this element of the conference, you will determine what the writer knows and can do independently, and what the writer can do with support, called the zone of proximal development (Vygotsky 1978). Begin by asking yourself:

- What do I already know about this student's developmental level of writing and past writing from my conference notes and previous observations?
- What can I learn from the student's current writing piece and writing behaviors?
- What can I learn through questioning and listening to the writer?

When asking students about their writing work, open-ended questions provide guidance and support for students to begin reflecting on their writing. A close-ended question, such as, "Is this you in the picture?" elicits a simple one- or two-word response. An open-ended question, such as, "What can you tell me about your picture?" offers opportunities for the writer to explain and describe ideas, motives, and feelings about his or her work, ultimately, gaining clarity and developing a deeper understanding of his or her writing. You might ask the writer:

- So, what are you working on in your writing today?
- What can you tell me about your important writing work?

Through your observation, you should determine a successful writing point and one teaching point that will help this child become a more independent writer. Selecting a teaching point can be daunting as we analyze a young writer's work. Teachers often ask, "How do you know what to work on when there are so many things?" The truth is there is no right answer. Here are some ideas to guide you as you select teaching points.

- Use what you know about the growth of this writer. Where is this writer developmentally?
- Consider what the student is working on at this time. What is the student's focus in his or her writing?
- Use the current writing curriculum and the Common Core State Standards.
- Use what is being taught in mini-lessons and whole-group instruction.

Where we ourselves are as writers, as well as where we are as teachers of writing, greatly affect our decisions. As you become more knowledgeable about the developmental phases of writers and the understanding of quality writing instruction, your decisions become more sophisticated. The more you confer with your writers, the more effective you become at making decisions during conferring. Most importantly, select one teaching point that will support each writer during your conference. Calkins (2003) reminds us to teach to the writer and not to the writing.

Conferring Step-by-Step *(cont.)*

Praise—Recognize the writer for work well done. Always begin a conference with a positive comment. This praise provides positive feedback intended to identify what the student is doing correctly and to encourage the writer to repeat that accomplishment in future writing. Isolate and identify the successful writing strategy in the student's writing piece. When praises are authentic and specific, they become a teachable moment. Below are some examples of powerful praise.

- "Something I really like that you've done is how you shared the setting with your reader. That's exactly what good writers do!"
- "I see here in your writing you chose to use color words to give your reader more details in your story. Wonderful words!"
- "Just like the authors we have been studying, you have an excellent picture that helps your reader visualize exactly what is happening in your story."
- "I am so impressed with the way you just got right to work and accomplished so much writing in such a short amount of time."

Guide—Personalize and scaffold instruction to meet the writer's needs. The instruction includes sharing the writing strategy you will teach the writer, demonstrating the strategy, and then guiding the writer through practicing the process. Teach the writer a personalized strategy based on your earlier decisions. When the decision is based on a previously taught mini-lesson, writers make additional connections and greater achievement is gained. As part of the routine of the mini-lesson, you must explicitly state what you will teach the student.

- Mentor texts and writing samples are excellent resources to weave into your conference instruction. Writers can visualize the craft you are teaching when they are exposed to concrete examples, particularly from real literature.
- Initial teaching remarks may include, "Let me show you something that good writers do…" and, "Sometimes in my writing, I try to…"

By offering support while the student practices the strategy, you increase the chances of success. Any time you engage students in the application of new strategies, you enhance the probability they will recall that strategy in future writing. Once the writer is engaged in practice, you may move on to confer with another writer. However, leave the writer with expectations until you return, such as, "When I get back, I want to see …" Upon your return, provide specific feedback relative to your expectations. For example, "Well done! Now I really have a picture in my mind of your character."

Conferring Step-by-Step *(cont.)*

Connect—Make connections between teaching and future writing. First, clearly restate what the writer learned and practiced. Then, remind and encourage the writer to use the strategy in future writing. As students become familiar with the conference structure, you may ask the student to share the new learning to get a sense of his or her understanding of your teaching. Making connections may begin as follows:

- "Remember, good writers always…"
- "Tell me what you just learned as a writer."

Writer's Workshop conferences will vary in length and type based on the time of year and the needs of your class. Conferences are most successful when routines and expectations have been established and young writers can manage their own writing time. At the beginning of the year, while establishing routines, drop-by conferences provide a quick glimpse into what each student is working on and what kind of help is needed. Once routines are established, meet with students in individual and/or small group conferences that are focused around specific needs. You may also include peer conferences, but this requires modeling, experience, and practice. For young writers, we use *Compliment and Question*. The compliment should be more than a general statement, such as, "I like your story." It should be specific to the writing, for example, "I like the way you ask a question to begin your story." A question should be something the peer would like to know more about or something that needs clarification.

The conference should be brief and reflect the child's age and development—usually not longer than 10–15 minutes in second grade. Small group conferences may be as long as 8–10 minutes as you will be checking in with each student. Hold the conference wherever you prefer. Some teachers prefer moving desk to desk or table to table while others prefer that students join them at a small conference table or on the floor. Remember these two points:

- *Have a seat!* Wherever you decide to hold your conferences, it is important that students know you are committed to giving them your attention. By sitting down, you are sending the message that you are there with them at that moment.
- *Be prepared!* Have materials readily available to you during the conference. You may wish to compile a Conferring Toolkit of essential materials (see page 234 of Appendix A) that can be carried with you or placed in your conference area.

Continuing to provide meaningful and relevant conferences requires some form of keeping notes during your writing conferences. A simple, but thorough conference summary can identify areas of writing deficiencies and strengths as you plan future mini-lessons, select students for small group conferences, and report student progress to parents. To support you as you make conferring a priority in Writer's Workshop, pages for the *Conferring Notebook* are included on pages 235–238.

Benchmark Assessment Overview

Administering a Benchmark (page 243) is a guide to assist you as you begin giving benchmarks. It is important that the prompt is uniform across classrooms when measuring growth at a school level. Second-grade benchmark prompts should be simple and attainable, for example:

- Draw a picture and write a story about your favorite food.
- Draw a picture and write a story about an animal. What does your animal look like? What does your animal eat? Where does it live? What is interesting about your animal?
- Write a story and tell about a special time you had with your mom (dad, grandma, grandpa, brother, friend). Be sure to include a beginning, middle, and end along with important details about your adventure.

The Writing Rubric (page 244; secondgradewritingrubric.pdf) is a tool to analyze student writing skills. You may refer to the Phases of Writing (pages 8–9) to further clarify your students' writing growth.

The Writing Report (page 245; secondgradewritingreport.pdf) serves as a summative report of a student's writing benchmarks. The completed form along with the beginning, middle, and end-of-year benchmarks are placed in the student's record folder at the end of the year.

The Grouping Mat (page 246 secondgradegroupingmat.pdf) is an at-a-glance chart showing which students in your classroom have attained particular benchmarks. Simply circle the current benchmark period, and complete the chart by recording your students' names in the boxes. Your goal is to see the students' names progressively move upward on the rubric report.

The core of writing instruction is the desire to support young writers as they explore, discover, and learn the writing process. It also involves determining what knowledge and skills young writers have developed over a period of time. Assessment is a continuous process and, when used properly, benefits teachers as well as students.

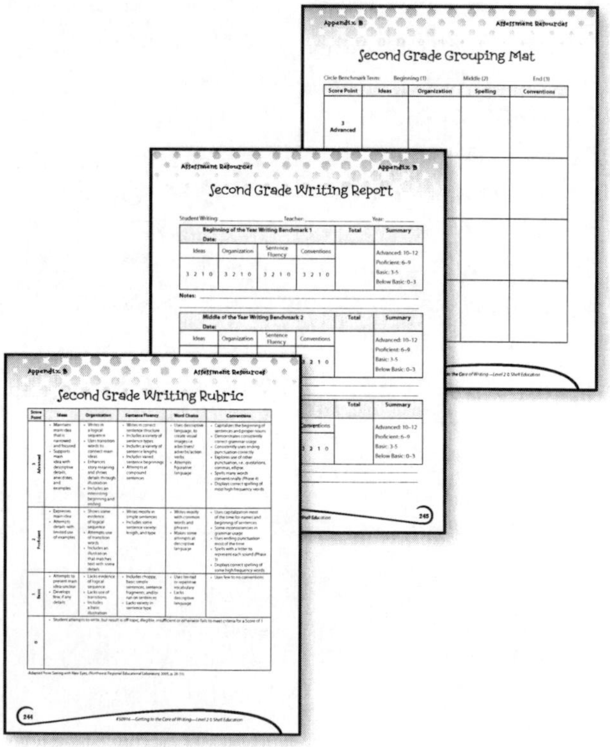

Administering a Benchmark

Writing Benchmarks are usually administered at the beginning, middle, and end of the school year to measure improvements and determine the writer's strengths and deficits in writing development. To get started, follow these guidelines:

- Administer the Writing Benchmark Prompt in small groups. This allows the teacher to observe and take anecdotal notes of individual student behaviors.
- It is important not to practice the prompt prior to the writing benchmark session.
- Do not provide teacher support. Your goal is to determine what students are able to do independently. If a student demonstrates frustration, he or she may just draw a picture, but you may wish to redirect the student to the prompt. Compliment the drawing and invite the student to write something about the drawing as best he or she can.
- Allow students to use classroom displays such as word walls. Note words copied from the word wall.
- Distribute paper to each student. Use paper familiar to the students. Students should write their name and the date on the back so that it is not seen prior to scoring the writing. This will help you to stay objective as you grade the writing piece .
- Supply pencils and crayons when necessary.
- Explain to your class that this process will show how much they have grown as writers and that a prompt will be given at the beginning, middle, and end of the year.
- Read the prompt to your students. Paraphrase the prompt when necessary to clarify understanding. You may wish to display the prompt on chart paper or on a whiteboard.
- Have each student read you his or her story upon completion. Keep a record of what each student wrote in your own writing so that you will be able to identify the words that he or she used. If some words are unreadable due to invented spelling, write them down at the bottom of the writing piece or on a sticky note.

Second Grade Writing Rubric

Score Point	Ideas	Organization	Sentence Fluency	Word Choice	Conventions
3 Advanced	• Maintains main idea that is narrowed and focused • Supports main idea with descriptive details, anecdotes, and examples	• Writes in a logical sequence • Uses transition words to connect main ideas • Enhances story meaning and shows details through illustration • Includes an interesting beginning and ending	• Writes in correct sentence structure • Includes a variety of sentence types • Includes a variety of sentence lengths • Includes varied sentence beginnings • Attempts at compound sentences	• Uses descriptive language, to create visual images i.e. adjectives/ adverbs/action verbs • Attempts figurative language	• Capitalizes the beginning of sentences and proper nouns • Demonstrates consistently correct grammar usage • Consistently uses ending punctuation correctly • Explores use of other punctuation, i.e., quotations, commas, ellipse. • Spells many words conventionally (Phase 4) • Displays correct spelling of most high frequency words
2 Proficient	• Expresses main idea • Attempts details with limited use of examples	• Shows some evidence of logical sequence • Attempts use of transition words • Includes an illustration that matches text with some details	• Writes mostly in simple sentences • Includes some sentence variety; length, and type	• Writes mostly with common words and phrases • Makes some attempts at descriptive language	• Uses capitalization most of the time for names and beginning of sentences • Some inconsistencies in grammar usage • Uses ending punctuation most of the time • Spells with a letter to represent each sound (Phase 3) • Displays correct spelling of some high frequency words
1 Basic	• Attempts to present main idea; unclear • Develops few, if any details	• Lacks evidence of logical sequence • Lacks use of transitions • Includes a basic illustration	• Includes choppy, basic simple sentences, sentence fragments, and/or run on sentences • Lacks variety in sentence type	• Uses limited or repetitive vocabulary • Lacks descriptive language	• Uses few to no conventions
0 Below Basic	Student attempts to write, but result is off topic, illegible, insufficient or otherwise fails to meet criteria for a Score of 1				

-Adapted from Seeing with New Eyes, (Northwest Regional Educational Laboratory, 2005, p. 28-31)

Second Grade Writing Report

Student Writing: ____________________ Teacher: ____________________ Year: __________

Beginning of the Year Writing Benchmark 1 Date:				Total	Summary
Ideas	Organization	Sentence Fluency	Conventions		Advanced: 10–12 Proficient: 7–9 Basic: 4–6 Below Basic: 0–3
3 2 1 0	3 2 1 0	3 2 1 0	3 2 1 0		

Notes: ____

____

Middle of the Year Writing Benchmark 2 Date:					Total	Summary
Ideas	Organization	Sentence Fluency	Word Choice	Conventions		Advanced: 13–15 Proficient: 10–12 Basic: 5–9 Below Basic: 0–4
3 2 1 0	3 2 1 0	3 2 1 0	3 2 1 0	3 2 1 0		

Notes: ____

____

Middle of the Year Writing Benchmark 3 Date:					Total	Summary
Ideas	Organization	Sentence Fluency	Word Choice	Conventions		Advanced: 13–15 Proficient: 10–12 Basic: 5–9 Below Basic: 0–4
3 2 1 0	3 2 1 0	3 2 1 0	3 2 1 0	3 2 1 0		

Notes: ____

____

Second Grade Grouping Mat

Circle Benchmark Term: Beginning (1) Middle (2) End (3)

Score Point	Ideas	Organization	Sentence Fluency	Word Choice	Conventions
3 Advanced					
2 Proficient					
1 Basic					
0 Below Basic					

Benchmark Writing Samples

Beginning of the Year

Prompt: Draw and write about something you enjoy doing with a friend.

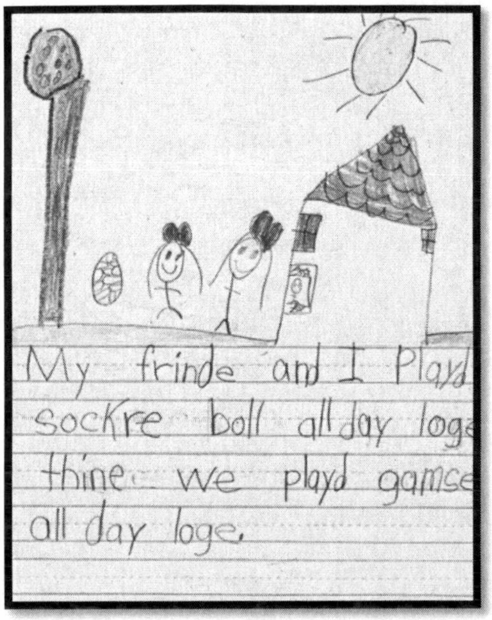

Text: My friend and I played soccer ball all day long. Then, we played games all day long.

Beginning of the Year Writing Benchmark 1 Date:				Total	Summary
Ideas	Organization	Sentence Fluency	Conventions	4 Basic	Advanced: 10–12 Proficient: 7–9 Basic: 4–6 Below Basic: 0–3
3 2 (1) 0	3 2 (1) 0	3 2 (1) 0	3 2 (1) 0		

Benchmark Writing Samples *(cont.)*

Middle of the Year

Prompt: Draw and write a story to tell what you do when it is cold outside.

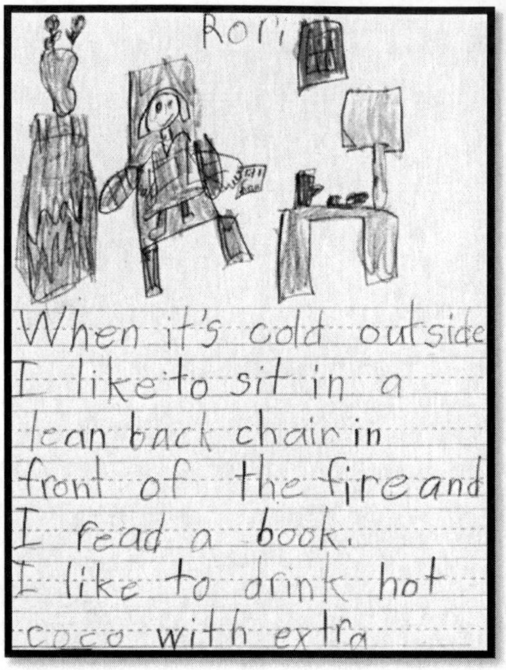

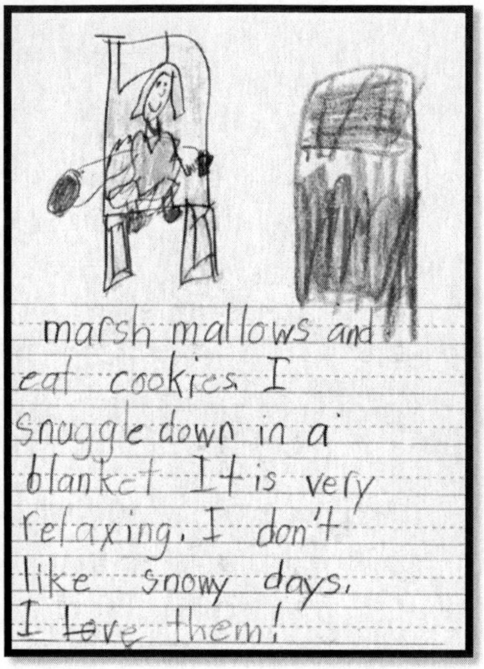

Text: When it's cold outside, I like to sit in a lean back chair in front of the fire and I read a book. I like to drink hot cocoa with extra marshmallows and eat cookies. I snuggle down in a blanket. It is very relaxing. I don't like snowy days. I love them!

Middle of the Year Writing Benchmark 2 **Date:**					**Total**	**Summary**
Ideas	Organization	Sentence Fluency	Word Choice	Conventions	10 Proficient	Advanced: 13–15 Proficient: 10–12 Basic: 5–9 Below Basic: 0–4
3 (2) 1 0	3 (2) 1 0	3 (2) 1 0	3 (2) 1 0	3 (2) 1 0		

Benchmark Writing Samples *(cont.)*

End of the Year

Prompt: Draw and write about a second grade adventure with a friend.

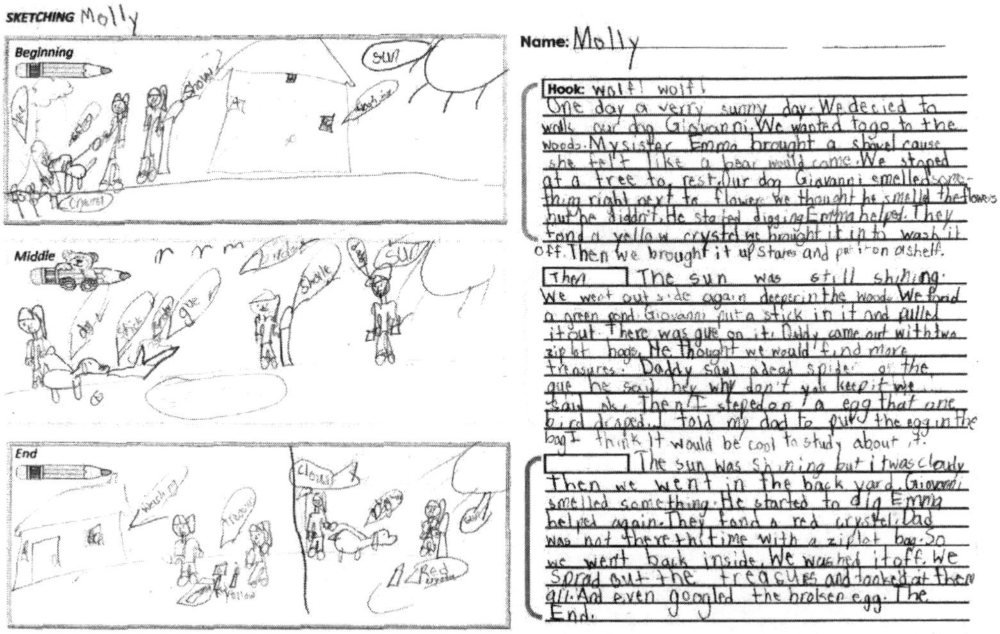

Text: Wolf! Wolf! One day a very sunny day, we decided to walk our dog, Giovanni. My sister Emma brought a shovel cause she felt like a bear could come. We stopped at a tree to rest. Our dog, Giovanni, smelled something right next to (the) flowers. We thought he smelled the flowers, but he didn't. He started digging, Emma helped. They found a yellow crystal. We brought it in to wash it off. Then, we brought it up stairs and put it on a shelf.

Then, the sun was still shining. We went outside again deeper in the words. We found a green pond. Giovanni put a stick in it and pulled it out. There was goo on it. Daddy came out with two Ziploc bags. He thought we would find more treasures. Daddy saw a dead spider on the goo. He said, "Hey, why don't you keep it? " We said, "Ok." Then, I stepped on an egg that one bird dropped. I told my dad to put the egg in the bag. I think it would be cool to study about it.

The sun was shining but it was cloudy. Then, we went in the back yard. Giovanni smelled something. He started to dig, Emma helped again. They found a red crystal. Dad was not there this time with a Ziploc bag. So, we went back inside. We washed it off. We spread out the treasures and looked at them all. And even googled the broken egg. The End.

Middle of the Year Writing Benchmark 3 **Date:**					**Total**	**Summary**
Ideas	Organization	Sentence Fluency	Word Choice	Conventions	15 Advanced	Advanced: 13–15 Proficient: 10–12 Basic: 5–9 Below Basic: 0–4
(3) 2 1 0	(3) 2 1 0	(3) 2 1 0	(3) 2 1 0	(3) 2 1 0		

Mentor Text List

Managing Writer's Workshop

Binkow, Howard. 2006. *Harold B. Wigglebottom Learns to Listen*. Minneapolis, MN: Lerner Publishing Group.

Cook, Julia. 2006. *My Mouth is a Volcano!* Chattanooga, TN: National Center for Youth Issues.

———. 2007. *Personal Space Camp*. Chattanooga, TN: National Center for Youth Issues.

———. 2011. *The Worst Day of My Life Ever!* Boys Town, NE: Boys Town Press.

Giff, Patricia Reilly. 1995. Today Was a Terrible Day. New York: Live Oak Media.

Kirk, Daniel. 2007 *Library Mouse*. New York: Harry N. Abrams.

Leedy, Loreen. 2005. *Look at My Book: How Kids Can Write & Illustrate Terrific Books.* New York: Holiday House.

LeSieg, Theo. 1993. *I Can Write*. New York: Random House Books for Young Readers.

Lester, Helen. 1995. *Me First*. Boston: Sandpiper.

———. 2012. *All for Me and None for All*. Boston: Houghton Mifflin Books for Children.

———. 2002. *Author: A True Story*. Boston Sandpiper.

———. 1997. *Listen, Buddy!* Boston: Sandpiper.

Lionni, Leo. 1973. *Swimmy*. New York: Dragonfly Books.

McGovern, Ann. 1992. *Too Much Noise*. Boston: Sandpiper.

Munsch, Robert. 2002. *We Share Everything*. New York: Cartwheel Books.

Reiss, Mike. 2008. *The Boy Who Wouldn't Share*. New York: HarperCollins.

Teague, Mark. 1997. *How I Spent My Summer Vacation*. New York: Dragonfly Books.

Watt, Mélanie. 2007. *Chester*. Tonawanda, NY: Kids Can Press Ltd.

———. 2008. *Chester's Back*. Tonawanda, NY: Kids Can Press Ltd.

Ideas

Aliki. 1987. *We Are Best Friends*. New York: Greenwillow Books.

Aylesworth, Jim. 1998. *The Gingerbread Man*. New York: Scholastic Press.

Beaumont, Karen. 2004. *I Like Myself!* Boston: Harcourt Children's Books.

Bottner, Barbara, and Gerald Kruglik. 2004. *Wallace's Lists*. New York: Katherine Tegen Books.

Boyd, Candy Dawson. 1998. *Daddy, Daddy, Be There*. New York: Puffin.

Bunting, Eve. 1989. *The Wednesday Surprise*. New York: Clarion Books.

Caseley, Judith. 1994. *Dear Annie*. New York: Greenwillow Books.

Cole, Joanna. 1991. *My Puppy Is Born*. New York: HarperCollins.

Mentor Text List *(cont.)*

Dr. Seuss. 1996. *There's a Wocket in My Pocket!* New York: Random House.

Gibbons, Gail. 1994. *Frogs*. New York: Holiday House.

———. 2000. *Bats*. New York: Holiday House.

———. 2004. *The Pumpkin Book*. Pine Plains, NY: Live Oak Media.

Harshman, Marc, Bonnie Collins, and Toni Goffe. 2002. *Rocks in My Pockets*. Charleston, WV: Quarrier Press.

Henkes, Kevin. 2007. *Chrysanthemum*. New York: Greenwillow Books.

Hest, Amy. 2007. *Mr. George Baker*. Somerville, MA: Candlewick.

Houston, Gloria. 1997. *My Great-Aunt Arizona*. New York: HarperCollins.

Howard, Elizabeth F. 2001. *Aunt Flossie's Hats (and Crab Cakes Later)*. New York: Clarion Books.

Kellogg, Steven. 1988. *Johnny Appleseed*. New York: HarperCollins.

———. 1992. *Best Friends*. New York: Puffin.

———. 1992. *Pecos Bill*. New York: HarperCollins.

Laden, Nina. 1994. *The Night I Followed the Dog*. San Francisco: Chronicle Books.

LeSieg, Theo. 1993. *I Can Write*. New York: Random House Books for Young Readers.

Lowry, Lois. 2004. *Gooney Bird Greene*. New York: Yearling.

MacLachlan, Patricia. 1994. *All the Places to Love*. New York: HarperCollins.

Marshall, James. 1993. *Little Red Riding Hood*. New York: Picture Puffins.

McGovern, Ann. 1992. *If You Grew Up with Abraham Lincoln*. Logan, IA: Perfection Learning.

Mercer, Mayer. 2001. *Just My Friend and Me*. New York: Random House Books for Young Readers.

Miller, Alice Ann. 2003. *Treasures of the Heart*. Chelsea, MI: Sleeping Bear Press.

Park, Barbara. 2000. *Junie B. Jones Has a Peep in Her Pocket*. New York: Random House.

Pfeffer, Wendy. 2004. *From Seed to Pumpkin*. New York: Collins.

Rosethal, Amy K. 2006. *One of Those Days*. New York: Putnam Juvenile.

Rylant, Cynthia. 2004. *The Relatives Came*. Pine Plains, NY: Live Oaks Media.

Sharmat, Mitchell. 2009. *Gregory the Terrible Eater*. New York: Scholastic Trade.

Shulevitz, Uri. 1986. *The Treasure*. New York: Farrar, Straus and Giroux.

Spinelli, Eileen. 2008. *The Best Story*. New York: Dial.

Wong, Janet S. 2002. *You Have to Write*. New York: Margaret K. McElderry Books.

Mentor Text List *(cont.)*

Sentence Fluency

Beaumont, Karen. 2005. *I Ain't Gonna Paint No More!* Boston: Harcourt Children's Books.

Brown, Margaret Wise. 1990. *The Important Book*. New York: HarperCollins.

———. 2005. *The Runaway Bunny*. New York: HarperCollins.

Bunting, Eve. 2004. *Whales Passing*. New York: Scholastic Inc.

Carle, Eric. 1994. *The Very Hungry Caterpillar*. New York: Philomel Books.

Charlip, Remy. 1993. *Fortunately*. New York: Aladdin.

Henkes, Kevin. 2007. *Chrysanthemum*. New York: Greenwillow Books.

Palatini, Margie. 2003. *Bedhead*. New York: Simon & Schuster Books for Young Readers.

Rylant, Cynthia. 2004. *The Relatives Came*. Pine Plains, NY: Live Oaks Media.

Smucker, Anna. 1994. *No Star Nights*. New York: Dragonfly Books.

———. 1995. *Outside the Window*. New York: Random House Value Publishing.

Williams, Vera B. 1984. *A Chair for My Mother*. New York: Greenwillow Books.

Yolen, Jane. 1987. *Owl Moon*. New York: Philomel.

Organization

Ada, Alma Flor. 2001. *Yours Truly, Goldilocks*. New York: Atheneum Books for Young Readers.

———. 2004. *With Love, Little Red Hen*. New York: Atheneum Books for Young Readers.

Arnosky, Jim. 2008. *All About Frogs*. New York: Scholastic Inc.

Bayer, Jane E. 1992. *A, My Name Is Alice*. New York: Puffin.

Brett, Jan. 1996. *Goldilocks and the Three Bears.* New York: Puffin.

Bunting, Eve. 1989. *The Wednesday Surprise*. New York: Clarion Books.

———. 1991. *Night Tree*. Boston: Harcourt Children's Books.

Carlson, Nancy. 1999. *ABC I Like Me!* New York: Puffin.

Cannon, Janell. 1993. *Stellaluna*. Orlando, FL: Harcourt Brace & Co.

Caseley, Judith. 1994. *Dear Annie.* New York: Greenwillow Books.

Crews, Donald. 1996. *Shortcut*. New York: Greenwillow Books.

Cronin, Doreen. 2011. *Click, Clack, Moo: Cows That Type.* New York: Little Simon.

Gray, Libba. 1999. *My Mama Had a Dancing Heart*. New York: Scholastic.

Harrison, Joanna. 1995. *Dear Bear.* Minneapolis, MN: Carolrhoda Books.

Mentor Text List *(cont.)*

Organization *(cont.)*

Henkes, Kevin. 1988. *Chester's Way*. New York: Greenwillow Books

———. 2007. *Chrysanthemum*. New York: Greenwillow Books.

Hoose, Phillip M., Hannah Hoose, and Debbie Tilley. 1998. *Hey, Little Ant*. New York: Tricycle Press.

Howard, Elizabeth F. 2001. *Aunt Flossie's Hats (and Crab Cakes Later)*. New York: Clarion Books

Houston, Gloria. 1997. *My Great-Aunt Arizona*. New York: HarperCollins.

Hummon, David. 1999. *Animal Acrostics*. Nevada City, CA: Dawn Publications.

James, Simon. 1997. *Dear Mr. Blueberry*. New York: Aladdin.

Jenkins, Steven. 2003. *What Do You Do With a Tail Like This?* Boston: Houghton Mifflin Books for Children 2003.

Jones, Sally. 2009. *How to Be a Baby by Me, the Big Sister*. New York: Bloomsbury Press.

Kasza, Keiko. 2005. *My Lucky Day*. New York: Puffin.

Keats, Ezra Jack. 1998. *A Letter to Amy*. New York: Puffin.

King-Smith, Dick. 2001. *I Love Guinea Pigs*. Somerville, MA: Candlewick.

Kitchen, Bert. 1992. *Animal Alphabet*. New York: Puffin.

Laminack, Lester. 2007. *Snow Day!* Atlanta, GA: Peachtree Publishers.

Leedy, Loreen. 2005. *Look at My Book: How Kids Can Write & Illustrate Terrific Books*. New York: Holiday House.

Noble, Trinka Hakes. 1980. *The Day Jimmy's Boa Ate the Wash*. New York: Putnam.

Numeroff, Laura. 1985. *If You Give a Mouse a Cookie*. New York: HarperCollins.

Palatini, Margie. 2003. *Bedhead*. New York: Simon & Schuster Books for Young Readers.

———. 2009. *The Perfect Pet*. New York: Katherine Tegen Books.

Pinkney, Jerry. 2009. *The Lion & the Mouse*. New York: Little, Brown Books for Young Readers.

Piven, Hanoch. 2012. *What Presidents Are Made Of*. New York: Atheneum Books for Young Readers.

Pretlutski, Jack. 1986. *Read Aloud Rhymes for the Very Young*. New York: Knopf Books for Young Readers.

Robbins, Ken. 2005. *Seeds*. New York: Atheneum Books for Young Readers.

Ryan, Pam Muñoz. 2001. *Hello Ocean*. Watertown, MA: Talewinds.

Rylant, Cynthia. 2004. *The Relatives Came*. Pine Plains, NY: Live Oaks Media.

Schnur, Steven. 1997. *Autumn: An Alphabet Acrostic*. New York: Clarion Books.

Shannon, David. 1998. *A Bad Case of Stripes*. New York: Blue Sky Press.

Silverstein, Shel. 2004. *Where the Sidewalk Ends*. New York: HarperCollins, 2004.

Mentor Text List (cont.)

Organization (cont.)

Rylant, Cynthia. 1993. *When I was Young in the Mountains*. New York: Puffin

Steig, William. 2009. *Amos & Boris*. New York: Square Fish.

Tuckfield, Liyala. 2000. *How to Make a Bird Feeder*. Boston: Rigby.

Viorst, Judith. 2009. *Alexander and the Terrible, Horrible, No Good, Very Bad Day.* New York: Atheneum Books for Young Readers.

Westcott, Nadine B. 1992. *Peanut Butter and Jelly*: A Play Rhyme. New York: Puffin.

White, E. B. 1952. *Charlotte's Web*. New York: HarperCollins.

Willems, Mo. 2003. *Don't Let the Pigeon Drive the Bus!* New York: Hyperion Press.

Yolen, Jane. 1987. *Owl Moon*. New York: Philomel

Word Choice

Arnofsky, Jim. 2000. *Rattlesnake Dance*. New York: Putnam Juvenile.

Banks, Kate. 2006. *Max's Words*. New York: Farrar, Straus and Giroux.

Boswell, Addie. 2008. *The Rain Stomper*. Tarrytown, NY: Marshall Cavendish Children's Books.

Cherry, Lynne. 2003. *How Groundhog's Garden Grew*. New York: Blue Sky Press.

Coffelt, Nancy. 2009. *Big, Bigger, Biggest!* New York: Henry Holt and Co.

Cole, Joanna. 2001. *Magic School Bus Explores the Senses*. New York: Scholastic.

Cronin, Doreen. 2011. *Click, Clack, Moo: Cow That Type*. New York: Little Simon.

Crummel, Susan S., and Janet Stevens. 2005. *The Great Fuzz Frenzy*. Boston: Harcourt Children's Books,.

Dahl, Michael. 2007. *If You Were a Synonym*. Mankato, MN: Picture Window Books.

Falwell, Cathryn. 2006. *Word Wizard*. Boston: Sandpiper, 2006.

Faulkner, Kevin. 1999. *The Big Yawn*. Minneapolis, MN: Millbrook Press.

Fox, Mem. 1994. *Tough Boris*. Boston: Harcourt Children's Books.

Haseley, Dennis. 2002. *A Story for Bear*. Boston: Harcourt Children's Books.

Henkes, Kevin. 2005. *Lily's Purple Plastic Purse*. Pine Plains, NY: Live Oak Media.

Jenkins, Steve. 1996. *Big and Little*. Boston: Houghton Mifflin Books for Children.

Jonas, Ann. 1989. *Color Dance*. New York: Greenwillow Books.

Keats, Ezra Jack. 1976. *The Snowy Day*. New York Puffin.

Lionni, Leo. 1973. *Swimmy*. New York: Dragonfly Books.

Litwin, Eric. 2010. *Pete the Cat: I Love My White Shoes*. New York: HarperCollins.

Mentor Text List (cont.)

Word Choice (cont.)

MacLachlan, Patricia. 1998. *What You Know First*. New York: HarperCollins.

Munsch, Robert. 2002. *Andrew's Loose Tooth*. New York: Cartwheel.

Munsch, Robert. 1985. *Mortimer*. Buffalo, NY: Annick Press.

O'Connor, Jane. 2008. *Fancy Nancy's Favorite Fancy Words: From Accessories to Zany*. New York: HarperCollins.

Palatini, Margie. 2000. *Zoom Broom*. New York: Hyperion Paperbacks for Children.

Ryan, Pam Muñoz. 2001. *Hello Ocean*. Watertown, MA: Talewinds.

Rylant, Cynthia. 1991. *Night in the Country*. New York: Atheneum Books for Young Readers.

Steinberg, Laya. 2005 *Thesaurus Rex*. Cambridge, MA: Barefoot Books.

Walton, Rick. 2001. *That's My Dog*. New York: Putnam Juvenile.

Wilson, Karma. 2002. *Bear Snores*. New York: Margaret K. EcElderry Books.

Wood, Audrey. 1996. *Quick as a Cricket*. Swindon, London: Child's Play International.

Yashima, Taro. 1987. *Umbrella*. Pine Plains, NY: Live Oak Media.

Yolen, Jane.1987. *Owl Moon*. New York: Philomel.

———. 2003. *Color Me a Rhyme: Nature Poems for Young People*. Honesdale, PA: Boyds Mills.

Voice

Aliki. 1986. *Feelings*. New York: Greenwillow Books.

Bang, Molly. 2004. *When Sophie Gets Angry, Really Really Angry*. New York: Scholastic Paperbacks.

Curtis, Jamie Lee. 1998. *Today I Feel Silly: & Other Moods That Make My Day*. New York: HarperCollins.

Davies, Nicola. 2004. *Bat Loves the Night*. Logan, IA: Perfection Learning.

Hall, Donald. 1994. *I Am the Dog I Am the Cat*. New York: Dial.

Hoose, Phillip M., Hannah Hoose, and Debbie Tilley. 1998. *Hey, Little Ant*. New York: Tricycle Press.

Kachenmeister, Cherryl. 2001. *On Monday When It Rained*. Boston, Sandpiper.

Kasza, Keiko. 2005. *My Lucky Day*. New York: Puffin.

Kirk, Daniel. 2003. *Dogs Rule!* New York: Hyperion.

Miranda, Anne. 1997. *Glad Monster, Sad Monster*. New York: LB Kids.

O'Malley, Kevin. 2005. *Once Upon a Cool Motorcycle Dude.* New York: Walker Childrens.

Orloff, Karen Kaufman. 2004. *I Wanna Iguana*. New York: Putnam.

———. 2010. *I Wanna New Room*. New York: Putnam

Mentor Text List (cont.)

Conventions

Beaumont, Karen. 2004. *I Like Myself!* Boston: Harcourt Children's Books.

Cleary, Brian. 2008. *The Frail Snail on the Trail*. Minneapolis, MN: Millbrook Press.

Crummel, Susan S., and J. Stevens. 2005. *The Great Fuzz Frenzy*. Boston: Harcourt Children's Books.

Dr. Seuss. *The Cat in the Hat*. 1957. New York: Random House Books for Young Readers.

Eastman, Phillip D. 1960. *Are You My Mother?* New York: Random House Books for Young Readers.

Hall, Pamela. 2009. *Punk-tuation Celebration*. Minneapolis, MN: Magic Wagon.

Kachenmeister, Cherryl. 2001. *On Monday When It Rained*. Boston, Sandpiper.

Karling, Nurit. 1998. *The Fat Cat Sat on the Mat*. New York: HarperCollins.

Keats, Ezra Jack. 2005. *Whistle for Willie*. Pine Plains, NY: Live Oak Media.

Leedy, Loreen. 2005. *Look at My Book: How Kids Can Write & Illustrate Terrific Books.* New York: Holiday House.

Numeroff, Laura. 1985. *If You Give a Mouse a Cookie*. New York: HarperCollins.

Palatini, Margie. 2003. *Bedhead*. New York: Simon & Schuster Books for Young Readers.

Pulver, Robin. 2008. *Punctuation Takes a Vacation*. Pine Plains, NY: Live Oak Media.

Rylant, Cynthia. 2004. *The Relatives Came*. Pine Plains, NY: Live Oaks Media.

Shannon, David. 1998. *No, David!* New York: Blue Sky Press.

Shaw, Nancy. 1997. *Sheep in a Jeep*. Boston: Houghton Mifflin Harcourt.

Shulevitz, Uri. 2003. *One Monday Morning*. New York: Farrar, Straus and Giroux.

Viorst, Judith. 2009. *Alexander and the Terrible, Horrible, No Good, Very Bad Day*. New York: Atheneum Books for Young Readers.

Ward, Cindy. 1997. *Cookie's Week*. New York: Puffin.

Willems, Mo. 2004. *Knuffle Bunny: A Cautionary Tale*. New York: Hyperion.

William, Vera B. 1984. *A Chair for My Mother*. New York: Greenwillow Books.

Writing Topics

There are many different topics that students can write about during Writer's Workshop. The chart below depicts the types of topics that students may be interested in, divided by months.

August/ September	October	November	December	January
summer fun apples community fall family favorites friends Grandparent's Day me pets school	animal habitats Christopher Columbus exercise fire prevention foods we eat germs Halloween healthy habits pumpkins spiders	Election Day Family farm animals habitats and needs harvest leaves The Mayflower Pilgrims Pocahontas Thanksgiving Veteran's Day	five senses gingerbread holiday winter visiting relatives	New Year's Day 100th Day cooperation fables helping others manners Martin Luther King Jr. penguins safety electricity snow/snow day
February	**March**	**April**	**May**	**June**
dental health feelings friends/friendship groundhogs pen pals presidents Valentine's Day	American heroes spring Dr. Seuss frogs space and solar system Saint Patrick's Day weather storms, wind, rain	art chicks Earth Day flowers poetry weather	gardens Mother's Day plants and trees life cycles our environment	Father's Day ocean/sea life other countries vacations

Ideas from Literature

The mini-lesson, *Getting Ideas from Literature* (page 61), can be adapted and used with numerous texts. Listed below are only a few favorites. Although this list contains only books, keep in mind that ideas can be found in other media as well, such as pictures, magazines, newspapers, videos, Internet exploration, and books online, as well as many other places.

Texts	Idea Topics
Best Friends by Steven Kellogg *Just My Friend and Me* by Mercer Mayer *We Are Best Friends* by Steven Kellogg	Draw or write about your best friend Write a "How to Be a Good Friend" book
Amos & Boris by William Steig *The Lion & the Mouse* by Jerry Pinkney	Write about a time when you helped someone or someone helped you
The Pumpkin Book by Gail Gibbons *The Apple Pie That Papa Baked* by Lauren Thompson	How do pumpkins grow? How to grow pumpkins Recipe for pumpkin pie, soup, or bread
The Relatives Came by Cynthia Rylant *My Great-Aunt Arizona* by Gloria Houston	Write about a visit to a relative's home, a special vacation, or a favorite relative
The Snowy Day by Ezra Jack Keats *A Stranger in the Woods* by Carl S. Sams	What do you like to do on a snowy day? How to get ready to go outside How to build a snowman How to make hot chocolate
The Hungry Caterpillar by Eric Carle *On Monday When It Rained* by Cherryl Kachenmeister	Draw/write a "Days of the Week" book Draw/write a "Months of the Year" book
Earrings! by Judith Viorst *I Wanna New Room* by Karen Kaufman Orloff	Write about something you want and why Write a letter
Bats by Gail Gibbons *Frogs* by Gail Gibbons	Write facts about an animal or insect of your choice
Alexander and the Terrible, Horrible, No Good Very Bad Day by Judith Viorst *One of Those Days* by Amy Rosenthal	Write about your worst day ever Write about your best day ever
If You Grew Up with Abraham Lincoln by Ann McGovern	Write about and compare the things you do to the things that Abraham Lincoln and George Washington did when they were young.
I Like Myself! by Karen Beaumont *I Like Me!* by Nancy Carlson	Write an "All About Me" or "I am Special!" book Write an "All About My Friend" book

Name: ____________________ Date: ____________

Writing Paper 1

Name: ______________________ Date: __________

Writing Paper 2

Name: ______________________ Date: ____________

Writing Paper 3

Supporting with Technology

Whether communicating via cell phones, texts, blogs, tweets, Facebook, email or gathering information via Internet, Google, and eBooks, today's students will live in a world increasingly shaped by technology. For this reason, Common Core State Standards highlight the effective use of technology-integrated instruction across the curriculum. Incorporating technology into instruction increases opportunities for students to be active learners, rather than passive receivers of information, and offers new ways of learning and sharing information.

The challenge for most teachers is how to seamlessly integrate technology use so that it does not take time away from writing instruction but enhances that instruction and increases students' interest and involvement. While uses of technology are seemingly limitless and constantly being updated, here are seven important ways teachers are successfully integrating technology into Writer's Workshop:

1. Digital and flip cameras can add excitement to any writing project. Student projects that capture pictures of the life cycle of a chick or a class field trip instantly invite students into a writing project. Digital photos can be used to generate a photo album of writing ideas, organize storyboards, promote language and vocabulary, illustrate student writing, and even be included in slide show presentations.
2. Document cameras are easily integrated in writing lessons and activities by both teachers and students. The benefits of using mentor texts for modeling are sometimes lost on students who may not be close enough to see the specific texts. Whether presenting photographs to gather writing ideas, sharing multiple beginnings from mentor texts, or displaying leaves and fossils to model descriptive language, the document camera offers a myriad of opportunities for modeling writing instruction for all students to see. Using the document camera allows you to zoom in on specific text features and details in illustrations. Students frequently volunteer to display their writing with the document camera and gather feedback from classmates on revising and editing. Teachers and students also enjoy presenting examples of good writing work and highlighting quality features in writing using the document camera.
3. Interactive whiteboards can serve a number of purposes for writing instruction. They provide the opportunity for student engagement and involvement of almost any materials or activity that can be viewed on a computer screen. Consider using the interactive whiteboard to teach whole group keyboarding skills, revising word choice by highlighting verbs or adjectives, using editing marks, building story webs, or reinforcing skills by accessing interactive websites. Of course, whiteboards are an excellent source to demonstrate and model lessons, present presentations and create class books and word banks.

Supporting with Technology *(cont.)*

4. Publishing tools abound in the technology realm. Students may be involved in illustrating their writing with Microsoft® Paint or a software program like KidPix®. Through word processing, students can create letters, essays, brochures, and even class newsletters. Many teachers use Microsoft® PowerPoint for publishing individual, team, or class writing projects, which can easily be printed and bound into classroom books or saved as eBooks. Podcasts are used to record students as they read their writing. This can support the revising and editing process as they listen carefully to their writing and add a special touch to a final published project. Technology enhances the writer's options for publishing their work. For example, parents and students enjoy viewing and listening to final projects on the school website.

5. Research has never been easier. Though writing teachers must be cognizant of Internet safety, misuse, plagiarism, and follow district policies, they know technology allows for new and purposeful ways to gather and synthesize research. Writing teachers demonstrate technology-driven research procedures and help students locate and bookmark trusted websites. Collaborating with colleagues about their student research websites can make research easy and accessible.

6. URLs (Uniform Resource Locator) are great to include in your classroom newsletter. Offer links for students to practice skills, view presentations, or learn about future topics like Arbor Day. And don't forget the authors! With activities like Ralph Fletcher's *Tips for Young Writers*, Patricia Pollacco's *Who Am I*, or *Poetry Writing with Jack Prelutsky*, author websites are filled with an assortment of information and activities to engage and motivate student writing. Visit author sites while teaching students how to create their own Author's Page. The possibilities are limitless.

7. Collaborative writing projects like ePals and virtual field trips open classroom boundaries to endless learning opportunities. EPals is a modern pen pal project in which students can collaborate on academic and cultural projects as well as establish everlasting friendships in other districts, states, or countries. Virtual field trips (VFT) offer learning opportunities that might otherwise be limited by distance and funding. Writing projects may be further enhanced by a virtual visit to the San Diego Zoo to learn about animal characteristics and habitats or to the National Aeronautics and Space Administration (NASA) to interview an astronaut.

Terminology Used

In order to adequately implement the lessons included in *Getting to the Core of Writing*, it is necessary to understand the terminology used throughout the resources.

Analytics—In order to be consistent with National Assessment of Educational Progress (NAEP) standards, the following analytics are used when describing writing proficiency:

- **Below Basic/Score 0**—Writing demonstrates an attempt to write, but the result is illegible, insufficient, or otherwise fails to meet the criteria for a score of 1.
- **Basic/Score 1**—Writing demonstrates little or marginal skill in responding to the writing benchmark tasks. Few traits of quality writing are present.
- **Proficient/Score 2**—Writing demonstrates developing skills in responding to the writing benchmark tasks. Most traits of quality writing are evident.
- **Advanced/Score 3**—Writing demonstrates effective skills in responding to the writing benchmark tasks. All traits of quality writing are obvious.

Anchor Charts—Anchor charts are used to track student thinking. In this resource, anchor charts are created cooperatively by the teacher and students. The charts are used to scaffold learning and chart key concepts of writing such as ideas for writing, vocabulary words, and examples of sentence structure. Anchor charts are displayed throughout the room to support a print-rich environment that promotes literacy acquisition.

Anecdotal Observations—Throughout Writer's Workshop, teachers practice the art of becoming astute observers of student writing behaviors. The teacher's Conferring Notebook is an excellent resource to store observations for the entire year of instruction (See Appendix A). As you observe, remember to present a statement of praise and develop a teaching point as this will guide future instructional decisions.

Author's Chair—Students are selected to share their writing with classmates. Usually students sit in a designated chair/stool. Classmates provide feedback to authors in the form of a question or a compliment.

Author's Tea/Author's Luncheon—An author's tea can be held anytime to support student writing efforts. Students invite parents and special loved ones to join them, sometimes with refreshments, to celebrate accomplishments in writing. Each student writes, illustrates, publishes, and presents a favorite piece of writing from the past year. It is important that every student has someone to listen to his or her especially planned presentation. You might invite the principal, cafeteria cook, librarian, or teacher specialists as part of the celebration.

Benchmark Assessments—The beginning-of-the-year benchmark serves as baseline information about a student's writing. Middle-of-the-year and end-of-the-year benchmarks represent a student's progress toward state, district, and/or school benchmark goals.

Terminology Used *(cont.)*

Heads-up, Stand-up, Partner-up—This is an activity in which the teacher gains students' attention, they stand up and quickly move to find partners, and they begin a discussion of focused writing talk. Partners can be assigned based upon the needs of the class or they can be chosen spontaneously. However, it is crucial that students move quickly and in an orderly fashion without any wasted time.

Mentor Texts—A mentor text is a book that offers multiple learning opportunities as both teacher and student develop writing skills. Mentor texts contain explicit and strong examples of the author's craft and are visited repeatedly to explore the traits of quality writing. Your favorite books to share often make the best mentor texts. You may wish to use the recommended mentor text as a read-aloud during your reading block with spirited discussions or quickly review it during Writer's Workshop. During writing block, focus on small samples of text that match the mini-lesson skill. A recommended list of mentor texts is provided as part of each lesson and additional titles are provided in Appendix C.

My Turn/Your Turn—*My Turn* indicates an individual teacher response with students not participating, but watching and listening. *Your Turn* indicates a whole-class group response with everyone participating. Use of hand gestures, with the hand sweeping across the group, palms up is an excellent signal to alert students to respond as a whole group. Recent research has shown that whole group responses eliminate poor behavior decisions, increase motivation, and improve participation. This management strategy is especially helpful for targeting specific writing strategies or having students respond to targeted concepts.

Pinch and Roll—This term refers to a strategy for the proper way to grip a pencil. Students hold their pencils in many positions that produce unnecessary stress on the body. Proper pencil grip requires a three-finger grip, with a roll of the pencil back into the space between the thumb and pointer finger. This is a relaxed, natural way to grip the pencil and eliminates undue writing fatigue.

Turn and Talk—*Turn and Talk* is a management tool for giving opportunities to students to have partner conversations. This procedure may take place at the meeting area or at desks. Students make eye contact, lean toward their partner, talk quietly, or listen attentively.

Triads and Quads—These are terms used to quickly divide the class into groups of three or four.

References

Anderson, Carl. 2000. *How's It Going? A Practical Guide to Conferring with Student Writers.* Portsmouth, NH: Heinemann.

Angelillo, Janet. 2005. *Writing to the Prompt: When Students Don't Have a Choice.* Portsmouth, NH: Heinemann.

Calkins, Lucy M. 1994. *The Art of Teaching Writing* (New ed.). Portsmouth, NH: Heinemann.

Calkins, Lucy M., Amanda Hartman, and Zoe White. 2003. *The Conferring Handbook.* Portsmouth, NH: Heinemann.

Calkins, Lucy M., Amanda Hartman, and Zoe White. 2005. *One to One: The Art of Conferring with Young Writers.* Portsmouth, NH: Heinemann.

Clay, Marie M. 1975. *What Did I Write?: Beginning Writing Behaviour.* Portsmouth, NH: Heinemann.

Hirsch, Eric, and John Holdren. 1996. *What Your Kindergartner Needs to Know: Preparing Your Child for a Lifetime of Learning.* New York: Dell Publishing.

Culham, Ruth. 2003. *6 + 1 Traits of Writing: The Complete Guide (Grades 3 and Up).* New York: Scholastic.

Culham, Ruth. 2008. *6 + 1 Traits of Writing: The Complete Guide for the Primary Grades.* New York: Scholastic.

Culham, Ruth. 2008. *Using Picture Books to Teach Writing with the Traits K–2.* New York: Scholastic.

Davis, Judy, and Sharon Hill. 2003. *The No-Nonsense Guide to Teaching Writing: Strategies, Structures, Solutions.* Portsmouth, NH: Heinemann.

Dolch, Edward W. 1941. *Teaching Primary Reading.* Champaign, IL: The Garrard Press.

Dorn, Linda J., and Carla Soffos. 2001. *Scaffolding Young Writers: A Writers' Workshop Approach.* Portland, ME: Stenhouse Publishers.

Ehri, Linnea C. 1997. "Learning to Read and Write Are One and the Same, Almost." In *Learning to Spell: Research, Theory, and Practice Across Languages*, eds. Charles A. Perfetti, Laurence Rieben, and Michael Fayol. London: Lawrence Erlbaum Associates.

Elkonin, Daniel B. 1973. "U.S.S.R." In *Comparative reading; cross-national studies of behavior and process in reading and writing*, ed. John A. Downing. New York: Macmillan.

Fletcher, Ralph, and JoAnn Portalupi. 1998. *Craft Lessons: Teaching Writing K–8.* Portland, ME: Stenhouse Publishers.

Fletcher, Ralph, and JoAnn Portalupi. 2001. *Writing Workshop: The Essential Guide.* Portsmouth, NH: Heinemann.

Frayer, Dorothy, Wayne Frederick, and Herbert Klausmeier. 1969. *A Schema for Testing the Level of Cognitive Mastery.* Madison, WI: Wisconsin Center for Education Research.

References *(cont.)*

Freeman, M. 1998. *Teaching the Youngest Writers: A Practical Guide.* Gainesville, FL: Maupin House Publishing, Inc.

——— 2001. *Non-Fiction Writing Strategies: Using Science Big Books as Models.* Gainesville, FL: Maupin House Publishing, Inc.

Gentry, J. Richard. 2000. *The Literacy Map: Guiding Children to Where They Need to Be (K–3).* New York: Mondo Publishing.

——— 2002. *The Literacy Map: Guiding Children to Where They Need to Be (4–6).* New York: Mondo Publishing.

——— 2004. *The Science of Spelling: The Explicit Specifics That Make Greater Readers and Writers (and Spellers!).* Portsmouth, NH: Heinemann.

——— 2006 *Breaking the Code: New Science of Beginning Reading and Writing.* Portsmouth, NH: Heinemann.

——— 2007. *Breakthrough in Beginning Reading and Writing.* New York: Scholastic, Inc.

——— 2008. *Step-by-Step: Assessment Guide to Code Breaking.* New York: Scholastic, Inc.

——— 2010. *Raising Confident Readers: How to Teach Your Child to Read and Write—from Baby to Age 7.* Cambridge, MA: Da Capo Lifelong Books.

Gentry, J. Richard, and Jean Gillet. 1993. *Teaching Kids to Spell.* Portsmouth, NH: Heinemann.

Gibson, V. P. 2004. *We Can! I Can Draw Pre-Writing Program.* Longmont, CO: Sorpris West Educational Services.

Gould, J. A. 1999. *Four Square Writing Method: A Unique Approach to Teaching Basic Writing Skills for Grades 1–3.* Carthage, IL: Teaching and Learning Company.

Graham, S., and Hebert, M. 2010, April. *Writing to Read: Evidence for How Writing Can Improve Reading (Report to the Carnegie Corporation).* Retrieved from http://carnegie.org/fileadmin/Media/Publications/WritingtoRead_01.pdf

Graves, D. H. 1994. *A Fresh Look at Writing.* Portsmouth, NH: Heinemann.

Graves, D. H. 2003. *Writing: Teachers and Children at Work 20th Anniversary Edition.* Portsmouth, NH : Heinemann.

Jensen, E. 2009. *Different Brains, Different Learners: How to Reach the Hard to Reach* (Second ed.). Thousand Oaks, CA: Corwin Press.

Johnston, P. H. 2004. *Choice Words.* Portland, OR: Stenhouse Publishers.

Koehler, S. 2007. *Crafting Expository Papers.* Gainesville, FL: Maupin House Publishing, Inc.

McMahon, C., and Warrick, P. 2005. *Wee Can Write: Using 6 + 1 Trait Writing Strategies with Renowned Children's Literature.* (P. Bellamy, Ed.) Portland, OR: Northwest Regional Educational Laboratory.

References *(cont.)*

Murray, David. 1984. *Write to Learn*. NY: Holt.

National Governors Association Center for Best Practices and Council of Chief State School Officers. 2011. *Common Core State Standards Initiative: The Standards*. Retrieved June 2011, from Common Core State Standards Initiative: http://www.corestandards.org

Olness, R. 2004. *Using Literature to Enhance Writing Instruction*. Newark, DE: International Reading Association.

Ray, K. W. 2001. *The Writing Workshop: Working Through the Hard Parts (And They're All Hard Parts).* Urbana, IL: National Council Of Teachers of English.

Ray, K. W., and Cleaveland, L. B. 2004. *About the Authors: Writing Workshop with Our Youngest Writers.* Portmouth, NH: Heinemann.

Routman, R. 1999. *Conversations: Strategies for Teaching, Learning and Evaluating*. Portsmouth, NH: Heinemann.

Routman, R. 2005. *Writing Essentials: Raising Expectations and Results While Simplifying Teaching.* Portsmouth, NH: Heinemann.

Spandel, V. 2001. *Books, Lessons, Ideas for Teaching the Six Traits: Writing in the Elementary and Middle Grades.* Wilmington, MA: Great Source Education Group.

——— 2005. *Seeing With New Eyes: A Guidebook on Teaching and Assessing Beginning Writers Using the Six-Trait Writing Model* (6th Edition ed.) Portland, OR: Northwest Regional Educational Laboratory.

Spandel, V. 2008. *Creating Young Writers: Using the Six Traits to Enrich Writing Process in Primary Classrooms* (2nd Edition ed.) New York: Allyn & Bacon.

Sprenger, M. 2007. *Becoming a "Wiz" at Brain-Based Teaching: How to Make Every Year Your Best Year.* Thousand Oaks, CA: Corwin Press.

Tate, M. L. 2004. *"Sit & Get" Won't Grow Dendrites: 20 Professional Learning Strategies that Engage the Adult Brain.* Thousand Oaks, CA: Corwin Press.

Vygotsky, L. 1978. *Mind in Society: The Development of Higher Psychological Processes.* (M. Cole, V. John-Steiner, S. Scribner, and E. and Souberman, Eds.) Cambridge, MA: Harvard University Press.

Contents of the Teacher Resource CD

Teacher Resources

Page Number	Title	Filename
N/A	Traits Team	traitsteam.pdf
N/A	Student Writing Samples	samples.doc
N/A	Year at a Glance	yearataglance.pdf
12–13	Suggested Pacing Guide	pacingguide.pdf
22–26	Correlation to Standards	standards.pdf
235	Conferring Notebook Cover	cover.pdf
236	Mini-Lesson Log	minilessonlog.pdf
237	Conference Log	conferencelog.pdf
238	Conference Countdown	conferencecountdown.pdf
244	Second Grade Writing Rubric	secondgradewritingrubric.pdf
245	Second Grade Writing Report	secondgradewritingreport.pdf
246	Second Grade Grouping Mat	secondgradegroupingmat.pdf
250–256	Mentor Text List	mentortextlist.pdf
259–261	Writing Paper	writingpaper.pdf

Managing Writer's Workshop

Page Number	Title	Filename
35	Sample Looks Like, Sounds Like, Feels Life Anchor Chart	lookssoundsfeelschart.pdf
38	Guidelines for Writer's Workshop	guidelineswritersws.pdf
45	Sample Partner Conversation Anchor Chart	partnerconversation.pdf
48	I Like/I Wonder Cards	likewondercards.pdf
51	Five-Step Writing Process	fivestepprocess.pdf

Ideas

Page Number	Title	Filename
54	Ida, Idea Creator	ida.pdf
57	Examples of Brainstorming	exbrainstorming.pdf
60	Ponder Pocket	ponderpocket.pdf
65	Important People in My Life	importantpeople.pdf
68	Important Places	importantplaces.pdf
71	My Heart Treasures	hearttreasures.pdf
74	Those Amazing Animals	amazinganimals.pdf

Contents of the Teacher Resource CD (cont.)

Ideas (cont.)

Page Number	Title	Filename
75–76	Animal Picture Cards	animalpiccards.pdf
79	Things I Know List	thingsknowlist.pdf

Sentence Fluency

Page Number	Title	Filename
82	Simon, Sentence Builder	simon.pdf
85	Sentence Builders	sentencebuilders.pdf
86	More Sentence Builders	moresentencebuilders.pdf
91–93	Parts of a Sentence Picture Cards	partssentencepiccards.pdf
96	Fragment Cards	fragmentcards.pdf
101	Question Cards	questioncards.pdf
106	Fun with Sentence Variety	funsentencevariety.pdf
109–110	Writing Detective Sentence Cards	detectivecards.pdf

Organization

Page Number	Title	Filename
112	Owen, Organization Conductor	owen.pdf
117	Triante Poem Organizer	poemorganizer.pdf
N/A	My Alphabet Book	abcbook.pdf
122–123	Hand Plan Samples	handplansamples.pdf
124	My Hand Plan	myhandplan.pdf
125	Topic Ideas	topicideas.pdf
128	My Story Mountain	mountainstory.pdf
129–130	Story Mountain Cards	storymountaincards.pdf
135	Organization Mentor Texts—Beginnings and Endings	organizationbegend.pdf
138	Sample Narratives	samplenarratives.pdf
139	Beginning, Middle, and End	begmidend.pdf
140	Beginning, Middle, and End Writing Paper	begmidendpaper.pdf
143	My Friendly Letter	myfriendlyletter.pdf
144	Letter Samples	lettersamples.pdf
149	Informative Report Sample	informreportsample.pdf

Contents of the Teacher Resource CD *(cont.)*

Organization *(cont.)*

Page Number	Title	Filename
150	My Report Planner	reportplanner123.pdf
153	How-to Planner	howtoplanner.pdf

Word Choice

Page Number	Title	Filename
156	Wally, Word Choice Detective	wally.pdf
159	Learn a Word Chart	learnwordchart.pdf
160	High Frequency Word List	highfreqwordlist.pdf
163	Using Our Senses Sample	usingsensessample.pdf
164	Using Our Senses	usingsenses.pdf
167	Action Words Sample	actionwordssample.pdf
172	A Rainbow of Writing Words	rainbowwriting.pdf
175–180	Onomatopoeia Dictionary	onomatopoeiadictionary.pdf
181–182	Teacher Resources for Onomatopoeia	teacheronomatopoeia.pdf
187	Sparkling Synonym Star	synonymstar.pdf
190	Transition Words Cards	transitioncards.pdf
191–192	Sequencing Picture Cards	sequencingpiccards.pdf
195	Simile Cards	similecards.pdf

Voice

Page Number	Title	Filename
198	Val and Van Voice	valvan.pdf
201	My Feelings	myfeelings.pdf

Conventions

Page Number	Title	Filename
206	Callie, Super Conventions Checker	callie.pdf
209	Sound Chart Word List	soundchartlist.pdf
210	Alphabet Chart	alphabetchart.pdf
211	Short Vowel Chart	shortvowelchart.pdf
212	Long Vowel Chart	longvowelchart.pdf
213–214	Digraphs and Consonant Blends Chart	blendschart.pdf
215–216	Vowel Team Chart	vowelteamchart.pdf

Contents of the Teacher Resource CD *(cont.)*

Conventions *(cont.)*

Page Number	Title	Filename
219	Sound Box Word List	soundboxwordlist.pdf
222	Capital Rap	capitalrap.pdf
225	Rockin' Editors	rockineditors.pdf
228	My Editing Tools	myeditingtools.pdf
233	CUPS	cups.pdf